IMAGINATION *in* ACTION

*thoughts on creativity*

*by painters, sculptors, musicians, poets, novelists, teachers, actors...*

BOOKS BY CAROL MALYON

*Cathedral Women*
*The Migration of Butterflies*
*Colville's People*
*The Adultery Handbook*
*Mixed-up Grandmas* (for children)
*Lovers & Other Strangers*
*If I Knew I'd Tell You*
*The Edge of the World*
*Emma's Dead*
*Headstand*

# IMAGINATION *in* ACTION
*thoughts on creativity*
*by painters, sculptors, musicians, poets, novelists, teachers, actors...*

EDITED BY CAROL MALYON

The Mercury Press

The publisher gratefully acknowledges the financial assistance of the Canada Council for the Arts, the
Ontario Arts Council, and the Ontario Book Publishing Tax Credit Program. The publisher further
acknowledges the financial support of the Government of Canada through the Department of Canadian
Heritage's Book Publishing Industry Development Program (BPIDP) for our publishing activities.

Cover, composition and page design: Beverley Daurio
Back cover: painting by Marjory Smart
Printed and bound in Canada
Printed on acid-free paper

1 2 3 4 5   11 10 09 08 07

Library and Archives Canada Cataloguing in Publication

Imagination in action / Carol Malyon [editor].
ISBN 1-55128-132-5
1. Creation (Literary, artistic, etc.) 2. Creative ability—Canada.
3. Artists—Canada. I. Malyon, Carol, 1933-
NX513.Z8I43 2007    700.92'271    C2007-904904-4

The Mercury Press
Box 672, Station P, Toronto, Ontario Canada M5S 2Y4
www.themercurypress.ca

in memory of Marjory Smart

where the conversation began

# CONTENTS

## CAROL MALYON

Malyon's latest novel, *Cathedral Women*, was published in 2006. Her other recent books are: the novels, *The Migration of Butterflies* and *The Adultery Handbook*; a poetry collection, *Colville's People*; and *Mixed-up Grandmas*, a picture-book for children. In her fiction Malyon writers of women — their relationships with lovers, mothers, children. She is interested in the fundamental and irreconcilable discord between men and women: their differing views of the world, of themselves, of others; their separate modes of communication. In the past she has been writer-in-residence at UNB, and owned a bookstore (Beaches Book Shop). She now writes full-time in Toronto, and is currently collaborating with bill bissett on a collection of discussions on topics ranging from religion, politics and world events to personal relationships.

## INTRODUCTION

The title of this book comes from a sentence in David Lee's article: "Creativity is imagination in action," For me the emphasis seems to be on the last word: action. Not merely having an idea, but doing something with it. Creative folks are the ones who start and then keep going. They don't stop. They are the ones who can't be stopped, no matter what.

This collection has been solicited from forty-four Canadians who are creative in more than one field: painters, sculptors, musicians, composers, poets, novelists, journalists, teachers, choreographers, actors, bookstore owners, cooks, farmers, needleworkers… They talk about what they do, and why, and how they do it.

Some examples: a poet and artist discuss their collaboration on a book. An artist compares the corporate and private world of art. While conducting a tour of her sculpture show, the artist tells what was happening in her life while the sculptures were being created. A poetics professor explains how the marking of essays makes him want to write poetry. A cellist's sentence structure is influenced by music. A writer compares the empty wall of her new bookstore to the blank page she faces when writing novels. (As a writer and ex-bookseller, I read this and gasped in recognition. I hope other readers will discover their own epiphanies.)

There's something here for everyone, from poems and a play to academic articles with footnotes.

Most of my friends write. We talk about it often: *What are you working on these days? How's it going?* Sometimes we try to figure out where the writing comes from, needing to know, curious, comparing notes. Hoping for some kind of communal feeling: we're not alone, other folks feel this way too. But on the other hand, suspecting we're all different, alone in how we go about our work; the process feels so completely our own. It seems instinctive, mysterious, defying verbalization. Sometimes we write poems, sometimes stories, and wonder why. Does the subject matter determine this? Or something else? What?

Wandering through art galleries I wondered whether it was the same for visual artists. All those media: oil, watercolour, acrylic, charcoal, clay; do they correspond to writing genres? Perhaps visual artists had reasons for choosing the medium they worked in, and knew what those reasons were. If I could find out about this, perhaps I could understand how we writers go about writing.

This was back in the 1990s. I decided to talk with two friends about it. Marjory Smart was a visual artist, then working in watercolour, who published two poetry collections; she had a keen eye for both detail and abstraction, and her poems were alive with imagery and colour. Milt Jewell, a sculptor and painter, was working mainly in encaustic at that time; in the seventies he had seen the need for an art-review magazine, so developed and edited a newsletter, for which he also wrote some reviews. I interviewed them both, asking lots of questions; excerpts from the interviews are included in this book.

This is the kind of thing I asked them about. When did you start writing? Painting? Do writing and painting help or influence each other? Do you go about them in the same way? Are you conscious of an audience when you're creating? How do you start? How do you decide on a subject? Do you paint and write about the same things? Are you conscious of this kind of thing when you're creating? Are the choices you make instinctive? Can you describe them for me at all?

Until that time I had placed artists in pigeon-holes and assumed they belonged there: poet, painter, cellist… It amazed me that these folks could create in more than one area. After all I can't paint or sculpt or make music, or do anything but write, but I feel *compelled* to do that. Writing is something I must do. I can't imagine being unable to write. I'm not sure I would feel alive.

I kept on wondering why people create, and how, and where it comes from, all those mysteries, as well as the relationship between different expressions of creativity, and finally, a decade later, I approached other artists who are creative in more than one medium, thinking they might have interesting insights on the topic. Some answered my questions directly, but others, being creative, did their own thing, and this book is richer as a result.

Visual artists and musicians were able to identify actual details of their process. Those who wrote about writing were less specific about technique, and this seems reasonable to me. Writers arrange and rearrange words to create stories and poems and essays, but everyone else uses these same tools every day. It's hard for writers to define just what is different about what we do.

Several contributors mentioned the creative mess, having to find one's way out of a disorganized situation: David Lee and Honey Novick referring to music, Milt Jewell and Sonja Dunn when discussing painting. When Sonja's son was in a highchair, smearing his food, she got out her paints, wanting to make a mess too. I can't imagine being tempted to do this.

I once watched a sculptor working in her studio and realized, well, it's no wonder I'm not artistic, my mother would never have given me permission to make a mess like this woman was making, and I would never have been disobedient to such an extent. My mother hadn't wanted the kind of child who stomped in mud puddles, whose clothes were covered with sand from making castles on the beach. She preferred a nice clean little girl who played with paper dolls on her bedroom floor. I've tried to shake this influence, but can't seem to.

All the same, the beauty that emerges from that mess fascinates me, and I recognize a relationship to the way I tell stories. For me, the actual writing is easier than putting the work together afterward. I keep moving sections about, sometimes throwing the pages around the room, scattering them on the floor, or shuffling them like a deck of cards — trying to figure out the best way to tell the story. What do I want the reader to know at this point, and at that? What if I tear up some of the pages so the reader will have to imagine those missing months or years?

I think I can't paint or sculpt; therefore I can't. But as a child I created families of paper dolls or green marbles and made up stories about them. I'm still doing this, four novels and two short-story collections later. I can trace the direct descent.

Artists create. How lucky for the rest of us. Perhaps we should simply celebrate that they spend their time this way. All the same, it would be wonderful to know more about how they go about it. People create in whatever ways work for them. Perhaps their methods are different, with little overlap. If so, it would be nice to know this, and it might be helpful to discover that there is no right way; we each need to develop ways that work for us. Guidelines exist, but there is no rule book. We can go ahead and read those how-to books and try their suggestions, but if they don't work for us, then we can forget them, be creative, and find our own method.

When I began writing, someone offered me back issues of a magazine for aspiring writers. They contained rules for everything: "Seven ways to make your characters zing;" "Guidelines for writing short stories;" "Ten rules for writing poems;" "Set the alarm for five o'clock; sit down at the computer and type nonsense until the words begin to make sense;" — that sort of thing. I followed the rules and was unable to write. Later I passed those magazines on to someone else, gradually forgot their content, and eventually began writing again. Perhaps a skull-and-crossbones warning should be printed on each cover: "These suggestions may not work for you. If so, throw away and try something else."

Writers write. Painters paint. Composers compose. All of us groping, learning the world however we can; using pens, paintbrushes, musical instruments, whatever we have. Trying to understand the world and our place in it; to bring order out of chaos; to figure out who we are and what we are doing here. Trying to communicate with others. *Who are you? What are you doing? Here's what I've been making. This is my version of the world. Is it similar to yours?*

Creating is the way we figure out things, explore our surroundings, learn the landscape, and the people who inhabit it.

The way a fetus gropes about inside a watery sac, the contours always shifting. Before one shape is learned, already it is changing. The thrum of the maternal heartbeat surrounds it: *lub dub, lub dub.* The infant finally learns the shape and feel of home, only to leave it and discover another. A cold dry atmosphere this time. The shock of emerging into it. Slap. Gasp. Yell. Discovering the outside of the mother's body, curve of shoulder, contour of breast, instinctively groping for a nipple, kneading the soft surrounding flesh like a kitten in order to feed. A primal instinct. Perhaps the creative urge is like that.

Observing. The way Inuit move across the tundra, carefully, trying not to leave footprints or disturb the scattering of lichens, tiny dots of colour in a grey land. Alert. Watching for changes, track of polar bear, scat of caribou. Cartographers chart each indentation of shoreline, the elevations of mountains, patterns of rock formation, the amount of soil on top of bedrock.

We are like earthworms, exploring the solidity of ground, testing it, chewing, creating pathways, inching along them; rootlets dangling above, like beaded ropes in doorways.

A cliché: writers write while staring out windows. The truth is, we are writing all the time. Words are always being linked together, unfastened, put together more effectively. That has become the way I live my life, stringing thoughts together, translating them into words, trying to make sense of things. In my head though, or on pieces of paper. So far I have not begun talking aloud to myself on streetcars and subways.

It's hard to write and do anything else. Once I start writing in my mind the story takes over: the soup boils over, the cookies burn.

Several respondents mentioned children. For me, developing children and developing characters in a story seem to tap into the same source. I didn't have enough of that energy to spare until my kids were well into their teens. I simply couldn't write and raise children, couldn't create both fictional characters and real ones. I've tried to imagine why the processes seem so similar, why I feel so strongly that this is true. Surely I have developed enough objectivity by now; my children are grown, and raising children of their own.

One similarity: the complete involvement. I am the mother of four. While they were growing up I was also a wife, daughter, sister, friend, neighbour, university student, freelancer working in health research... I wandered through those other aspects of my life, but the children were my focus, what really mattered. Whatever else I might be doing, they were always on my mind. Raising children seemed to be by far the most important way to spend my time. I still believe this.

But they are grown now. Other stories have taken over, and the fictional people I live with seem terribly real and compelling. I live for years with the protagonists of my novels; perhaps it would be more surprising if they didn't seem important to me.

That concentration, obsession, the sense that time is fleeting, and everything that happens matters so terribly and must be reported.

The same way it felt all those years ago when a helpless babe was swaddled by a flannelette receiving-blanket and my arms. Knowing it was up to me do it right, whatever *it* was. Knowing nothing else mattered in the world. The infant would never get another chance at childhood. I had taken on this awful responsibility, and now I'd better get it right.

Of course those youngsters weren't empty slates. Genetics had laid foundations, and a myriad of other folks would influence their lives: father, grandparents, babysitters, playmates, teachers..., but all the same I felt a terrible maternal responsibility. I had made a conscious decision to grow those youngsters inside me. They hadn't existed before, but now they did.

And now, all these fictional characters I live with. I love them all. They enrich my life. I want things to go well for them, but just as in real life, am not able to make this happen. I try to be true to them as I tell their stories, try at least to be accurate, get it right. Nothing seems more important.

Artists move off into other worlds; they grab our hands and pull us along. They create imaginary places: stories and paintings we can climb into and explore; music we get lost inside. All the folks in this collection create. I am grateful that they do.

# ADAM DICKINSON

Adam Dickinson was born in Bracebridge, Ontario. His poems and reviews have appeared in a number of Canadian literary journals and in anthologies such as *Breathing Fire 2: Canada's New Poets*, and *Post Prairie*. He has published academic articles on Canadian literature and film. His first book of poetry, *Cartography and Walking*, was published by Brick Books in 2002 and was short-listed for an Alberta Book Award. The collection that became this book won the 1999 Alfred G. Bailey Prize from the Writers' Federation of New Brunswick for the best unpublished poetry manuscript. His second book of poetry, *Kingdom, Phylum,* was published by Brick Books in 2006 and was a finalist for the 2007 Trillium Book Award for Poetry. Adam received an MA in creative writing from the University of New Brunswick before moving on to Edmonton where he completed his PhD in English at the University of Alberta. He is currently professor of poetics at Brock University in St. Catharines, Ontario, where he teaches poetry, creative writing, and literary theory.

## OTHER MINDS:
## THE POETICS OF TEACHING AND WRITING POETRY

I keep a notebook close at hand when marking student essays. It took me a while to realize it, but marking essays makes me want to write poetry. I don't mean this as an escapist impulse; I mean it rather as a genuinely creative response. I write not to record humorous malapropisms, or the strange, unintentional metaphors of the automatic spellchecker and thesaurus (though these are certainly worthy of record), but to explore my own metaphorical threads, my own poetic projects that are always emerging and re-emerging at the margins and limits of my thinking.

Why should that most ostensibly numbing aspect of teaching be so creatively generative? No one looks forward to marking; it requires intense concentration and it can often be discouraging to see repeated errors. Indeed, I would not claim, even in light of these remarks, that I enjoy marking; it is very hard work. I have come to realize, however, that the relationship between creativity and marking is part of the larger relationship between creativity and teaching. I studied to become a professor because I wanted a job that would allow me to combine my career as a writer with immersion in the material and study of writing itself. Given this intimacy between art and job, I used to worry that teaching poetry would make me sick of writing poetry. I sometimes struggle for time to write, given the commitments of teaching and the other responsibilities of a university professor; however, I never feel creatively diminished — if anything, I feel pushed, I feel compelled, I feel sympathetically attuned. Why?

It goes without saying that teaching is a creative art. The best teachers I have had in my life have been artists. A lecture is a performance. Directing a discussion is alchemical, crystallographic. Coming to realize the shape a problem assumes in a student's mind can be transformative. More fundamentally, however, I would like to propose that the reason marking papers or preparing for a lecture is so creatively generative is because teaching and writing poetry share a key site of productive tension: the intersection between aesthetics and ethics. Aesthetic decisions are always in tension with the openness to what one doesn't know — and there is much a teacher doesn't know (texts, students, and classrooms all have their own constantly retreating horizons of discrete intelligibility). In many respects, teaching, like poetry, is a way of standing in relation to the limits of knowing. The art is in how you stand. Like poets, teachers are constantly shifting their weight.

It might appear that, for teaching, aesthetic concerns are confined to questions pertaining to the organization of the class or lecture; the euphonious delivery, and resonant critical analysis. This is superficially the case. More significantly, the very act of attempting to "see as" a student while trying to give meaningful feedback on a term paper, for example, requires all of one's aesthetic resources. In *Wisdom and Metaphor* Jan Zwicky extends Ludwig Wittgenstein's concept of "seeing-as" to account for the pattern recognition that underlies the experience of understanding. To understand something, according to Zwicky, is to "see how things hang together. Even in cases that involve analysis, *understanding* is not knowing *that* if you follow a series of steps, you will get results, but seeing *how* the result is contained in that series of steps" (24). Zwicky turns to examples drawn from geometrical proofs in order to demonstrate that understanding involves a gestalt shift where "the dawning of an aspect...is simultaneously a perception or reperception of a whole" (2). Similarly, teaching is irrevocably concerned with pattern recognition and the ability to distinguish how it is that things hang together — both from the perspective of the student and from that of the teacher.

One of the greatest challenges in teaching literature is to help students learn how to write a successful essay, how to communicate the patterns they discern in texts. Part of the difficulty is that such a task requires imagination, which is not something conventionally teachable — imagination is, rather, employed; it is discovered in its use. Thus, I continually find myself trying (imaginatively) to discover different ways to enact the gestalt shift, to elicit the metaphorical thinking that reveals the play of patterns. In addition, grading essays is often an imaginative exercise in trying to inhabit the mind of a student struggling with an argument. That sublime moment when an essay reveals its strange and convoluted architecture is exhilarating both for the unique perspective that it represents, but also for the insight it allows in how to communicate assistance. Teaching, like poetry, compels one to look at things otherwise, to bring to bear all of the resources of the imagination, all of the senses tuned to the contradictions in the patterns of writing, the patterns of people, and the patterns of people writing about writing. It is here that teaching is poetically generative.

Balancing the aestheticism of "seeing-as," however, is the fact that teaching, like poetry, exists at the limits of thinking — that very moment when we are open to the other. The unknown is always folded within any event of learning. Poetry and teaching have in common the ethical implications of this relationship with difference. In *Vis à Vis* Don McKay talks about the "poetic attention" that precedes the poem, the humble openness to the "wilderness" of things that resists the mind's appropriations (21). Similarly, for Emmanuel Levinas it is in the act of teaching that a relationship with the infinite is apprehended. He points out in *Totality and Infinity* that "The first teaching teaches…the ethical" (171). The poem, as an object of study or as an artistic production, requires that one face the limitations of one's capacities, intellectually, temporally, and physically. This encounter with the "otherness" of the poem can, of course, provoke great anxiety when students feel an essential meaning has escaped them and they simply "do not get it." By encouraging students to employ all of their seemingly unrelated sensual and intellectual resources (the various patterns) when encountering poetry, it is incumbent upon the teacher to be open to difference. The ethics of the encounter encompasses more than simply the reader and the poem, but also the teacher and the infinite perspectives of the readers. For the teacher, as for the student, the challenge is to avoid the closed assumptions of systematic thinking, and yet engage with the text (and the class) in a meaningful way. This is the tension inherent in poetry. Even when poems ostensibly resist meaning, they nonetheless mean; yet they do so in a way that is not reducible to the logical strictures of making sense. Consider the etymological links between the words "study" and "stupefy"…the scholar and the poet are at once stupefied and engaged.

I sought to become a professor, as I mentioned, in order to integrate my creative writing career with immersion in the study of writing. The result has been that, even as I teach, I am also a perpetual student. I am a student of the texts I read, but also a student of my students. They challenge me aesthetically and ethically to respond as an artist to their imaginations and their differences, to the things they build and the ladders, mirrors, and fires they use to build. This is the generative tension from which poetry emerges and with which I am constantly testing my limits as a writer and as a teacher. The medium of teaching is other minds…the author's, the student's, or one's own conflicted readings. This is not, of course, a fully intelligible or consistent medium. The frequencies vary, the centres cannot hold. Teaching, therefore, like poetry, stands here and then stands there, but always in relation.

# WORKS CITED

Levinas, Emmanuel. *Totality and Infinity*. Translator Alphonso Lingis. Pittsburgh: Duquesne University Press, 2001. Trans. of *Totalité Et Infini*. 1969.

McKay, Don. *Vis à Vis: Fieldnotes on Poetry &Wilderness*. Wolfville, NS: Gaspereau Press, 2001.

Zwicky, Jan. *Wisdom and Metaphor*. Kentville, NS: Gaspereau Press, 2003.

# ADRIAN

Adrian is an inventor who works primarily in glass and metal, as well as any other media he can think of: dryer lint, door knobs, whatever.

## INVENTING: IN BUSINESS AND IN ART

Inventing in business: Someone presents you with a problem. You have a parameter to work with, a problem, and a time limit. I just concentrate: this is the problem, this is what I'm going to do. Everything I do is focused on that. Often I even forget to eat.

One company hired 4,000 graduate engineers every year, but it took two years to really know where they would fit in, so they wanted an instrument to get it down to six months or so. The company wanted something to recognize the leaders and followers and sub-leaders and so on.

Because of their training, their discipline, it's hard for engineers to think out of the box. Well, I created this toy, this instrument, a tactile internet. There were three groups of ten engineers, and each group got the same materials and was given a task: to create satellite cities and connect them in such a way that each city could send messages back and forth, going through a cleaner, or not going through a cleaner. As they proceeded the company could see who was taking leadership and who wasn't. It only took three months to get these people sorted out instead of two years, so the company was very happy with the instrument.

Other companies wanted similar instruments. They wanted something and I created it.

One took place during a weekend seminar and involved various games that I invented. They are like creative educational tools. They work because they're tactile, and engineers love to go there. It gets them thinking out of the box. It worked very well, and other companies wanted a similar type of thing.

I always had to join things together. Probably the first art I formed was as a child during the war. Cuttlefish and squid were washing ashore all the time, and they were broken and had been dead for a while so weren't any good to eat. We would take the cuttle-bone as the hull of the boat, and then stick in the transparent squid skeletal structures to make sails. The wind would catch them and away they'd go, nice little sailboats. All the kids did it. Well I was always using the material differently, and I was never satisfied with just using one or two sails. That was probably my first experience of artistic assembly.

My family has pictures of me in a playpen in a kind of courtyard, My basic toys were tin cans, stones, varying shapes of wood — blocks, dowels, and so on. In the baby pictures that's what I'm always doing, playing with these things.

IMAGINATION *in* ACTION

I'm still doing it. I've never stopped. Some of the materials have changed a little bit, but basically I use stone and wood and clay and steel and glass, and also charcoal for drawing material.

We had a beautiful well-head in the courtyard, like the top of a corinthian pillar. As a kid I would get hold of some colours of soft stone, like clay tile from the roof, a nice red colour, and I would get some yellows and white chalky stuff and black charcoal, and paint all the characters and designs on the coats of arms around this well-head. That was my colouring book. I always worked with things like that. I just couldn't help myself. That was what occupied me. It still does.

It's like the old cliché, necessity is the mother of invention. It happens with everything in art, because art is inventing. They call it creating, but it's really inventing.

When you're inventing you set parameters as to what you want something to do, the mechanism or the compound, whatever. You have an outline to work with, and you're working within this parameter. But with art you're being creative just for the sake of it. It has nothing to do with a problem. You may have a problem with the particular medium you're using, so then you become inventive in your creation. That's all.

If it were words you were smithing, instead of iron, you'd describe the work as cryptic, enigmatic. It's very cryptic, you know, when you create, and it just comes together. All of the sudden it has a flow, it has a step.

It starts out cryptic, extremely abstract. There's no rhyme nor reason to any of it, and then it gradually begins to take shape. It starts to flow. You can see where it's going. It takes on a life of its own.

It's always different. Every time you do something it's different.

I'm just creating art for my own satisfaction. To bend, meld metals, put different materials together, different mediums, to force mediums together that aren't normally put together in art. That's the challenge. I need to do it. It has to happen.

With metal you're working with heat ranges. With glass, you're working with heat ranges and colours, flame colours and so on. With clays it's the same thing. It's always from the forge; from the fire comes pretty well anything I make, other than ink, pencil drawings, and even with those sometimes I have this tendency to introduce them to fire if I don't like them.

With my art I never know who's going to pay me so I do it for myself. That's one of the other differences between inventing for others and creating art for yourself.

Sometimes I think I need clay and then start out and find this is all wrong. As soon as I get my hands into it I start to realize that this is not what it needs. Sometimes it needs something I don't have, and I don't know what it is. Then I have to build and destroy, build and destroy, until I find some way to express the thought.

I once envisioned a futuristic-looking giraffe in my mind, with bubbly markings. Now, when I first got the idea I wanted to start forming this thing in clay, but it just wasn't working. It wasn't doing what I wanted it to do, what I really envisioned. I eventually ended up making the giraffe out of automotive chrome. I went to a wrecking yard and took bumpers and bumperettes and large bits of chrome and just kept working with them until I had an enormous chrome-bumper giraffe. It worked. There are artists who do things like that on paper and make it look like it's chrome. There's one Japanese artist that does just unbelievable work. He makes robots, usually in the female form, but they're very metallic. Gorgeous, beautiful stuff. They look like photographs. And he can't do it on anything except paper. Apparently he has tried to sculpt it but it just doesn't work for him. He used silver polymer clays, very expensive to work with, and very toxic, but he still had no luck. It wasn't what he wanted. The only way he could capture his thoughts was on paper.

The medium isn't always what you think it's going to be. You envision a piece, something you want to create, and it almost never ends up the way you expect. It just doesn't happen.

When I sculpt clay I'm very rough with it, and then don't like to see it rough so start trying to smooth it. Then I'm in a mess and have to simplify it. My original thoughts are no longer there, so I find that I have to do it in glass or something, a whole other process.

What I've learned on my own has been the most productive. Everything that I've been taught, well, I guess it's been productive in a way, because it's been what not to do.

I've taught creative thinking. That's a different thing. I didn't teach art.

But, with teaching blacksmithing, there's such an old way. Very little has changed in the last thousand years. It's still done the same way. Now they weld with electronic welders, so that has changed. One form of joinery has changed, but that's only because of the invention of square tubing. Other than that, blacksmithing is still done the same way. It is such an old art that pretty well everything has been tried already.

I love multimedia, junk; that's one of my favourites. It could be anything, coffee cups, spools, you name it, old watch faces, junk. I call it recycled art. It really is, because all of these different things are art. Door knobs are forms of art, but then recycled into some other depiction, to become a large face, whatever.

I've used wood, clay, glass, ink on linen, ink on paper, multicolour inks, watercolours, oils, acrylics, egg tempura, chalk, pastels, grease sticks... I've even peed in the snow. I think that's more of a guy thing though. But when the snow is white and bright and crisp, if we can add a little colour to it, a design, why not?

So, anything. Textiles, cloth. Recently I happened to go into a shop where they sell skeins of wool. I couldn't get over the wild colours and materials they had there. I went crazy and bought one of these and one of those and one of those. I took this huge bag of stuff home and started snipping little bits of it. I got into doing felt pieces using carded wool and soaping it out using Murphy's Oil Soap. That's how to make felt, 100% wool felt, in different plys. Then I added some of these bits of wool to it, got different

IMAGINATION *in* ACTION

textures and rises and feelings coming out of it, putting some design into it. I had a lot of fun, but didn't really make anything with it, just flat pieces of art, I didn't make belts or purses or shirts. but you could. You could make the material large enough.

Sometimes I do a drawing on an 8 1/2" by 11", and I fill it right to the edge with ink, so it's a line drawing, and it's very very intricate, then I print it on stock, half-way between bond and card, and make envelopes out of it. I turn it so I have a lighter area for the address. I press gold letters into the envelope and then put a piece of red cel-luloid tape over top so it stands out for the postman. I stick a stamp on it, and mail a piece of art.

Dollar stores sell confetti that looks like musical notes or angels or christmas trees or wreaths, a dollar for a whole bag, so why not use it? I can't be there at their party to throw confetti, so make a little card for an occasion, whatever it may be. I booby-trap it with a paper clip, an elastic and confetti, so as soon as they open it confetti flies out. To me it's fun. I don't know whether the people receiving it find it so much fun because they have to clean up the mess. I can only do it once though. After that, they open their mail very gingerly over the wastepaper basket.

Once, for someone who was into angels, I got a punch-out stamp and punched out thousands of angels in different colours. They opened it in the summertime when the fan was on, and the angels became airborne and filled the house. They told me that they were seeing these angels for over a year in their house. Damned angels, I think they called them.

Things like that have always been of interest to me, to do something that's differ-ent. I can't make something the same all the time. I just cannot do it.

Once I worked in my cousin's glass factory. My job there was polishing the break, where they break off the piece, putting it in the annealing oven, sandblasting the logo on the bottom, stuff like that, very menial-type work, but in my spare time, in the evenings, as long as the artists were still working I could take my chances and do what-ever. So I learned how to pull and play with the glass. I made a dixieland band there, a six-piece band in all different colours, one-foot-tall figures, with striped jackets and straw hats and big shoes. They worked out very well.

I took courses, but they never taught me what those artists taught me, and I learned so much by error on my own. I learned what not to do. I learned a lot of what not to do.

Sometimes I look at other artist's work and I see aspects I would like to use, not all of it, just certain aspects. Then I'll see someone else's and I'll combine some bor-rowed highlights and adapt them into something else, my own thing, in a different medium with a different focus.

Once I saw a painting done with strips of wood, stained snow-fence pieces. You see art like this at the seaside, a marquetry sort of thing. Well, I saw a basic idea that looked good. There was a moon looking like a galleon travelling behind the trees. It was just these flat sticks, straight-looking, more like cacti than trees, and I thought that's great. So what I did, I stretched out a big piece of canvas. First I put a moon on the canvas. I took a large piece of plastic doily, those plastic doilies that look like filigree, and cut a chunk out of it so it was off-set, and then I put a yellow piece of cloth over it so some of this doily telecast through, and then I stapled it on the canvas using gold staples. Then I took bark from different-coloured dogwood trees, some reds and yellows and greens, and sewed it into the canvas like the bark of trees, so they looked more like trees, superimposed on this moon. So I borrowed the basic idea but it's totally different. I liked the whole idea of the movement of the moon. You could almost see it moving through the trees, and I tried to create the same idea and it worked. I actually used a needle and wool. I made wooden needles, and ran into all kinds of problems, a medium I never tried before, but I figured it out and it worked. I used beeswax to seal up all the holes. Things were starting to unravel on me, but you work with it, you get there. It's fun. And once you're done it someone says, "Oh I would really like one of those," but there's only that one and there won't be any more. They're a true one of a kind. I don't make two of the same thing.

Some artists seem to produce painting after painting, but something's always different. Changes are always made.

Well, with iron I do that, variations. I do mokami, a Japanese art which uses dissimilar metals. Making little vessels, vases, things like that. You bring up the colours of the metals. You make some coppers truly red, and make really yellow brasses. You put them together in a forge, forge-weld them together, and then you twist, mutilate, whatever, until you have a pattern that you want. Then you expand, roll the pattern around to the shape you want. So all of a sudden this vase looks like a checker-board. All these little dissimilar metals have come together. That's what mokami is. You do these layers, then you fold them, so you end up with more layers, then you may twist it, hammer it flat again, fold it. All different metals, and you put them together in one billet and you keep working the billet until you have the pattern and shape you want. In mokami you're never going to make another one the same. You can have a similar pattern, similar colours, but it would not be the same, ever. It's impossible, because every hammer blow is changing it, and, as good as you can get with a hammer, the blows are never the same.

I don't do something twice, even if I really like it. Once I've done something that I'm satisfied with that's all that I need. That's it. I move on to something else.

# ALLAN and HOLLY BRIESMASTER

Allan Briesmaster is a freelance editor, micro publisher (www.aeo-lushouse.com), and literary consultant specializing in poetry and non-fiction. He has a PhD in English from the University of Toronto and taught briefly but left academia for a career in I.T. which lasted until 2005. He was centrally involved in the weekly Art Bar Poetry Reading Series from 1991 until 2002, and since January, 2006 has been one of the organizers of the popular monthly reading series, Toronto WordStage. As an editor, Allan has been instrumental in the production of over forty books from a number of literary presses, including watershedBooks (1997-2000) and Seraphim Editions (from 2000 on). He is the author of nine books of poetry, including *Galactic Music* (Lyricalmyrical Press, 2005), *The Other Seasons* (Hidden Brook Press, 2006), and *Interstellar* (Quattro Books, 2007). His poetry has appeared in many anthologies, and he has given numerous readings, in venues from Victoria to Halifax. He lives in Thornhill, Ontario with his wife Holly, a visual artist.

Holly Briesmaster was born in Toronto and received a BA in Fine Art from the University of Toronto. Afterward, she was a tour guide for the Art Gallery of Ontario and spent a year studying at the University of Leiden, Holland. She has exhibited her watercolour landscapes and collages in many group and juried shows (Toronto Outdoor Art Exhibition, Art Gallery of Mississauga, Art Gallery of Peel in Brampton), and has had several solo and duo shows in recent years: at the Illuminary Art Gallery in Toronto, at the McKay Art Centre in Unionville, and at Pteros Gallery and Gallery Hittite in Toronto. The shows at the latter two galleries involved Holly's paintings in acrylic on large folding paper fans of various sizes — a new and unexpected development. For several years Holly has also collaborated with her husband Allan on several books featuring her pen-and-ink drawings and collages together with his poems, and she has provided the cover art for a number of other works of poetry and fiction.

## GALACTIC MUSIC: A COLLABORATION IN POETRY AND ART

Our work in visual art and poetry has always had deep affinities, and we have been collaborating in image-text projects since 1999. We are both interested in the landscape, with ecological concerns; and we share a fascination with astronomy and cosmology. In style, we both favour relative density, complexity, and richness of texture; and while we like to appeal to the senses, we prefer taking an expressive rather than a literal approach. Having worked together in the summer of 2004 on texts and art relating to landscapes in walking distance of our Thornhill, ON home — most of which were sketched on-site — we were ready for a radically different project when our friend and publisher Luciano Iacobelli approached us with an intriguing idea.

Under the Lyricalmyrical imprint, Luciano had been producing hand-made hard-cover books in limited editions. *Urban-Pastoral*, the book we created for his press that same year (2004), was very well received and went into a fourth printing. We were grateful to be allowed the scope to bring together poems and artwork of widely different forms and styles. Those were enlisted in conveying our sense of an inextricable overlap: the sphere of woods and fields encroached on by grids of suburban development, all the while green space and wildlife still persist in the hearts of Canadian cities. Holly's pen-and-ink drawings and collages for that book covered the spectrum of abstract and representational, and my poems did something similar: interspersing the non-objective (or metaphorical) and the imagistic. What was especially exciting about the new project was the publisher's invitation to explore, not the typical dimensions of a poetry book, but an 8 ½" x 11" format.

For a poet who has many texts fifty to sixty lines long, the possibility of placing such poems on single pages without overflow had obvious appeal, as did the extra width. I took fullest advantage of this with the poem "Earth Two and the Nature of May," which consists of thirteen-syllable lines stretched comfortably, without wrap-arounds, onto three whole pages. For Holly, these larger dimensions permitted the creation of work that did not need to be shrunken down much or at all from its original size, as was often the case in our previous book, *Pomona Summer*. The roomier size also encouraged us to extend our practice of sometimes juxtaposing a very small piece of text with a much larger art image, and vice versa. Thus, for example, I could write nine- or eleven-line poems and anticipate an eye-pleasing accompaniment, and know that a poem spilling over onto two-thirds of a second, facing page would be sure to have a small-scale image to cap it. In any case, the varying shapes of the poems, and of the images that could potentially go with them, held out many possibilities.

Best of all about Luciano's invitation was the free rein given. What a great thing for a writer and an artist — to have a publisher who understands what they are all about! We likewise left each other almost unlimited scope. No restrictions or definite expectations came into play when we began, and we proceeded independently until near the end. As with *Urban-Pastoral,* we had the basic confidence derived from knowing that this book-to-be, whose working title became *Galactic Music*, had a theme in which both of us had a long-standing keen interest. And, too, some of the poems that would go in the book had already been written. In previous books the same was true of some of the artwork, though not this time. There was one entirely new and exciting direction now. For some months we had regularly been visiting the NASA website to view the latest findings from the two robot vehicles that were exploring Mars, plus the latest from the Cassini probe orbiting Saturn. (Both of these had already made brief appearances in my poem "Interplanetary" in *Urban-Pastoral*.) We were also checking the images from the Spitzer Space Telescope. These showed strange, enormous phenomena never before detected, surrounding the birth and death of stars, sometimes written up with extraordinarily poetic phrases.

There was a lot more, of course, to our conception of this cosmologically-oriented book. We felt an equal but not ultimately unrelated pull in directions opposite to the immense starry spaces. We were drawn in particular to earthboundness, both in the sense of human limits and as regards our affectionate bonds to this planet: even while envisaging connections with things far beyond. (One example: the theory that earth and everyone on it is made of the stuff of exploded stars.) Neither of us intended to mime astronomical images which are often enhanced with "false colour" and always come synthesized. Not any more than we meant to simulate what had best be archived on the Web or might go in a textbook. My poems do sample an assortment of scientific terms — ones which can be deliciously odd, and evocative — and they do borrow some of the startling metaphors science writers have used ("a stellar nursery," "methane rain"), but they don't take them straight. They tend to temper a rapt wonderment at the cosmos with scepticism about the human part in it all.

The artwork, meanwhile, makes no attempt to mirror the planetscapes and nebulae; and in some instances it is the "raw images," which include static and the empty slats where transmitted data went missing, that are referenced. The collages, in particular, utilize a splicing that recalls the incomplete, broken images that first arrived from Mars and Titan: with some portions left blank. Along with this, there is a suggestion of a lay person's inquisitive awareness grappling with, and transposing in its own terms, the *feel* of an often bizarre lore.

In a somewhat similar vein, the poetry, although word-processed very soon after a first draft in pen on paper, resorts at times to traditional forms and metres. But then, there are also four "found poems" whose wording was selectively cut and pasted from the Spitzer website. Then, as well, because these other things, too, are cosmic, there are poems about the mortal body, music, the coming of night, and the afterlife of names. Some of this latter group originated, not from extraterrestrial sources, but as homages and rejoinders to work by other expansive-minded poets who have, in different ways, excited my awe. The accompanying artwork has a less literal interaction with these pages, and did additional service in simply separating relatively dissimilar poems.

What was generated in both media had, in fact, no conscious plan behind it. Sometimes images, either from astronomy sources or from the mind's eye, and sometimes words, were the poetic jumping-off points. Occasionally a title like "Winds of Neptune" would of its own accord set things in motion. It so happened that no poem originated as a direct response to any of the artwork. Still, I did see each piece as soon as it was completed, and subliminal influences undoubtedly came into play. The art-work, on the other hand, was sometimes triggered by a specific phrase or image in a poem. However, every piece of work in both media was conceived as, and remains, an independent creation able to speak for itself, unsupported.

The principal area of direct collaboration in all our books *is* the fitting of poems and art on the pages. Such ordering and placement occurs only in the final weeks of the project, and here the larger creative process truly culminates. We often make some surprising discoveries: of parallels and connections not noticed before. This phase does not even begin until we are close to having produced the totality of work intended: in this case, about twenty images, and enough poems to occupy some twenty pages. It has been my experience, whenever I have nearly completed a manuscript, that a few gaps inevitably emerge which need to be filled. For instance, I'll see that two distantly-related poems could benefit from having a third poem between them, which would act as a bridge. Or, the posturing of one atypical poem will suit a book better if a new poem can offer a counter-stance. A late spurt invariably ensues with the artwork as well. Some of the strongest results each of us achieves come about in the home stretch because by then we have gained a grasp of the whole. Thus we keep open to possibilities up to the end.

Another influence on the final phase of construction is a desire to vary and distribute the images throughout the book, while ensuring that their dialogue with the texts happens optimally on page after page. Texts and images alike should also give the reader the sense of a subtle progression, even a journey of sorts. This may not have a precise beginning and end, conceptually speaking, or any narrative thread, yet we do want a certain flow and momentum. In my own sequencing I interleave short gnomic and lyrical pieces with more discursive, reflective ones, and might follow something fairly lofty with something tongue-in-cheek. I'll place a sonnet or other constraint-based poem next to one that's free-form. Similarly, some of Holly's images are recognizably rocks and hills and watercourses, while others are entirely abstract yet may nonetheless suggest various forms of "celestial mechanics."

The writing and art which both of us gravitate toward is of a kind that, in an exuberant, playful way, gives off energy. Or so we believe. Feeling fully, and drawing on, the energy of creation, enables the collaborative making of a book like *Galactic Music* to be a process having a life of its own. For the most part our sense of this process was of something thoroughly intuitive, and incalculable, and we would not have wanted it any other way. It has been like that from the onset of our first seven-year cycle: joining forces with new ideas, never knowing quite what to expect, beyond surprise.

The following poem from the book, which is adapted from the German of Rilke, can stand as an analogy for Holly's and my artistic outlook, both independently and together:

## Only,

       not to stay blocked-off,
not be cut by the trivial wall
from the measure of stars...

What innerness? except
a lofted sky, the moved heaven
birds plunge through:
                      deepened
with the clear, homing gusts.

# ANTANAS SILEIKA

Antanas Sileika's most recent novel is *Woman in Bronze*. He is also artistic director of the Humber School for Writers.

## CREATIVITY DEMYSTIFIED

When I was asked to write about creativity, my answer was short: "I don't believe in creativity. I believe in work."

But there's more to it than that, and all sorts of oddities about creativity in writing.

The first oddity is that my most creative writing, arguably, is the work I do for freelance jobs, often magazine work or "hack" work. Someone calls me on the phone and says, "Can you write a thousand words on the subject of neighbourhoods in light of a recent murder of one neighbour by another? We need it in eight hours."

Can I? Just watch me. My creativity has been spurred.

Four hundred funny words on the hibachi in thirty-six hours? No problem. I can have it in four.

One morning I discovered my son had backed into someone else's car ($850) and I needed special, orthopedic shoes ($350). That afternoon, I was offered a job to write about dogs at summer cottages for *Cottage Life*. I don't even like people who fawn on their dogs, but I needed the money, found a way to do the job, and managed to pick up a silver National Magazine Award for my part of the work. And I had a lot of fun doing it. So much so, that I delight in any call from *Cottage Life*.

Fun is important.

The ability to write "instantly" on a subject, otherwise known as occasional writing, has never been valued all that much, and I don't value it as much as my fiction. But for a non-sportsman with very little competitive sense to him, I find these offers a delicious challenge, a glove thrown down to my intellect and wit. Because the stakes are relatively low, I take delight in this kind of work and can do it fast and unselfconsciously.

This is the sort of creativity that is really mysterious to me, but it is not the sort of creativity that interests most writers.

Creativity in fiction is far more fraught both for me and most of the people I know, largely because one writes from nothing when one writes a story or a novel. There is no occasion, no editor, and no assignment. No one hands you a theme. Unless you have a reputation, no one phones, asking for a piece of fiction, and even if someone does, it is often part of an open call, a brutal invitation for you to audition as if you were just starting out.

I was once on a TV show, in the unenviable position of defending the superiority of fiction over non-fiction against Charlotte Gray, a wonderful non-fiction writer, one of the best. As I groped to find an argument, I said that a non-fiction writer is like a tailor. He makes a suit to fit the man. The fiction writer must not only create the suit, he must also create the man. That's harder.

How does one create a novel or a story from nothing? My reflex is still to say it is all work, but that work, or "creative process" to use a phrase I can barely stand (for its pretentiousness, its bureaucratic/psychological pseudo-scientific ring) can be broken down into at least four steps: watching, reflecting, writing, and editing.

The first step to being a writer is simply watching. The writer is a voyeur, more interested in observing than acting unselfconsciously. That's worth a little thought in itself, but it's a theme not germane to the rest of this essay. It's amazing what you see if you just pay attention, both with your eyes and your ears. Lenin once said, memorably, that power was lying in streets, waiting for someone to pick it up. The same can be said of characters and stories. They are all around us, all the time. Pay attention. Say to yourself, as Christopher Isherwood did in the title of his collection of stories, "I am a camera."

Gifts of scenes, characters, and stories are lying about us. Pick them up by noticing them.

I was once filmed for a spot on ethnic television in a ludicrously overwrought, almost feverish session that lasted two hours. What saved me from exploding with frustration at all the fuss was the knowledge that I could *use* these characters, ones who needed to act more like TV producers than CBC producers because they had to make up for the smallness of their market. I would get revenge on them in print. (The value of revenge as a motive for writing has been much understated.) The scene "happened" to me. I just needed to notice it.

Here's another example. I share cigarettes with a colleague who is a lesbian comic. In telling me of her world, she once described a comedy club scene in which she was trying to impress another, important comic, while all she really wanted was to jump into a metaphorical mosh pit with the twelve-member lesbian hockey team which had cheered her on from the audience. This is a world I ordinarily have no access to, and I stored the lesbian hockey team for future use. What fun I will have with that once I find a place for it in my fiction.

Yet another example. My late mother once took a pensioners' bus tour to Maine. At the motel the first night, one of the pensioners spied a discount liquor store on the other side of the four-lane highway. Always eager for a deal, these pensioners wanted to get there, but how to do it when the youngest was seventy-five and the oldest ninety? They paired up, one young pensioner to one old pensioner, and hobbled across the highway in couples as the others stood around, keeping watch and cheering them on.

Pure narrative gold.

When you are watching, you also need to observe small tics that are useful in describing characters — the smile that rises so high up the gums it looks grotesque, the boss who will only drink coffee less than twenty minutes old, the colleague who is so insanely generous, he will buy for himself a cordless circular saw in case you might ever want to borrow it. These are the oddities of taste and expression that go into fictional characters, and we can see samples of them all around us if we just look carefully, practising mindful watching of the world around us.

Watch your past as well. Think back on your childhood. Try to remember the taste of the air on a spring morning in the country / suburbs / city. Remember the lady who called you a low-class immigrant, and picture the worn housecoat she was wearing that made her words less an attack on you than a defense of that worn piece of clothing. Feel the itchy wool of the scarf on your neck, taste the sandwich spread with pork drippings and both imagine why it tasted so good then and why it would taste so repulsive now. Your past needs to be watched, not as a repository of facts, but as a repository of sensations and feelings.

It might be worth mentioning here that your job in watching is not necessarily to report directly on the world you see. Your responsibility as a fiction writer is to breathe life into a piece of writing, and straight delivery of an anecdote is rarely enough, a straight sketch of a funny character is rarely sufficient. You will need to recombine what you see into some sort of artistic whole, which will have its own demands. But if you watch carefully all the time, you will collect bits of Lego. How you assemble them will be up to you.

The second step, after watching, is reflecting. It comes, though, almost at the same time as writing, because it is hard to reflect on nothing. I'll often start a novel, getting down a few pages, and then sit on it for weeks, going back to it every few days to keep the mulling refreshed.

Since I have so little time in life, with a family, a day job, and freelance work in print and broadcast, I can not afford to reflect at the writing desk. That place is reserved for tapping on keys.

Actually, I do stare out the window a lot when I should be tapping away, but I do most of my thinking, my reflecting, my mulling, while I am doing something else. Driving the car is good for this. Keep the radio off, and see what your mind starts to do. Doris Lessing once said we need to be slightly bored to write, so get yourself slightly bored. Wash dishes, peel potatoes, fiddle around on a musical keyboard, go for long walks (or even short ones), make risotto, pies, stuffed red peppers, cabbage rolls, puff pastry, beef stock, cassoulet. Sand a canoe. Make a quilt. Go fishing.

The two enemies of mulling, in my case, are television and music. I can not afford to watch television any more. If someone tells you the Sopranos are great, wait until you can rent the series on DVD. Take off the ipod headphones. Unless you do all your work to music, it will fill up the space reserved for reflection. Ride the bus and sub-

IMAGINATION *in* ACTION

way without book or magazine. Not only will you see things, you'll reflect on things you have seen. Get slightly bored.

One must mull and write at the same time, but the hardest mulling is at the beginning, the idea for the story or novel, and the fleshing out of the details. I can not help you with this. I wrote my first published novel because I used to daydream about a polar bear in the vicinity of a beach umbrella, and needed to explain to myself how they got into the same scene. I don't know where that scene came from or why it need to be purged by writing a novel.

Writing is work, and I deal with work this way: try to do the hardest thing first to get it out of the way. When I have writing times, fixed ones in the week, I go to them and refuse myself the pleasure of e-mail or the newspaper until I have 800 words or so. (600 words are acceptable; 400 OK; 200? At least it's something; 1,500? A banner day — break open the champagne!) Even with only three writing slots a week, I can still get a first draft of a novel written in one year at this rate.

The regularity of the writing helps the reflecting, because one feeds off the other. If you write often enough, you keep thinking about your work as you are doing other things. I hate to take two weeks off for a bout of concerted writing because I find it too hard. I can usually get 800 words down in about three hours. After that, I want to play. My one experience at a writers' retreat found me watching films every afternoon, taking over dessert production from the chef in the evening, and drinking far too much each night. Give me a day job with a couple of hours free in the morning and on weekends, and I'm chugging along happily. Make me write all day long and I become self-absorbed and grumpy.

Writing a first draft is the hardest part of all for me. Getting those words down, even when I know what they should be, is hard labour. I've been putting off this essay for weeks. I had it framed in my mind at least twelve days ago. I could have found the time, but I put it off because it was so hard. In other words, I can give advice, but sometimes I don't follow it. I'm human, and I forgive myself. Forgive yourself as well if your creativity is not quite up to *Wuthering Heights* standards today. Maybe it will be tomorrow.

Of all the writing-related jobs, I find editing the most fun. Once I have finished a story or a novel and then come back to it, I see what's wrong with it all too clearly. Whole chapters must be cut or reorganized. Phrases are wrong, wrong, wrong. Darlings need to be killed. This job is easiest for me with small pieces: stories or magazine work; pieces that can be read at one sitting are usually improved if I reread them and rewrite them twenty times (over twenty days) before I hand them in.

Novels are too big for this, and they are therefore harder. My hardest editing job was fourteen major rewrites of a novel that started out at over two hundred thousand words. In that case, I had the help of an editor who was very tough indeed. We argued over five phone calls concerning one apostrophe, and not about its grammatical correctness. We had differences of opinion about connotation.

If you are lucky enough to have an editor, treat him or her as an angel. If you wrestle with angels, your literary value rises. Put another way, an editor is like a physiotherapist, the one who makes you do what you did not want to do, and gives you literary abs that will be the envy of the hacks.

"Creativity" as a concept is a whore — it attaches itself to every activity to give it panache, to give it status. I am far fonder of craft, which is less pretentious. I do not deny the mystical aspect of writing, but I can't know it because it lies in the realm of the unknowable, along with God and life after death.

I prefer to think of my work the way Dylan Thomas did, as "My craft and sullen art." And for me, my work often is "sullen." Creativity implies joy and freedom, but the experience of writing has more to do with concentration, and turning a sullen face to the distractions of the world, which interfere with that concentration.

Let the advertising executives and salesmen be creative. I think of a book as something like a box, and I like to think *inside* that box.

The muses visit far too infrequently for me to bother invoking them all the time. I'm too busy working, though I always do it with sensitivity to the breath of creation that sometimes stirs my pages.

IMAGINATION *in* ACTION

# bill bissett

originalee from lunaria a far distant galaxee    sent to erth on frst childrns shut-
tel from that goldn planet thru halifax    travl a lot on erth dewing reedings &
art shows    usd 2 hope 2 undrstand erthling wayze    now seems less likelee
most recent cd    *deth interrupts th dansing/a strangr space*    with pete dako
from red deer press    most recent book *this is erth thees ar peopul*    from
talon books

## painting n writing  sirka 2006

i create art n poetree bcoz eye cudint danse aftr having manee operaysyuns n 2 make
up 4 that loss    th gain uv writing n painting needs 2 aktivate as oftn as possibul    n
bcoz i delite in dewing n need 2    2 feel komfortablee alive    fullee reel    n responding

    i can write in th midst uv events n such happning    on a street car wher i wrote
recentlee    *xtreem blu balls*    n it developd furthr with composr pete dako    with whom
i rekordid it whn i got 2 th studio    i can write on planes wher i wrote a lot uv *lunaria*

    whn i paint tho    not drawings    wch i can dew almost aneewher 4 me    is whn ium
by myself    usualee late at nite    whn iuv dun all or most uv th langwage things    soshul
skills    if i have lernd anee    n papr work iuv renamed papr play    all that    n ium in th
world uv colour n line    fluiditee composisyun    n th danse uv th strokes on th canvas
painting is not langwage based    n most likelee preseedid words n may b th basis uv let-
trs n words    its xciting 2 see th picktographik resonans in langwage

    painting is not 4 me sew soshulee based    painting late at nite is veree physikul    n
like a bit swimming    is wher i get 2 b part uv th kniting 2gethr uv all th places in uv
me    motor fakulteez    painting is    can b    veree physikul    eyez    breth    mind    spirit    th sunshine cumming out in all our levls    evn legs n chest ar involvd in painting
yes    i bcum whol 4 that time at leest

    sew i dew go abt painting n writing quite diffrentlee nor dew they reelee kontain
th same subjekt mattr    subjekt mattrs    if th idea that cums 2 me    is inside langwage i
write    if its not    i paint    its kind uv like that    n uv kours image n word ar intrtwind
in th wiring    yet if th painting is going well it reelee feels outside uv langwage

    th choices i make in both disciplines    writing n painting    ar mor instinktiv    built
on xperiens n nu ness    th touches    th nuanse    th main bodee    ornamentaysyun    trope
in th writing wch may b sirtinlee based mor on ideaz n word konsciousness    n paintings based on kolour    form    n strokes    th mewsik n dans uv    line    n    images

    all ths is how it kurrentlee is    sirka 2006    uv kours it will change    tho its bin
wher th fire is    thees wayze    4 quite a whil

# DAVID LIVINGSTONE CLINK

David Clink was born in Medicine Hat, Alberta, and grew up in West Hartford, Connecticut, and Toronto, Ontario. He is the webmaster of poetry-machine.com, a resource for poets. He is a past Artistic Director of the Art Bar Poetry Series. He is the author of five poetry chapbooks, including *One Dozen*, published in May 2007. David's poetry has appeared recently in *The Antigonish Review*, *Asimov's Science Fiction*, *The Dalhousie Review*, *The Fiddlehead*, *Grain*, and *The Literary Review of Canada*. He has a poetry collection forthcoming from Tightrope Books in 2008.

## THE MECHANICS OF CREATION

After the number of poetry readings I have attended, and given, I sometimes think the act of creation should be left to a higher power. But sometimes one can go to a reading and be mesmerized, or one can produce something that is memorable and original, that says something in a way that has not been done before, and it is for these moments that I live for poetry. This essay is supposed to be about creativity: how one creates, why one creates, where one gets ideas from, and it is also supposed to compare and contrast the different approaches to the creative process when employing different art forms. Since I am a poet first and foremost, I will wax poetic first.

### 1. How I Create (the poetry perspective)

When it comes to poetry, most of my writing is done on the bus or subway. I get an idea and I write it down. This leads to other lines and I write these all out in longhand, on a letter-sized yellow figuring pad that I liberated from the storage cabinet in the library where I work. The pad has green lines that are 5/16" apart. I use a pen, not a pencil.

I use the margins of the page, if necessary. (It always seems necessary.) I keep this copy with me, and work on it for the next few days or longer, editing, adding and subtracting until I can't do any more or I am in danger of not being able to read my own scribble. The page looks like someone ate alphabet cereal, including the punctuation and proofreading symbols, and then upchucked on the page. It's not pretty; it looks like garbage I could sell to a museum of modern art for a hefty sum, pun intended.

At this point I'll either have to hire an exorcist, or I'll write out a fresh copy, on a figuring pad, in block letters, as clearly as I can, a version of the poem that includes all the changes. I work on this copy for a number of days or more, making many editorial changes until the page is either a ruddy mess, or I can't think of any more changes to make.

For the first time I enter the poem on the computer. I print it out in Garamond 14 or 16 or 18 pt., because the font is easier to read, usually with a line-spacing of 1.5 or 2. I will, again, make changes to this version, over a week or several weeks, doing the whole editing thing, and I may do this step one more time. Note: I rarely compose poems on the computer. I do edit on the computer when preparing poems to send out to a market. I also prepare larger font printouts for when I do readings, or when I want to workshop a poem. I usually work on several poems at once.

At a certain point, when I think the poem is pretty much done, (what poem is really done?) I will workshop it. I belong to three writing workshops and a reading circle. Getting feedback from people you respect is a great way to improve your poetry; other people will have different perspectives about what works and what doesn't. I don't make changes to a poem unless I think the suggestion improves the poem. Sometimes a workshop will homogenize a poem, getting rid of all its rough edges. There is a middle-of-the-road thing that happens, so be aware of this, and make sure the heart of the poem remains intact.

At most workshops the poet reads their poem aloud. You can catch some things at this stage — better to catch them then than on the stage! It is the easiest way to know if something flags or is weak, or tripping on the tongue. Trust your own judgment. When you read a poem aloud in front of a crowd, you can tell, based on your own impatience with it, and the stinking feeling you get when you want to crawl under a goose turd and wish the pain would end, that the poem is too long, that all the exposition at the beginning and/or middle was not necessary. They were necessary when you first wrote the piece, but they did their work. Usually the tendency to go on too long affects beginning writers more than a writer who has been around the writer's block a few times. For me, poetry is about getting to the heat of an emotion, feeling, moment, mood, idea, and if a line does not serve that purpose, it must go.

2. Why I create (three reasons, two of which are true)

    1. I create because Yahtzee and Projectile Vomit belong on the same line.
    2. I write poetry to meet women.
    3. I began writing poetry in a dedicated fashion when my sister, Carolyn, invited me to join the Algonquin Square Table Poetry Workshop in November 1995. Since then I have tried to improve my writing and to use poetry as an outlet for my creative expression. I want to get what is in my head down on the page, without losing anything. I think I am successful one in every twenty poems or so.

## 3. Where ideas come from (eight places)

People rarely ask (thank God), "Where do you get your ideas from?" Here are a few places where ideas come from. You may want to check these out:

1. Inside gum that does not stick to most dental work.
2. In and around ant farms.
3. On the surface of lemon drops and at the base of chimney tops.
4. Beside the shadows of ice sculptures.
5. Underneath dirty clothing collecting in stinky hampers.
6. Inside food that contains MSG.
7. In places where you find cream-coloured ponies and warm woolen mittens.
8. Beneath the retinas of eagles that have had their vision corrected through a technology reverse-engineered from a possible future.

In summary, ideas come from all sorts of places. Recently I wrote a poem when I was heading home on the bus about a man I saw vacuuming a carpet in an office building. When I was writing, I thought, what is his story? Does he talk to the security guard? What if he doesn't work there, what if he breaks in, tries to blend in? What if he dons the uniform of a cleaner, and vacuums, and he doesn't steal anything? What if he has an obsessive compulsive disorder to clean other places, but has no energy afterwards, so his own place starts to turn to rat shit? This is the idea I had and I turned this into a prose poem titled: "Clean." I later added a second stanza that has him get caught, and the people that ended up catching him wondering why he did this.

## 4. Seven exercises to aid in the act of creation

Here are a few exercises/suggestions that may help you with your ability to write new, interesting and original poems. (They may also help you write uninspired, derivative poems, so watch out!)

1. I write down ideas, phrases, thoughts on scraps of paper, most of which are disconnected, and write a poem that combines a number of these. The result is usually something that you would not have come up with if you started with a blank piece of paper, usually something very inventive, and unusual. I wrote a piece in January 2002, which combined a bunch of these, titled: "My Latest Poem." I was doing this to see if I could get a good poem out of it, and, in all modesty, without beating around the bush, I can proudly say: "Mission accomplished."

2. I have taken a whack of poems that are so bad a fifteen-year-old performance poet with acne would disown them, and I excised the best one or two lines from each

poem, and created a poem from them, titled: "Beyond the Eastern Edges of the World." This worked out well.

3. *The Practice of Poetry: Writing Exercises from Poets Who Teach*, (Harper Collins) by Robin Behn and Chase Twitchell has a number of exercises. I recommend picking up a copy and trying some! I used an exercise by Jim Simmerman to write a poem titled: "Black Sun."

4. Take paid workshops where an instructor gets you to write. For example, Stuart Ross has an all-day workshop called a "poetry boot camp," that he does once or twice a year, and is taught usually in downtown Toronto just above This Ain't the Rosedale Library. Find a workshop in your area and try it out!

5. Two words: Poetry Magnets.

6. Try writing in one of the poetic forms you have not tried. Some examples of poetic forms include villanelle, glossa, pantoum, sestina, prose poem, ghazal, and sonnet. There are books available that go into detail about the various poetic forms.

7. Become a member of a poetry workshop or circle that meets regularly. You may find yourself composing a poem the night before or the morning of, but at least you wrote a poem! There is nothing like a deadline to compel one to action.

## 5. Different approaches, different art forms

Part of the purpose of this essay is to compare the creative process to more than one artistic form, and there are other things I have done in an artistic manner that may have some relevance. I am the webmaster of poetrymachine.com, a resource for poets. I was the Artistic Director of the Art Bar Poetry Series for three years, ending in June 2005. I run a cheese-doodle contest at Eeriecon, a convention held annually in the spring in Niagara Falls (on the American side). I am co-publisher of "believe your own press," a poetry chapbook publisher. All of these endeavors require different acts of creation. As with all of these, there is a framework that one has for artistic expression, like the proverbial artist that begins with a blank canvas, or the proverbial writer who starts with a blank page.

When taking on a creative process, you may want to ask, "Is there a framework?" If yes, what is it, and do you have to strictly follow it? Is there wiggle room, and more importantly, do you want to wiggle? And, why are there always questions? The framework for the Art Bar Poetry Series is that there are three features every week, along with the occasional theme nights. I organized an annual theme night called "The Dead Poets Society Night" where a group of poets each read for five or six minutes from a dead poet. I also organized an "Art Bar Poetry Idol," and asked Paul Vermeersch and Sandra Kasturi to host it with me, where we listened to the work of poets and gave constructive criticism. Even given a framework, given bounds or limitations, one can be creative within these limits. The cheese-doodle sculptures turned into a contest, with themes, and prizes for the winner. With the press, Myna Wallin and I choose who we want to publish; we also edit chapbooks, and invite guest editors as well. We have tried different formats; for example, not a standard 8½" x 11" folded sheet, which makes chapbooks the standard size of 8½" x 5 1/2", but ones that are square, and taller, thinner ones. We work with Carleton Wilson, who has designed the books for us through Junction Design and Typography (www.junctionbooks.com).

The creative process is hindered/helped by things that take you away from your creative writing, things like writing grant applications, organizing events, readings. The business side of writing can get in the way of writing as well. In starting "believe your own press," we got a master business licence from the Ontario Government, allowing us to open a business bank account, and be able to deposit cheques made out to "believe your own press." With poetrymachine.com, I had to get the domain name, and register the site, and design the site, and work on the content. Grant-writing itself is a lot of work, and doing this for a series requires financial statements, and an accounting of the previous year's work, and plans for the future.

In conclusion, it is not necessary to know the mechanics of creation to create, but every little bit helps. Don't let too many things get in the way of your reading and writing time, or whatever it is you do to help you create. Keep at it, and I wish you success with your creations.

# DAVID LEE

After graduating from UBC, David Lee lived in Toronto for fourteen years, where he became known as a double bassist and cellist, working with artists as diverse as playwright Eugene Stickland, choreographer Robert Desrosiers, and poets Steve McCaffery and Paul Dutton. He also toured and recorded with the well-known improvising group The Bill Smith Ensemble, worked for the jazz magazine *Coda* and, with his wife Maureen Cochrane, ran the publishing house Nightwood Editions. Moving back to the west coast he played in community bands, co-founded the Pender Harbour Jazz Festival, wrote a Vancouver Island guidebook and co-authored the autobiography of jazz pianist Paul Bley. After receiving his MA in Music Criticism from McMaster University, he wrote *The Battle of the Five Spot: Ornette Coleman and the New York Jazz Field* (The Mercury Press 2006) and *Chainsaws: A History* (Harbour Publishing 2006). David currently lives with his family in Hamilton, Ontario.

## HATRED, PROCRASTINATION, ACCEPTANCE

One thing I hated about writing this essay was the ridiculous level of anxiety and convolutedness that, with no good reason, I brought to writing it. After weeks toying with good intentions, running into dead ends and copying out lengthy quotes from better writers, the best thing I came up with was an ironic, even self-defeating epigraph: "Creativity is ten percent inspiration and ninety percent procrastination."

Finally, I made it work for me. From the start I wanted to show the ways that improvisation, as I have learned about it in music, works in writing, and by extension works in all our daily actions. One good thing about procrastination is that, providing you haven't given up altogether, it can get you into a state where you're open to whatever influences might help you get the job done. For example: a dozen or so rotten drafts into this essay, given a rare hour with the house to myself, instead of sitting down at the keyboard I sank into the couch with some food and turned on the TV. There, purely by chance, was composer/saxophonist Benny Golson defining for a PBS interviewer the two ingredients necessary to create jazz music.

Creativity and imagination, Golson said and my first reaction was, aren't those the same thing? But Golson was speaking of the tradition in which a jazz artist begins with a theme and improvises more music based on that theme. Building something new from given material is an imaginative process and in this case, if the music is judged to be "original" — if it sounds distinctly different from what other players might build from the same material — then it is also a creative process.

If creativity is imagination in action, the most rewarding art can be that which calls upon — even demands — the creative input of its audience, be it Rorschachian connections elicited by an abstract painting or the effect of rhythm in the spoken word or written text, layering the work with feelings that might be quite different from the "meanings" of the words.

In improvised music we have "erasure phrases." In the course of an improvisation one can arrive too soon at the fulfillment of an idea, or run out of ideas completely. That can be the time to insert an "erasure phrase" — several bars of sudden, possibly atonal, musical non-sequitur to fill in the time before some more good ideas arrive. There may be no "logical" connection between the preceding music, the erasure phrase, and the music that follows, but creativity and imagination are of course not confined to the player. The nature of the human brain is such that we are always trying to make connections, and in this case, the listener will make connections that the players themselves never perceived or intended, fusing the sinking improvisation, the erasure phrases, and the new material into a coherent, even an inspired, whole.

But here's another thing I hated about writing this essay: I feel like I'm buying into a frame of mind that classifies — in fact, segregates — creativity together with the arts and only the arts. I am quite okay with the Art Is Good for You model that convinces us to appreciate creativity in all its facets whenever we regard a great work of art or architecture, but I see no reason that, for example, a lawnmower engine shouldn't be looked at the same way. Creativity, after all, infuses every part of human existence. Without it, some of the best things in life — education, self-employment, parties, festivals — become the worst things. So in writing about "creativity in the arts" I feel like I'm buying into a stereotype that privileges the dullest poet over the most dynamic shop teacher. But what can I do? — I am, after all, writing an essay not planning a moon launch.

My editor specifically wanted something about music, and I've often found that the most revealing writing about improvised music is often anecdotal rather than theoretical: concrete and personal, no footnotes. Lol Coxhill saying that when he got into music, the important thing was to have his picture taken wearing a hip suit and holding a saxophone. Charles Mingus writing that when a fellow bassist first showed up with an amplifier, Mingus raised the action on his own instrument, played as loudly as he could and shamed the other bassist into giving up — these anecdotes become snapshots, in a few words revealing important facets of music-making. Facets of ego, of display, of competitiveness. Rather than trying to deduce timeless verities from one's artistic goals, it can be more instructive to confess why the fashion of the season or the passion of the moment seemed so important at the time.

I was the class "writer" during my high school years and music didn't start to seem necessary until I was eighteen and in my first year at UBC. For Christmas my parents gave me a portable record player. I asked them to take it back, and we traded it in for an actual instrument. The territory covered by the six strings of the guitar looked impossibly vast, so I chose a five-string banjo, which has only four fretted strings.

I took a few lessons on banjo and otherwise taught myself. The texts I used were *Earl Scruggs and the 5-String Banjo*, *How to Play the 5-String Banjo* by Pete Seeger, and issues of *Guitar Player* magazine that I borrowed from the Vancouver library.

If at some point I acquired a firm grasp of, for example, the differences between major and minor scales, the credit probably goes to *Guitar Player*, which had a page of musical basics in every issue. Once the banjo had broken the ice of my musical reticence, I added guitar and taught myself to play the C and the F, and the open-string scales, but I knew that to get really good at them, I would have to practice. Practice them over and over. And over and over and over, faster and faster until I could play them as fast as the guys in *Guitar Player* magazine could play them.

Unfortunately I lacked the steely resolve to do this — did the path to artistry have to be so damn boring? Without a teacher to inspire me into finding scales interesting, or to bully me into playing them anyway, I hit upon what I thought was a better approach to teaching myself scales.

From the banjo I had learned the basics of playing different strings at the same time with my thumb and fingers. I put this to use practicing scales. If I played an E major scale on the first string of the guitar (the highest string), it sounded like an E major scale: E, F#, G#, A, B, C#, D#, E. If however, every time I plucked one of those notes with my index finger, I also plucked the open E sixth string (the lowest string) with my thumb, the scale sounded completely different, since each of those notes had a completely different interval with that open E. In fact, because of those changing relationships, the open E itself seemed to change, taking on a different character in contrast to each different note.

Reasoning that all the notes on the scale harmonize with each other (this is well, kind of true) I developed a more fun way of practicing scales. As I went up and down that E scale on the first string, I plucked, either together or fingerpicking sequentially, notes of the E scale on one or more of the other strings — whatever notes I could reach. It was soon apparent that rather than fast, clean scales, my forte was to work my way up and down the neck, dramatizing each note with whatever intervals and harmonies I could come up with from the other strings.

Somewhere in this process I turned a page in the Earl Scruggs book and hit a staggering revelation: that the notes and chords I was playing on banjo and guitar were *the same notes and chords that were on the piano*! By this time I was living at UBC's least upscale student residence, a former World War II barracks just down the hill from the university music building. At night I would sneak up to the piano rooms and practice chords, bringing songbooks by Scruggs, Bob Dylan, Donovan, and Crosby, Stills, Nash and Young. There are few drippier songs than Graham Nash's "Our House," but you don't need to be a pianist to play it perfectly on the piano. Occasionally an actual UBC music student would blunder into the practice room, even claiming that they had booked it, but they immediately saw how hard I was working and retreated.

These were my nascent songwriter days, but I kept coming back to my own way of playing — meditative improvisations over a shifting landscape of scales, intervals and chords. I loved some of the sounds that came out this way, and was liable to fall into this style no matter what instrument I picked up — piano, guitar, banjo, mandolin — and play that way for hours. One day playing an electric bass I thought wouldn't it be cool to play an entire piece this way — in public — and just make everything up, make it up on the spot?

At the time what little I had seen of jazz — Louis Armstrong singing "Hello Dolly" with Carol Channing on the Ed Sullivan Show — included no such notions. My examplars of creativity were the pop musicians of the time. A completely free improvisation — there was a piece on the Jefferson Airplane album *After Bathing at Baxter's* with Jack Casady, Jorma Kaukonen and Spencer Dryden that I suspected was completely improvised, and I had read that Casady (35 years later, I still think of him as the greatest thing to ever happen to the electric bass) would take long unaccompanied solos during Airplane concerts. I wondered if I would ever get that good.

Group free improvisation — that was the obvious next step, but when I got together with other musicians, they always wanted to work out of songbooks or play the blues. My shy suggestions — "Why don't we just start in A minor and just, you know, just play?" struck them as puzzling and perverse.

Perhaps because of this, I didn't get very good at playing with other people in the conventional ways. I had dropped out of grade-nine band because I thought I wasn't interested in music (then I became really interested in music). Although my solo explorations of scales and harmonies were fun and sometimes even sounded like real music, they were not much good for honing a time sense or an ear for chord progressions. Plus, although I kept working on writing songs, I had no show-business personality — the ability to enjoy being in front of an audience for its own sake (I have since developed this particular taste). I took songwriting very seriously and the thought of singing a lyric that was not deeply heartfelt made me blush. Or playing music that wasn't loaded with personal or social significance — outrageous (and to be honest, considering my haphazard musical background, difficult). With so many big issues to tackle, how could anyone just play music for fun? So I was not one for jam sessions or singalongs, which now seem to me to be an essential part of the developing singer/songwriter's palette.

All this time, I was getting interested in the acoustic string bass. I was fascinated by its sound as played by Donny Thompson with John Martyn and Pentangle, and by Ron Carter on my one jazz record, "Out of the Cool." Of course, I also loved Jack Casady's playing, but I was ecology-minded and didn't want to need electricity to play music (I also didn't like very loud music, a taste that has not changed over the years).

IMAGINATION *in* ACTION

After university I moved to Toronto. For a while, at the Charley Farley Art Studio on Queen Street, I took free guitar lessons from Danny Marks. Towards the end of our sessions together, Danny advised me to consider playing bass — perhaps this is standard advice that responsible guitar teachers give to students who seem to have no prospects of ever playing fast.

Sometimes at the studio I heard an improvising group called the CCMC. At the time the group seemed to have eight or nine regular members. Like most large improvising groups the music was mostly chaos, but there would be a few interesting minutes in every set, and the players were obviously trying for something even freer than the "free" improvisations I'd been playing by myself.

Later that same summer, I walked into the Jazz & Blues Centre on Yonge Street, which as it happened was run by one of the CCMC's saxophonists, Bill Smith, and his partner John Norris. Bill invited me to the Saturday afternoon sessions he played in at the Sandpiper Tavern on St. Clair Avenue. The band was Bill, Maury Coles, Stu Broomer and Larry Dubin. Various musicians would come by and sit in, but there was no regular bass player.

Not only was this a music that seemed to have a future (unlike the folk and rock musicians I was meeting, older than myself and keenly aware that the sixties were over and they had not become The Next Big Thing), but the people who played it were really interesting — witty, erudite and knowledgeable about a wide range of subjects, especially in the arts. Besides playing music these guys seemed to like sitting around in bars and talking. I was up for this.

One day I saw an acoustic bass advertised in the Toronto *Buy & Sell*. I took the bus out to Mississauga, looked at the bass — an old plywood Hohner, held together by metal patches and staples from a hard life on the road — and bought it from a retired country & western musician for $150. For about ten months I took lessons from John Gowen of the Toronto Symphony.

Soon I was getting together for private sessions with Bill, Maury, Andy Haas, and other musicians. The way of playing I'd developed on string instruments and piano — somewhat-free, open to shifting tonalities and key centres, but still very much based on standard scales and intervals — fit pretty much perfectly into an improvised music scene that, if not exactly burgeoning, was growing in fits and starts.

Finally, for the summer of 1978 I played Monday nights upstairs at the Beverley Tavern on Queen Street West. The regulars were Bill, Maury, Andy, John Oswald saxophones, Larry Cramer trumpet, myself on bass, Geoff Stewart drums, and various musicians who came by and sat in.

I had acquired a heavy tube Ampeg B15 bass amplifier. To get to the gig I would carry the amplifier and my gear from my apartment at Bay and Davenport to the bar via subway, then I would take the subway home and get the bass.

On the way with my bass to the first night at the Beverley, I got off the subway on the north side of Queen and made immediate eye contact with a handsome, middle-aged black man who was crossing the street towards me, wearing an immaculate three-piece pin-stripe suit and carrying a tenor saxophone case.

We shook hands and introduced ourselves. The tenor saxophonist was Buddy Tate. He was on his way to the first night of a week's gig at Bourbon Street, and he assumed I was his bass player. I quickly set him straight and told him I was playing a block or two down the street, at the Beverley.

"I've only been playing two years," I gushed. "This is my first gig."

"Ah." Tate thought for a moment. Then he said, "I played on Charles Mingus's first gig. It was a big band, 1938. Gene Norman's Concerts By The Sea. Mingus was so nervous. We played a couple of numbers and then I looked back at him and I said, 'Hey son, you sound good' — and he just *beamed*." Tate chuckled. "Mingus still tells that story."

Thus started my musical career. Another thing I hated about writing this essay is that I wanted to write about the big picture — improvisation in daily life, the links between music and writing, even something called "the genius of the hand." Instead I've just come up with some teensy snapshots, faded polaroids of small parts of my own musical past. But maybe, as I suggested earlier, the anecdotal can be more revealing than the theoretical. Anyway, over time life's information tends to converge. Sometimes when you think you have something, you actually have nothing; and sometimes when you think you can do nothing, you can actually do anything.

# DAVID PEACOCK

David Peacock studied at the Banff School of Fine Arts and graduated with honours and a scholarship from the Ontario College of Art before he commenced a thirty-year career in the field of advertising. During those years he won both national and international awards as an Art Director and Creative Director with many of Canada's leading advertising agencies. In addition to teaching positions at the Ontario College of Art and at Sheridan College in Oakville, he has written and illustrated numerous books. In 1991 Peacock began to paint. The subject matter of his paintings is primarily derived from regular visits abroad. He has had eight solo exhibitions since that time, and has been represented in more than a dozen group shows. His work is held in corporate and private collections in Canada and the U.S.A.

## ART: CORPORATE CONSENSUS VS. PERSONAL PASSION

When I was fifteen years old I attended the Banff School of Fine Arts and I did a painting a day for six weeks. That was an incredibly stimulating creative experience for a kid. I suppose I was a geek of sorts because for a couple of years after that my weekend activity was painting with a like-minded friend. We would set up our easels, winter and summer, on the main street of Markham or Unionville, on the banks of a creek, or beside an old barn, and produce oil sketches.

My heroes were the magazine illustrators of *Maclean's*, *McCall's* and the other popular magazines of the fifties. When I finished high school I went to the Ontario College of Art to study illustration.

I never did become an illustrator. Instead I joined an advertising agency upon completion of college, and for the next thirty years my creativity was channelled and disciplined to meet the considerable constraints of the advertising world.

First as an artist, then as art director, then as creative director, through many job changes, to finally as a freelance creative consultant, my creativity was confined by agreed-upon objectives and strategies. Words and pictures had to work together to communicate, not just the desired message, but in the desired tone and manner, and it always (it seemed) had to be done for a meeting at nine a.m. tomorrow morning.

And of course, we had to produce at least half a dozen concepts, all meeting the prerequisite requirements, which were then put before several focus groups. After which we would have another go at it and turn out another five or six concepts before finally presenting three concepts to the client. The client, naturally, always had the final say, no matter how hard we pushed for the one idea we believed in, and needless to say, the focus groups rarely allowed for brilliant ideas to survive — only the safe ones.

This procedure applied to all media — newspaper, magazine, outdoor, radio and television. It made little difference. The creative process was the same. This was creativity on demand. No room here for writer's block. Not permitted. No room here for temperamental artists. They just weren't allowed. Like Nike — just do it.

I always thought I wanted to paint, but never had the time, or so I said. Perhaps I was afraid to find the time. However, I guess I whined about it so often, one Christmas I was presented with some oils and blank canvases.

A blank canvas can be very intimidating when you've been schooled in structured discipline for so long. The canvas said freedom to do as I wished, the way I wished, but I had no idea what to paint or even what style or manner to paint. Would I paint simple colour field abstractions? Expressionistic pieces? Surrealistic or impressionistic works? Would I paint some imaginary being or a fantasy place? What to paint?

As an old advertising man I turned to product. I pulled out a mirror and painted myself. And I've done that every year or so ever since — whenever I get in a dry spell. I find it usually gets me going again. One year I completed thirty-nine paintings. (I paint reasonably big — 36" by 36"). One year I did just twelve. I've painted for as long as eighteen months without a pause of more than a week or two, and I've gone as long as three months without painting at all.

When I'm on a roll I do a painting in a day, or two or three days, and at least one painting a week. That's because when I'm on a roll I have a direction. I have a focus. I have a subject I wish to explore and I can't stop until I've practically beaten it to death. I have to check out every avenue, explore every turn, every possible twist. This one direction may take ten or twenty paintings until I feel it's complete. And then I've done it and I'm done. There is no going back to revisit that subject again.

I usually don't paint more than four or five hours a day. I may stop after the first hour or two, go make a coffee and sit for a while and look at what I've done. Then I'll go back in fits and starts for an hour at a time. The next day I may only change some small thing and spend no more than half an hour with it. On the third day I might take a longer run at it and even finish it off.

While I'm painting I may have a follow-up painting in the back of my head, but I rarely start on one before finishing another — unless I have to wait for the paint to dry, which is seldom something I worry about. That's why I like oils — they're very forgiving. You can wipe something off and do it again or delete it forever.

In my advertising days I always did thumb-nail sketches for an ad. Then I'd do a series of roughs, and finally comprehensive layouts for presentation. Now I just start. I draw directly on the canvas with a brush loaded with red paint. Why red? For two reasons. First, because it's a bold decisive move that reassures me that I know what I'm doing. Secondly, the red often continues to show through as an under-paint, providing the appearance, happily, not unlike the orange-red air burn on the pine panels that the Group of Seven painted on. Not that I emulate The Group of Seven any more than I emulate the Cobra Group or Painters Eleven or the Hudson Valley School. I just like the look of it, and drawing in red paint is just something I do. Immediately following the red paint, when it is still wet, I put a colour wash over the whole canvas, or a good part of it, before blocking areas of solid colour here and there. When the canvas has some visual weight to it, and a colour direction, I stop and make that coffee.

Often I know after the first day that if I don't stop now I'm going to kill the painting. That is, I will work it over and over and clarify it to the point it has lost all its life. Perhaps I can blame this problem of over-painting on my past career. I have this urge to clean up my spontaneous brush strokes and refine them, until everything appears as it truly is, as opposed to leaving much for the viewer to think about. I'm working on this.

I have no close painter friends. No one to confide in. No one to help me solve a problem. Sure, I have acquaintances who paint that I might have a word with. But I don't paint with anyone or share studio space. I enjoy the solitude of painting and solving my problems my way. I would have great trouble talking about what I'm painting or what the meaning of it is to me. In fact this is the first time I've ever thought about even the process of painting, and even that is difficult to write about.

When I worked in advertising and I used to sit behind the one-way mirror listening to the people in the focus groups discuss the merits, or more likely the weaknesses of my endeavours — I always felt it was a bit like pulling your pants down in front of a crowd. They got to see who you really were through your work, and you got to hear what they really thought of you. Maybe that's why I find the subject of my painting too personal to share, because often the object or objects in the painting are not necessarily the actual subject of my painting.

My paintings come very easily once I've hit upon a subject matter — and this is invariably influenced by a trip abroad. We've been fortunate, in that for many years we've gone to France on holiday, and I would come back with oil sketches, (too heavy and cumbersome to do now), ink and chalk drawings, photos (which my wife took), brochures, booklets, maps, CDs, ticket stubs and posters. All of this, plus supplementary reading, would be the sources I could draw upon to sustain me for a year or so or until the next trip.

For me, a series of paintings can number as high as two dozen canvases. It's impossible to see them all at one time in a small studio space, or even in part, as I'm working on them. For that reason, among others, it's rewarding to see them as a completed body of work on the walls of a gallery.

I'm fortunate in that the gallery currently representing my work has been kind enough to provide two exhibitions recently, and shown two large series of my paintings in their entirety. Unlike a previous gallery where I exhibited, whose dealer would drop by the studio every four or five months and select a few pieces to take away for show, leaving most of my work sitting in the studio unseen.

Now I know commercial galleries are just that — commercial. I know they prefer to carry only product they believe they can sell, but I've found a gallery that instead believes in me. For that I'm very grateful.

It's as if you wrote a book that required eighteen chapters to tell the story. You would like the publisher to take the whole book, not just select a few chapters for publication and expect the reader to make sense of it. It's the same with a series of paintings. Unfortunately, or fortunately, when the gallery begins selling one here and a couple there, holes appear in the series and the story is no longer complete. It's not that each painting can't stand on its own, but for that time, however brief, when they are all there together on the walls, I feel completely satisfied and fulfilled.

I enjoy painting. Advertising was work. Now it's my product and I'm the focus group and the client rolled into one. There's no second guessing or wondering what the client's wife will think of it. There's no deadline. And I don't even have to complete the sale myself. This is unfettered creativity. Now if I could just figure out what to paint next...

# DEBORAH STILES

Deborah Stiles was born and raised in Appalachia. From the University of Maine she received a Master's in English (1988) and a PhD in Canadian rural and gender history. During a sojourn to Fredericton, Stiles fell in love with the Maritimes; she's been in the region pretty much ever since. Now an Associate Professor, Humanities, at the Nova Scotia Agricultural College in Truro, Stiles divides her time between writing, farming, gardening, conducting rural research of divers sorts, teaching literature, history, and writing, and worrying about the planet. She has published articles, fiction, and two poetry collections, *Riding Limestone* (Northern Lights Press, 1991) and *Movement Catalogued* (BrickHouse Books, 2002). She's presently at work on several projects, including a novel and a social history of masculinity via the life and writings of New Brunswick radical and poet, Martin Butler.

## AGAINST THE SILENCING

"Not science." That's how my students — at the mainly applied and hard-science Nova Scotia Agricultural College — describe the courses I teach, which involve things like creative writing, history, literature. "Fun."

I imagine they also, truly, find the problems they solve in physics, ecology, chemistry, and soil, plant and animal sciences "fun," or they would not be in the sciences to begin with. Yet, there is something to the idea that creative and other writing-intensive courses are mind-liberating, soul-satisfying — fun — for all their marginalization in our techno-heavy culture. Myself, I can't fathom doing other than what others call "creative," the action of creation. But that may have to do with being a poet, and having, but also wanting, to do other things to nurture the art and stock the pantry. Three things I've done a lot of, the past two decades, are writing, cooking, and farming; the trio range (or, rather, lounge) across that spectrum of what it is possible to do, creatively, and so in this essay, I'd like to explore the connections between these activities, and the creative impulse that (for me) underpins them all.

Why create?

A defense against the silencing...

I am standing in the kitchen of the second West Virginia farmhouse with the cordless pinned to my bad ear, listening to myself committing to another writing project I don't know how in the world I'll finish, opening up a can of mandarin oranges for a pitiful, mid-winter fruit bowl.

Comfort food: dinner of sloppy-joes, canned corn. Dessert is a cut-glass bowl swimming with the plump quarter suns of little mandarins. They're bumping up against the last banana in the house — sliced — and all of it is now speckled in flaked coconut because IT'S PRETTY and when will I have time, really, to make a coconut cream pie?

In my poem, "hold fast," the central organizing idea is the "subtle desperation/of late afternoon, mid-*hiver*." This is the state of mind when the can-opener comes out, in suicidally-seductive late January. But the warm colours of yams, chickpeas, my winter-type Long Island cheese and butternut squashes (holding out in cold storage), the hopeful green of cabbage, the pungent purity of onions, well-kept: all of them cheer. As I'm cheered it becomes possible to transition from anxiety and inertia to cooking up African stews with steaming millet or couscous on top, and finding hopefulness in the action.

The creative impulse in cookery intersects with the act of writing and its creative impulse, in the sense that both have audiences. But with cooking, compared to writing, there is much more attention paid to that pesky notion, audience. I'm sure the degree of attention varies with all cooks, poets, writers; some may have to imagine an audience, but for writing that act of creation mostly has to do with having something to say and the drive to say it. With cooking, the audience may, similarly, be just me, but food demands an audience, if only of one, and it needs it fairly soon after the fact (unless, of course you're making cheese, or rotted shark, or melomel, or something crafted to eat or drink, but that's not in the cooking category, in my book). There's an expiry date, so to speak, with the creative products of cookery, while we poets can create holding tightly to the comfort that if no one gets it in our lifetime, maybe, just maybe, it'll make sense to someone in the next generation, who comes along after we're dead. It is the same persistence to create that keeps me at a poem, off and on, for usually a year before it's to the final first draft stage. Thank the gods that poems have no expiry date.

Cooking, by contrast, offers a rush of creative expression, demands an audience (and usually commands one: do you know anyone who can cook who doesn't have friends?), and it's all so lovely and immediate. Hence the cheer factor, in late winter or anytime a pick-me-up is needed. If I can cheer myself — or others — by making the simple menus of childhood; if I can delight the dearest by taking the hours to cut in lard to flour to make crust, separate yolks from clears (why should they be called "whites" when they're not white to begin with?), and stir endlessly the cauldron of custard, finally beating and beating those remains of egg for the finishing flourish of meringue, then, why shouldn't I? Why shouldn't I, in the cause of pie?

This past year I've not written as much as I expected to, being on sabbatical, and so freed, mostly, from the demands of teaching. There was a subtle silencing at work; the two families I'm a part of lost two valuable and beloved members within five months' time. I just felt too sad to write, and as I think back on it, the silence was similar to when I would approach the end of a semester in grad school, and was feeling totally, totally drained of words, words that I HAD to produce, in order to get by.

Back then, I recall, I would find an old colourful *Geographic* or home/garden magazine with lots of interesting pictures of nature, and I would cut up a selection of pictures and construct intricate mosaics of the pieces...butterflies and wart hogs, sunsets and tree frogs, mixes like that. I remember that somehow it comforted me, when I was unable to work on my poetry because I'd been so drained by academic writing.

These past few months, when I've been too sad to write, I've had the blessing to be able to dive into another creative act, that of farming, and it has been a comfort to help my husband, who's a farmer, and to remember the joy in my dying father's face as we told him, "The barley's up." Both of the men we lost, my father, and my father-in-law, were farmers, and consequently I have felt that I was being creative as well as consoled by preparing the soil with Dad's tiller, directing the cows into the barn with Carl's cane.

Irrespective of these losses, however, I would argue that farming requires a type of creativity that sustains itself, over seasons, and sod, and involves the same type of planning and good instincts needed for crafting fine poems. Both farming and writing involve a creativity bound up in a series of choices. Iambic or trochaic? Plant now, or wait another week? Endstopped? Enjambed? Barley, or spring wheat? Should the character who's contemplating standing up to the bully in her office *imagine* the whole big blow-out with the bully as it's unfolding at the neighbourhood Tim Horton's the day before Christmas Eve (and what she actually does is chew her nails and sabotage the bully's work in some small way), OR should the blow-out actually occur on page eight of the story?

What comes before matters after, in the creative act of writing, as well as in agriculture. A simple example of this can be had in the thing called crop rotations. To maintain fertility, avoid insect and disease problems, and manage weeds, crop rotations must be adhered to, though there is some flexibility in what goes into the rotations, meaning that in a particular field you would grow nitrogen-fixing legumes one year or two or three, for example, followed by nitrogen-hungry corn being grown the next year in that field, to take advantage of the set-up to success that's been given by those previous years of nitrogen-fixing crops in the rotation. Naturally, these principles of planning hold true for poetry and fiction, and other creative ventures as well. Ernest can't digest the well-prepared speech of his elderly aunt, if, in the writing, he's not been set up to be in the same room with her, right?

Of all the ways I express/convey/fashion/find out/share with/ — *create* — the results can be seen as all similarly conceived but differently executed. Two items that seem to me to define (and also perhaps defy) creation are the time and the sheer desire to craft SOMETHING. Mary Wollstonecraft Shelley, in introducing a subsequent edition of her novel *Frankenstein*, wrote that, "Invention, it must be humbly admitted, does not consist in creating out of void, but out of chaos…Invention consists in the capacity of seizing on the capabilities of a subject, and in the power of moulding and fashioning ideas suggested to it."

Those who are much more adept than I, as farmers, writers, and cooks know that this sentiment expressed by Shelley encapsulates the drive, instincts, purposeful planning and sheer joy that is creating. And this as it attaches to each of the endeavours I'm talking about. For the farmer, it is "seizing on the capabilities of" the land and the livestock; for the art of the best cookery, I'm convinced, it's attaching a creative purpose to those ingredients you have on hand or that you find in-season.

One late summer I was going to have guests and so I ordered a pork loin roast from our village hog farmer. Usually, roasts to me are for special, fall or winter occasion meals. But the tide had turned on summer, the nights were getting cooler. I determined to have a roast. But I was at a loss — no cranberries yet, no apples; what would I do for a fruit accompaniment? I went for a walk along Fundy Bay, and it was August, so of course I hit upon the solution. Blueberries. A blueberry sauce with sage and other flavourings would pair well with the fresh leaves of sage in the onion stuffing and the pork, and the preceding salad, which included lemon-scented geranium leaves, was light enough to carry us through that rather heavy main pork event to a raspberry and blueberry echo in the shortcake ending.

In farming, that spark of creativity is in the planning stages all the way to harvest, but especially in January, the season of the seed catalogue. Brightly beaming dahlias, roses, lilacs in the bulb version, happy people with harlequin gourds or shimmering red peppers in their grasp, multiple, sometimes magenta depictions of the best ground-cover money can buy — all of this helps me abandon inaction and get those creative waters flowing. It is also of course time to plan field crops and (if the conditions are right) spread manure. Feeding the ground some more, and preparing for the coming plantings help the farmer in this hemisphere to feel a particular affinity with February, if not January. *Spring will be here before we know it!*

If invention, as Shelley understood it, is creating, then creating is not creating something from nothing, but rather out of the mud, blood, chaos and joy that surround us. There sounds a trumpet against the silencing of ordinary life; it may be only a mute morning-glory trumpet of violet or blue, or the trumpet of a four o'clock flower, whose scent is only with us in the mid-afternoon, when it blooms (sort of like my son, and some writers I know, who are definitely NOT morning people or morning glory-ers)…, but a trumpet, all the same. And this is in a sense how and why we create, as writers, but the sane holds true for farmers and those who create in the kitchen. Take the time to imagine, experiment, and craft/tend/shape, and that creative bone in the body, in my body at least, is happy.

IMAGINATION *in* ACTION

# EDITH HODKINSON

Edith Hodkinson was born in Kirkland Lake and grew up in Crystal Beach. She has a BA in English from Queen's University. While at Queen's, she was a soloist in the Queen's Revue, danced with the Highland Dancers, did choreography for the Drama Guild and a musical for Dr. Graham George. Dance teachers included Helen Peacock, Jean Spear, and Betty Oliphant. She studied choreography with Nesta Brooking in London, England. After attending many teachers' courses at the National Ballet Summer School, she received her ballet teacher's certificate, Cecchetti Method. Edith taught ballet in Red Lake and Dryden. Her ballets for children were performed at schools and fairs in Red Lake, Sioux Lookout, Ignace, and Dryden. She currently lives in Owen Sound.

## DANCE

"If your revolution doesn't include dancing, I'm not interested."
— Emma Goldman

Dance is a natural response of children to the world around them. Wind swirling, autumn leaves, softly falling snow, or the pure joy of a summer morning make children skip, jump and twirl. Why do some of us continue to dance for the rest of our lives? Why do we see patterns of movement in the everyday world and use dance to express our feelings about that world? I can only relate my own experiences.

Dance is intimate and private and allows one to express the deepest joys or sorrows. Dance, as a performance is public and exposed. Reconciling these can be rewarding or excruciating.

All dance is private in the beginning. In my rural childhood no one danced and music was heard only at school or church. Many dancers tell of seeing a dance performance at an early age and then begging for dance lessons. I didn't know that dancers existed. I just loved to move in response to my small world. Trees, grasses, and flowers moved as the wind blew and each swayed in a different way. Insects that flew or crawled were fascinating with their unique ways of moving. I danced to imitate these things. Dancing for children is pretending. It is story telling using movement instead of words.

When music entered my world, it was magical, all that movement expressed in sound and rhythm. Rhythm was something not found in the imitation of nature. It gave a new shape to dancing, especially quick footwork. Music expressed emotions in a way I had never experienced. Longing to hear more, I got a radio and a record player. Now

I began to make up structured dances with beginnings and endings. I chose music that expressed my personal feelings. These dances were poems in movement.

I was twelve when a movie theatre opened in our village. A new way of dancing was revealed to me. Every Hollywood musical made me try to imitate those glamorous dancers. Two years later I danced my own version of a gypsy dance for a high school assembly. Maybe ignorance really is bliss. All I remember of that dance is lots of kicks and twirls and a large red skirt. My fellow students applauded. I discovered I could make other people happy when I danced. Their approval made me feel good too. My private dance world had started to become public. For the rest of my dancing life, I would question if what I danced in private was going to please other people.

The following year a dance school opened in our village. The teacher was an acrobat and tap dancer but also taught ballet. I loved it all, but especially the acrobatic dancing. Making someone else's technique and choreography express my feelings was difficult. It was a struggle that never ended as long as I danced. I would look at what the teacher showed us and get an idea about a different move, pattern, or shape of movement that felt better to me.

Later, I got a chance to study ballet at the National Ballet Summer School. In those days, the National Ballet had huge summer classes in the St. Lawrence Hall in Toronto. Celia Franca included classical mime in her classes. I was entranced. Dancing could talk! As a result of these classes, I enrolled in Betty Oliphant's studio on Sherbourne Street. Classical ballet technique was difficult, but so beautiful — the long lines of turned out legs, elegant stretched feet and curved arms. All the struggle was worthwhile when a ballet combination felt like dancing, instead of doing steps.

Later, when I taught ballet in Red Lake and Dryden in North-western Ontario, I tried to remember how I felt as a child who loved to move. To teach ballet technique and not destroy a child's love of movement was my goal. Making a child aware of what his body is doing is necessary, but not stifling his creativity is vital. I encouraged imitation of animals, flowers growing, the wind, the rain, and emotional response to music and rhythm. I learned from the children too. One child preferred to imitate machines. Her moves later inspired my choreography for a modern dance.

Gradually, my dance students enjoyed using their ballet technique to express their response to music or to tell a story in our performances. Watching this happen was the most fulfilling part of teaching.

After a few years of teaching in Dryden, my interest in choreography grew to the point where I felt I needed to concentrate on it and be with other choreographers. Life in the north inspired many ballets for children using French-Canadian folk music, stories of pioneer families, and dances based on the European traditions of the immigrants that lived in the mining and paper mill towns. But I felt stale and wanted something more.

IMAGINATION *in* ACTION

After a five-week choreography course with the Nesta Brooking Studio in London, England, I came back to Dryden with all kinds of new ideas about movement. I had seen other choreographers using dance in new ways, especially for large groups. Just as one can read a phrase in a story and say "That says exactly what I feel, but I would never have thought to say it that way," so can someone else's choreography inspire a new way of moving.

My choreography produced different kinds of dances. There were short dances, or variations as dancers call them, which expressed pure emotion inspired by the music and using classical ballet technique. If some movement didn't look right, I would say to the dancers "Do you have any ideas? I don't like mine." Often they came up with good moves. One of these students went on to have a dance school and choreograph many ballets for children.

Another type of dance was for short performances. My school was often asked to provide entertainment for civic functions. These dances were all modeled on European folk dances and set to appropriate music with colourful costumes. We could even perform outdoors because we had an accordionist to provide the music.

The most satisfying and challenging choreography was for the two-act ballets that my students performed throughout North-western Ontario. The stories were often fairy tales, but the most popular one was about the settling of Western Canada. It included scenes of the settlers leaving Europe, farmers, cowboys, Indians and even a Russia-Canada hockey game, as well as dances representing modern day Canada. We presented this ballet at schools in Sioux Lookout, Dryden, and Ignace, and at fall fairs. Our audiences were the people of the north — townspeople, bush workers, Indians and immigrants. They were looking at their children dancing a ballet they had inspired.

Dancers, like story tellers and painters, have always reacted to the world around them. Nature, emotions, people, past and present events, and always, music, inspires dancers to move and create new dances. For those who love dance, it is the most rewarding expression of life experiences.

# GEORGE SWEDE

George Swede has published twenty-nine collections of poetry, most of them involving short-form poetry, the two latest being *Almost Unseen: Selected Haiku of George Swede* (Decatur, IL: Brooks Books, 2000) and *First Light, First Shadows* (Liverpool, U.K.: Snapshot Press, 2006) He has also published books and articles on creativity, the latest being a chapter, "Poetic Development" in *The International Handbook on Innovation* (Shavinina, L.V. ed., Oxford: Pergamon, 2003). A former professor of psychology at Ryerson, he lives in downtown Toronto.

## TRACKS IN THE SAND*

### Why Do We Write?

Novelists, already rich and famous as a result of their work, continue to write into old age while established poets, with almost no financial reward or fame for their work, also continue to write for a lifetime. Clearly, neither group devotes decades to their chosen vocation for only fame and glory. What, then, motivates them to keep going?

A number of psychologists have tried to explain this persistently high level of motivation. Sigmund Freud felt that it came from the sublimation of pent-up emotion resulting from unconscious conflict. Carl Jung thought it was an inborn drive of the collective unconscious. Alfred Adler believed it stemmed from feelings of inferiority, while Otto Rank considered it to be the result of a desire for individuality. Eric Fromm hypothesized a need for transcendence, and Max Wertheimer an inborn need to construct patterns (or gestalts). Both Carl Rogers and Abraham Maslow felt it came from a need for self-actualization (Woodman, 1981).

All of these theories strike a chord; they all are appealing explanations for the consistently high motivation shown by writers. But, after decades of studying this phenomenon from two perspectives, that of a poet and that of an academic psychologist, I believe the most complete answer lies with a combination of the theories of Kornei Chukovsky and Albert Bandura (Swede, 2003).

Chukovsky (1971) believed that children from the ages of two to five are linguistic geniuses. Children at this age, in their attempts to master their first language, invent words and experiment with rhyme, rhythm and metaphor. They see this learning as play, not work. Chukovsky provides numerous examples, such as this poem by a four-year-old boy:

The raven looked at the moon—oon—oon
And saw in the sky a yellow balloon
With eyes, nose, and mouth in a round face,
Swimming with clouds at a slow pace (p. 76).

With Chukovsky as my inspiration, I took notes whenever my sons said something unusual during their early years. Here are two utterances that startle with their poetic inventiveness:

16/7/1972, Andris, age 3 years, 10 months (in anger to his brother Juris):
   "I'm going to pull your bones out and swim in you."
19/1/1973, Juris, age 5 years four months:
   "I had a bad dream last night, a nightmirror." (Swede, 1976, 2003).

Note that Chukovsky's example, as well as the metaphors from my sons, show a connectedness with the immediate environment, i.e., a haiku-like directness with current experience. I believe that children between two and five are not only linguistic geniuses, but also blessed with the capacity for the haiku way of seeing.

When children begin school, their interest in poetic wordplay and perception declines as their attention becomes focused on how to read and write, do arithmetic, science and history, as well as how to deal with the social challenges of a school environment. A few students, however, continue to express their poetic outlook into adulthood, in spite of the many distractions along the way. They consider poetry important and believe in their capacities to grow and develop as poets. How does this happen in a world that considers athletes, actors, bankers, broadcasters, CEOs, cops, doctors, filmmakers, journalists, politicians, singers, soldiers and tycoons much more important than poets? In my opinion, Bandura's (1997) self-efficacy theory best explains how this can happen:

Self-efficacy beliefs are constructed from four principal sources of information: enactive mastery experiences that serve as indicators of capability; vicarious experiences that alter efficacy beliefs through transmission of competencies and comparison with the attainments of others; verbal persuasion and allied types of social influences that one possesses certain capabilities; and physiological and affective states from which people partly judge their capableness, strength, and vulnerability to dysfunction. Any given influence, depending on its form, may operate through one or more of these sources of efficacy information (p. 79).

In Bandura's terms, the students who insist on becoming poets, despite the fact that they cannot make a living writing poetry (other than for greeting card companies), must have had repeated positive feedback about their talent. This can occur in a number of ways: from the personal satisfaction of having finished a poem one considers successful; from comparisons of one's work with that of peers; from praising comments by respected others, especially established poets; and from the exhilaration and excitement one feels while engaged in the process of writing poetry.

Biographical sources are replete with examples of such forces at work to shape a person's destiny for poetry. I will focus only on William Carlos Williams, someone with a recognized kinship to haiku. In his autobiography (1967), Williams states that at age 16, when a heart murmur forced him to give up baseball and running, he turned to poetry:

> I was forced back on myself. I had to think about myself, look
> into myself. And I began to read (p. 1).

Another person might have begun to read about archeology or astronomy, but Williams from early childhood had been raised in a family that valued language and literature:

> My father was an Englishman who never got over being an
> Englishman. He had a love of the written word. Shakespeare
> meant everything to him. He read the plays to my mother and
> my brother and myself. He read well. I was deeply impressed (p. 2).

Williams took the sense of self-efficacy formed by success in baseball and track and redirected it toward other areas for which he was also well-prepared — reading and, eventually, writing poems — pursuits that continued even during the rigors of medical school. According to Bandura's formulation, this persistence was likely maintained by Williams' sense of accomplishment when a poem was finished; by positive feedback from his peers; and, in time, from editors for literary magazines and book publishers as well as established poets.

Those of us who write haiku are even more unknown to the general public than mainstream poets such as Williams, and thus are even less likely to be motivated by money and fame. We too must have maintained a love of language long after Chukovsky's linguistic genius stage. Most of us, however, also developed an interest in observing nature together with a Far-Eastern-based philosophical outlook involving reflective detachment. Among writers of poetry, we seem to be a group made distinct by influences in addition to the love of language.

# Why Haiku?

Once in a while I ask myself how it happened that I ended up writing mainly Japanese short-form poetry. To date, I've been able to identify a number of possible reasons. Taken together, they seem to explain why, almost. Since some readers have probably asked themselves the same question, I thought one person's search for connecting strands might be interesting.

I started out as a free verse poet, publishing my first poem in 1968 and my first collection in 1974. Then in 1976 I was asked by the editor of a literary journal to review a just-released book by the University of Toronto Press, *Modern Japanese Haiku* by Makoto Ueda. As I read the four hundred anthologized haiku, I felt as if blinders were being taken from my eyes. I learned that it was possible to write objectively about everyday experience without serious intrusions of the ego. Such work was a tonic for someone grown weary of reading about personal obsessions, including those in my own work.

In order to review the book fairly, I read as much about haiku as I could. Fortunately, the University of Toronto library had many publications dealing with the form and, a few weeks later, I sent in a review that appears, to me, even now, to have been written by someone relatively knowledgeable. While studying and working on the review, I also began to write haiku. The form seemed to fit me like a favorite pair of walking shoes and, in 1977, I published my first haiku in *Bonsai*, a U.S. haiku periodical. To my surprise and delight, it won an award for that particular issue:

> Still noticeable
> among the bare trees
> a TV antenna

I then became obsessed with writing haiku, churning out over a thousand a year for a while and publishing around ten percent of them. In terms of time and effort spent, I had become a dedicated haiku poet.

I felt I had a natural predilection for the haiku and a few years later discovered one for the tanka form as well. But from where did this affinity come? To me, Ueda's book was merely the spark that set it off. I suspected some other possible causes. One explanation did leap out at me. When my mother and stepfather and I emigrated to Canada from post-WW II Europe, we settled near the village of Oyama, British Columbia for three years. Oyama was named after a Japanese general who commanded forces in Manchuria during a war with Russia in the early twentieth century. Prior to WW II, Japanese came to the region to engage in fruit farming and gave the village its name. But, upon our arrival in 1947 to live with my mother's parents on their fruit farm, no Japanese lived there anymore. When Japan entered WW II, practically all Japanese-

Canadians were interned in camps with the result that their farms around Oyama were left abandoned, even for years after the war.

One of the empty, but still locked, farmhouses was across the road from that of my grandparents. I recall going by the mailbox with a Japanese name to look in the windows from which I could glimpse furniture and decorations that were of Eastern design. Perhaps this early experience helped to sensitize me subconsciously to Japanese things. And it was not the only one. When I was ten, my family moved to Kamloops, a small city about two hours drive away, in order for my stepfather to receive treatment for tuberculosis at a sanatorium. During the two-year stay, I became best friends with the two sons of a Japanese dentist and spent much time at their home that was full of the things reflecting their heritage. Today, Kamloops has a sister city — Uji, Japan — and, according to the Kamloops city web site, the relationship was initiated by the Kamloops Japanese Canadian Association.

My stepfather's illness was too advanced for successful treatment and when he died in 1952, my mother and I moved to Vancouver, which then already had a large Asian population. During high school, two of my best friends were of Chinese heritage. In hindsight, after strong friendships with Japanese and Chinese Canadians, it was not surprising that at the University of British Columbia I studied Japanese and Chinese history for two years. To go any further, I would have had to study the Chinese and Japanese languages and decided that psychology was more in line with my abilities.

The connection to things Japanese continued after I graduated with a BA in psychology in 1964 and got married shortly thereafter. Although my wife and her family were British-Canadians, their lives were imbued with Japanese culture. The father was a house-builder, whose homes reflected his strong interest in Japanese design. All were built with interior Zen gardens and I recall with fondness spending time in the lovely one in the middle of the family home. Even today, one can see the father's Japanese-style roofs and facades dotting the landscape in West Vancouver.

In the following years, the hippie culture began to blossom in Canada and, of course, it was interwoven with Asian religion and philosophy. While never a true hippie, I did espouse some of its Eastern-based values, especially after moving to Toronto, which by the late 1960s and early 1970s, had become more avant-garde than Vancouver. After my first wife and I divorced in 1969, I grew interested in writing poetry and was at first influenced by poets such as Lawrence Ferlinghetti, Kenneth Patchen, Richard Brautigan, Allen Ginsberg and Jack Kerouac and later by Walt Whitman, William Carlos Williams and Wallace Stevens. For the most part, the work of these poets was accessible and full of strong images and was the kind of poetry to which I aspired in my writing. It also prepared me, I think, to appreciate, a few years later, the haiku in Ueda's anthology.

But do the childhood and adulthood influences described above really explain my strong attraction to haiku? Why was I not drawn to other types of Japanese or Chinese poetry? Most likely, another aspect of my early life also helped to direct me towards short, sensory-based poetry. In Oyama I was a lonely child with the closest playmate two-and-a-half miles away. For hours several times a week, I wandered with my dog through the wild hills beyond the farm, my attention riveted by hundreds of arresting things: wildflowers, grasses, thick woods with overgrown pathways, dozens of different birds, deer, skulls of range cattle, the lake in the valley below, cloudless days, stormy ones, and so on. I never formed an overarching view of the things I encountered. I simply experienced. Individual, direct memories of that time remain vivid, even now, over fifty years later, and have been the source of many haiku.

I like to believe that I have identified my main reasons for writing haiku. For me, they lead like spider threads to the center of a web. Then again, no one can ever understand him- or herself completely and other explanations doubtlessly lie hidden to me and perhaps obvious to others.

## REFERENCES

Bandura, A. (1997). *Self-efficacy: The exercise of control*. New York: W.H. Freeman and Company.

Chukovsky, K. (1971). *From two to five* (M. Morton, Trans.). Berkeley, CA: University of California Press. (Original work published in 1925).

Swede, G. (1976). (Metaphoric utterances by my two sons prior to the age of seven). Unpublished raw data.

Swede, G. (2003). Poetic innovation. In: L. Shavinina (Ed.), *The International Handbook on Innovation* (pp. 471-484). Cambridge, U.K.: Pergamon.

Williams, W.C. (1967). *I wanted to write a poem: The autobiography of the works of a poet* (Reported and edited by Edith Heal). Boston, MA: Beacon Press.

Woodman, R.W. (1981). Creativity as a construct in personality theory. *Journal of Creative Behavior*, 15 (1), 43-66.

* From two columns in the online periodical, *Simply Haiku: A Quarterly of Japanese Short-form Poetry*.

      "Why Do We Write?" appeared in 2006, Vol. 4, No. 1

      "Why Haiku?" appeared in 2005, Vol. 3, No. 4

# HONEY NOVICK

> Honey Novick is a singer/songwriter/voice teacher and evolving poet. She lives in Toronto where she found an oasis of delight on the shores of Lake Ontario. There she communes with four families — swans, geese, ducks and gulls. The nesting spot of these birds offers comfort from the hustle and bustle of everyday living. Honey Novick has created "Sing Your Way" for Sheena's Place and Spark of Brilliance (Guelph). She has lovingly been called "Poet Laureate of Yorkville's Hippies" and wears that badge with honour and joy. www.honeynovick.com

## THIS SIDE OF CRAZY

The late, great, jazz singer, Joe Williams, once told me, "Jazz is being in a situation, and then how you get out of it — that's Jazz." I've gotten through life with the help of Jazz. Improvising, thinking fast on my feet, being in the moment, making something out of nothing, taking risks, pulling the invisible out of the air, being creative, spontaneous, resourceful, taking the initiative, daring, trying, surviving. Jazz can be a metaphor for life.

I was in my twenties the first time someone called me "creative," "unique." Up to that point, I had no idea why I did the things I did. I figured I'm damned if I do and damned if I don't so I'd rather do, and did. (I should have had a clue because as a teenager I got fired from my clerical job at Eaton's Department Store for singing along with the Muzak!!!). I am many things, including: Miss General Idea Performance Artist, scat singer, folk singer, jazz singer, wannabe. I have become a successful, accomplished human being — a vocalist, songwriter, voice teacher, poet, producer, and evolving humanist.

As a child and teenager, I got lost in thought, in time and in reality. As a teenager, I was considered "incorrigible," "uncontrollable," "crazy," especially in school. I wasn't mean-spirited, just bored and uninvolved. I was devoted to watching TV, going to movies, listening to music, being in solitude, "tripping," and fantasizing during daylight. As a young adult, I didn't pursue finding a husband, being a mother, traveling to Europe, accumulating financial wealth or building security of any kind. I had other ambitions. I wanted to sing and hopefully have an effect on the world and have an audience appreciate the sound of my music.

Very early in life, maybe at four or five, I was clearly attracted to certain things — language and sound, ballet lessons, drawing freely, imaginatively for hours on end, and being alone where I could create games like "See What I Could Find Today While Walking On The Street." My cache might be a beautiful maple leaf, discarded candy wrapper, crayon, or interestingly-shaped stones. These would come home, be put in a doll's house and then have a story or adventure made up to go with them. I also wrote songs and poems.

At nine I began traditional, private piano lessons in a teacher's home, then switched from piano to singing. WOW! I felt a twinge of liberation through vocal expression. My first repertoire was gospel music. Since my parents were Paul Robeson fans, the music was not only welcomed but also discussed.

After only a few months, the teacher said it was time for me to move on to the Royal Conservatory of Music. The big time! My mother saved the baby bonus cheques for the lessons and to buy a second-hand piano. I tried learning "La donna è mobile." When I asked, still nine years old, what the words meant, I was told, "Woman Is Fickle." Since I didn't know fickle women and couldn't relate, I suspected that my time at the conservatory would be limited.

American Bandstand, Annette Funicello of the Mickey Mouse Club, Motown, Rhythm and Blues, Doo-wop music were all happening throughout North America at that time. I would scour record stores for obscure Doo-wop, American R & B, and Motown LPs — even going so far as Buffalo, alone on the bus at twelve years old, in pursuit of my pleasures.

My musical education was very broad. Elvis was part of my earliest consciousness; it seemed everyone was into "Hound Dog" and "All Shook Up." I had a penchant for Hank Williams and old-time country music. At synagogue I heard the blissful ecstasy of the men in vocal, melodic prayer. Saturday afternoons my parents listened to the Metropolitan Opera on the radio. I hated opera. I couldn't relate, but since that time opera has become a beloved, acquired taste. I also discovered Pete Seeger and the Weavers. They had a radio hit with "On Top of Old Smoky." A message song, sung simply and with integrity.

Looking back, my ears became a guiding light, a "seeing-ear." Even though I had a lot of lessons, no one seriously encouraged me to consider a career in music. Out of the question for a girl who should be married or employed as a secretary, nurse or teacher. The older I got, the more miserable I became.

By 1963 when John F. Kennedy was shot, I was going deep inside myself. I was only going through the motions of teen stuff — parties, boys, clothes, but mainly writing a private diary and playing hookey where I would hide in the church next door to school. I liked the silence of the church and the solitude. Because I looked different and my thoughts were unusual for my generation, I really didn't fit in. I was short, buxom with a thin waistline, had severe acne, long black hair, and glasses, and couldn't handle being stared at.

Then I heard "Like a Rollin' Stone." A new cultural revolution was dawning. I was introduced to the music and ideas of Bob Dylan and Joan Baez. It really wasn't only Dylan's words that caught my attention, it was his voice as well — a natural voice, unique, puncturingly honest, committed to something big and significant. I thought if Dylan could express himself and get heard, why not me?

I volunteered at the Mariposa Folk Festival and was placed in the Aboriginal Section. I heard leaves rustling in the wind in the sounds of native singing, drumming, dancing and speaking. I studied guitar and tried to emulate what I heard and how I felt, eventually writing "Where Does A Man Go To Be Free?"

> Listen to the leaves, as they rustle in the wind, (repeat)
> Where does a man go, when he wants to be free?
> Alex and Ed belong to an army but they don't know their enemy
>     (repeat)
> If you feel the need to compete, you must remember one must
>     always lose.

I kept hearing things, listening to sounds, sounds and more sounds, rhythmic sounds, traffic sounds, symphonies of typewriter keys, choirs of birdsongs, haunting wind airs, poetry in footsteps. Conversations didn't mean a whole lot and gossip was good only if there was a great story.

I became one of Charles Jordan's singing students. His technique was based on the use of the abdomen as control centre of the vocal instrument, and he used "Barbara Allen," the old English folk song, as his method for each and every class. I sang that song developing my breath control, every lesson, for two and a half years!

Simultaneously, I became involved with the General Idea Performance Art group. As Miss General Idea, Beauty Contestant winner, I improvised my title acceptance speech, flying by the seat of my pants. I had pulled off a coup, out of thin air and in front of a live, important audience! To this day, I have no idea what I said. Still, I wasn't yet singing. I would sit at the General Idea kitchen table and put music to the poetry of Tennessee Williams. When Jorge Saia, of General Idea, encouraged me to contact Mr. Williams, to tell him his poems were becoming songs, I did! Tennessee Williams' legal team was not happy, and wouldn't give me permission to perform his poetry to my music. Later, I would do the same with a song of Pete Seeger, "River of My People," — recorded it and sent it to him. He actually sent me a contract! A trickle of something started flowing.

Looking back, it seems that the significant subliminal message I was getting is this: it is important to speak out, reach out, and express yourself.

My parents came from Palestine (Israel), to the "New World" and had to learn Yiddish as well as European Jewish culture. In time, this also would serve me very well for I researched, produced and recorded a collection of beautiful Yiddish songs from a feminist perspective, "Rising Towards the Seraphim."

The 1970s were the heyday of the General Idea group. At night, in the General Idea studio, in the stillness of the dark, I would secretly write my feelings, hour after hour and day into month. At this point, I started to take my songwriting seriously. After all, Bob Dylan was doing it!!! I collected some poems, songs, and thoughts in a folder and called York University Poet-in-Residence, Irving Layton. He drove from York U. in the northern part of the city to my apartment downtown, took the folder, read everything and pronounced, "My dear, these aren't poems, these are songs!" Closed the folder, and promptly left. I was devastated and hid the folder in a closet for many years. But what a lesson! I hadn't seriously imagined myself a songwriter. Could it be true?

It should be mentioned that General Idea formed in the controversial, free-thinking, revolutionary Rochdale College. Yet, for me, Rochdale did what it was supposed to do. It gave me freedom and permission to learn through experimentation, socialization and process.

In time, many schools and libraries invited me to sing for the children. I developed a repertoire that was diverse — scatting, nonsense sounds, stories through songs, international folk songs and inclusive, sing-a-long songs. Why not try to write my own? And I did.

*A Kiss Without A Hug Is Like A Donut Without A Hole*
*And a donut without a hole is like a mushroom without a puff*
*A mushroom without a puff is like a wolf without a huff and*
*A wolf without a huff is no wolf at all!!!*
*A kiss without a hug is like a donut without a hole*
*And a donut without a hole is like fish without a bowl*
*A fish without a bowl, uh-uh, is no fish at all!!!*
*You could walk a cat or a dog, or even a monk*
*You could have anything that you want, but*
*If you've got a kiss without a hug,*
*Then you've got no kiss at all!!!*
(Improvised scat singing to rhythm of the words)

The 1970s presented many things to me: the idea that I could write and sing songs; knowledge that I was comfortable in artistic, creative circles and the realization that I was physically sick. The latter was the most generous gift of all. Slowly my kidneys were failing. I was constantly cold, with hair falling out, no energy, I weighed eighty-two pounds at my worst, suffered excruciating pain that would come and go unannounced, and developed an ability to look at time slowing down.

During my illness, I began to pay attention, to focus. I made a commitment that if I were going to die, then I would die as a singer doing work that was important to me.

While in bed, I would hear my pulse beating by placing a thumb on my wrist vein or cupping my ear with my palm. Music was a constant, guaranteed pulse, rather like the Rhythm of the Universe — constant as day flowing into night and dependable as winter becoming spring.

From my sickbed, I began having hope. I lucked into meeting the great American composer, David Amram. When "SOLID," my first LP (a collaboration of voice and kit drums), was played for him, he said the music was "primitive," a great compliment, like aboriginal music or African tribal communication or Yiddish cantorial improvisational prayers or urban street expressions.

A mystical thing happened on this particular part of my journey. Chris Henderson, American drummer extraordinaire, and collaborator on "SOLID," introduced me to the Buddhism of Nichiren. The primary practice is chanting "NAM MYOHO RENGE KYO." I loved listening to the sound of people chanting this mantra. It was like a human symphony. When adding my voice, my energy changed. With eyes open and a sonorous voice, I plugged into this eternal cantata.

I am now convinced that creativity is about faith, as in, "having faith" means that if you try it, you will make it. It is faith in being alive and communicating that experience. Song, melody, words, rhythms, sounds, ideas, poems, text, and stories are the media that I understand. The process is like reaching into the ether or Neverneverland and pulling out a gift of song, story, rhythm, idea, something. If I believe what I'm doing or feeling or thinking is important, it is up to me to convey that through some kind of expression. We are all stories, reflections, lessons and gifts to one another.

I developed my vocal studio, "The Creative Vocalization Studio," as a means of sharing my experience with others. My teaching methods are different than the norm. I have become the kind of singing teacher I always wanted to study with. I use scatting; vocal improvisation; composition; listening to the body and recognizing its obligation to wholeness; and the realization that all of our abilities are worth exploring and sharing. It is vital to allow people the freedom to sound ugly and untraditional. These are all means of expression. All of it is valuable because we are all valuable.

I had to research, record and produce my own recordings because I could never attract a producer. My recording of "SOLID," a collection of song/poems. garnered me an invitation to appear at the famed Carnegie Recital Hall in New York City and a paragraph in the New York Times, comparing me to Yma Sumac. I've recorded six major CDs and have been a guest on the collaborative "Darn Folksinger" produced by Fat Albert's, Canada's longest-running folk club. The CD, *New Songs for Peace*, became the basis and fundraiser for the New Songs for Peace project, which grew out of the United Nations proclamation that the first decade of the millennium be the Decade for the Culture of Peace and Non-violence for the Children of the World. Our mandate is to encourage people to write new songs that we would collect for our website www.new-songsforpeace.org or on paper for a book.

As I grow comfortable in my mantle of middle age, I'm being serendipitously, invisibly guided to include writing in my daily life. I never thought of myself as a writer, per se. I'd considered myself a singer who questions where lyrics begin and poetry ends. I still consider myself a singer who loves to share some of my personal stories.

When I write a song or poem, I'm usually sitting down. Then I tune everything else out of my awareness and concentrate on what I want to say, what I'm feeling. For a song, either I'm at the piano and I tinkle with sounds until something speaks to me in sound, or else I've got my guitar in my hands and I strum, or pluck, and search for a sound. If I'm writing a poem, I focus my attention — laser-light almost, and allow a rhythm to come to me, or try to find words that rhyme, or else just write freely, striving to express something I think needs to be communicated.

Creativity, by its very nature, is being flexible and making room for development, using all our senses. We must pay attention to the visible and the invisible — energy lives all around and inside and upside and through and through. There is give and take and recognition in offering and accepting. Nothing is mutually exclusive. Creativity lives and guides and teaches and hurts and cultivates. We are the canvas, the baton, the colours, the saga, each and all things. When I open myself to me, I reveal a wealth that is private, symbiotic and I can choose to honour that by offering myself to you or keeping myself for me. Creativity is the larder that anyone can access, if we want to.

I'd like to give the last word to Herbie Hancock who says, "Creativity implies the ability to change." So let's change; it is the only thing that is absolutely constant!

# JACQUELINE DUMAS

Jacqueline Dumas has been in the book business since 1963. She has worked in new and second-hand bookstores in Edmonton, Red Deer, Calgary, and Montreal, and has owned and operated two bookstores of her own, notably Aspen Books (co-owner) and Orlando Books in Edmonton. Between its opening in 1994 and its closing in 2002, Orlando Books hosted more than 500 readings, video presentations, theatre workshops, drumming circles, and other community events. She has also published numerous articles and is the author of three books, including two novels. In 1989, *Madeleine and the Angel* won the Georges Bugnet Award for best novel and was short-listed for the Books in Canada Best First Novel Award. She lives in Edmonton where she is currently at work on her third novel.

## THE TERROR OF THE EMPTY SPACE

I stood in the middle of the empty space, seized by the same mixture of terror and anticipation often experienced while seated at my desk before the blank page. Where to even begin the transformation of this bare grey room into an appealing bookshop that would attract members of the community on a regular basis? I had just signed a five-year lease and was determined to fill these 1200 square feet with books from floor to ceiling. But once I did so, would there be enough people out there who cared?

I already had a name for the bookshop: Orlando Books. A few weeks earlier I had been struggling to come up with a name, listing relevant natural landmarks in the area, waking up in the night to add a beloved fictional character to the list, rereading Virginia Woolf's essays, searching for the one word or phrase that would accurately depict the bookshop and yet be straightforward enough for customers to readily pronounce, spell, and remember. Then one morning I wandered into my favourite second-hand bookshop, and there on the special shelf behind the antique sales desk was a signed first edition of *Orlando*. I immediately recognized the name of my new bookshop, and purchased the book on the spot.

The vision for my store was inspired by the cafés and literary salons that had flourished in the great cities of Europe between the two World Wars: the Bloomsbury Circle of Leonard and Virginia Woolf in London; the Weimar Berlin of Christopher Isherwood's day; and in Paris, Natalie Barney's Friday nights and Gertrude Stein's Saturdays. The writers, artists, composers, dancers, and actors who gathered in these circles had seemed to feed off each other's creative energy, an energy that stimulated original thinking and free expression.

Some twelve years earlier I had sold my interest in another bookshop to focus on writing. But writing is a lonely business, and I had come to miss the daily contact with people that bookselling provides. Writing agreed with my hermit tendencies, but bookselling had satisfied my daily people fix, as well as the need for involvement in a common cause.

As a bookseller, I had always carried a particular fascination with Shakespeare and Company, the bookshop Sylvia Beach founded in Paris in 1917 (the same year as Leonard and Virginia Woolf started the Hogarth Press). It wasn't long before Beach's passion for literature and support of writers and other artists positioned her bookshop at the heart of the contemporary cultural scene. Expatriate American writers Ernest Hemingway and Ezra Pound hung out in her bookshop, as did French writers André Gide and Paul Valéry, composer George Antheil, and photographers Man Ray and Berenice Abbott. Even Canadian writers Morley Callaghan and John Glassco passed through, Glassco being the author of one of the finest accounts of those years, *Memoirs of Montparnasse*.

I had no illusions, or even desire, of creating another Shakespeare and Company — for one thing I was hoping to earn a living. (Sylvia Beach is perhaps best known for going broke publishing James Joyce's *Ulysses* when no mainstream publisher would touch it.) But in the context of carrying on the tradition in 1994 Western Canada, I hoped to create a space that reflected my own literary passions and activist interests at the same time as it complemented other like-minded concerns in the community. The impetus to write and be published and the one to sell books share a common desire to exchange ideas with others. In this regard, both writers and booksellers are interested in selling books and having them read.

So I had a lease, a name, and a vision. Now what?

Setting up a good bookshop requires the same panache, resourcefulness, perseverance, discipline, and attention to detail required in the writing of a novel. The brightest idea is worth little until expanded upon and brought to completion. I wanted Orlando to have a tranquil yet stimulating atmosphere. I wanted people to come into the store for the first time and be impelled to return, and, as in a good novel, I wanted the bookstore's construction lines to be invisible.

While in the process of being seduced, readers of a novel are complicit in the seduction, consensually suspending disbelief so as to be drawn into the narrative, not wanting to be distracted by a technique that draws attention to itself. Participants of a book club, for example, will debate the merits and demerits of a particular novel, objecting to flaws in the plot should they arise, but if the plot works, they don't usually care to examine *why* it works. A book club discussion can be as intense and intimate as a kitchen gossip session, with its participants at variance about the qualities of a particular character, but most readers are not particularly interested in the techniques used to create the character, or in analysing how plot and pace and time might be related to each other. They are not interested in *how* they are being seduced: they just want to be seduced.

The challenge, then, was to create a space in which the books themselves stood out, but not the bookshelves on which they were displayed. Success would be measured by the number of customers who would be drawn in time and again, yet be unable to later report if the bookshelves had been oak or pine or the walls green or white.

To achieve this effect, every detail required attention, from the height and slant of the shelves, to the width of the aisles, to the lighting, to the amount of space allotted to shipping and receiving. Could room be spared for a few inviting nooks and crannies? Cozy chairs for the customers? A small table? Where to place the cash desk so that potential shoplifters could be monitored without making browsers feel unwelcome? I constructed cardboard models of potential fixtures and moved them around on a grid drawn to scale. Once satisfied that a particular configuration would work, I contacted a carpenter friend who agreed to build the fixtures. He attached casters to the bottom of four of the aisle bookcases so they could be rolled aside to create ample space for author readings. Then, while the fixtures were being built, I spent a couple of happy afternoons in the Special Collections Room at the University Library leafing through books on the art of Bloomsbury, searching for the appropriate palette, as well as inspiration for the bookstore logo. Now the sign could be ordered, the carpet chosen, and volunteers rounded up for the painting of the walls and fixtures.

Once the physical space was organized, it was time for the most important job of all: the selection of the opening inventory. Should my first customers be greeted by an inadequate selection of books, it might be a long time before they returned. A dazzling array of interesting titles, on the other hand, would surely entice them back for more. To create the all-important first impression, I set about ordering books that both reflected my own literary interests and reached beyond them. The trick was to find a balance between integrity and practicality, to attract and keep a clientele that was like-minded yet diverse.

Luckily there was a general bookstore down the street, which meant that I was free to ignore the Stephen Kings and Danielle Steeles and concentrate on Canadian prose writers and poets, a commitment that would be supported by a proposed weekly reading series. I eagerly worked my way through stacks of publisher catalogues, beginning with those from the small presses. I ploughed through the blurbs in the University Press catalogues, determined to build solid sections in Philosophy, Politics, Cultural Studies, Women's Studies, and Queer Studies. These subject areas would be displayed close to the entrance, thus signalling the presence of a serious bookshop with progressive leanings.

Augmenting one's personal selection of titles with interesting books that fall outside one's own purview is an art. Just as it is limiting for a writer to say, "I write for myself and myself alone," a bookseller cannot stock a bookshop uniquely with cherished books. Else you might as well confine yourself to writing a diary or sit reading in your book-lined study all day long and be done with it. Writers must respect their audience and booksellers must acknowledge the wishes of their customers.

Much of bookselling involves matching readers up with the unread books they didn't know they were looking for — a process that requires intuitive leaps on the part of the bookseller. Just as novelists must be observers of people, so too must booksellers be able to size up their customers. A person might enter the bookshop and ask for "a good read." What's "a good read?" What does "this" customer mean by it? Oh, she loved *The Lord of the Rings* but thought *The Shipping News* was boring. Then don't suggest *The Stone Diaries*, even if it did win a Pulitzer Prize. Hand her a copy of *Gormenghast* to consider: you yourself never managed to get through more than twenty pages of Tolkien, and you liked Mervyn Peake even less. There's a particular, bent satisfaction in pleasing a customer with a book that left you cold.

Selecting forthcoming titles is riskier but more exciting than reordering backlist. A strong and balanced backlist may be the backbone of a good bookshop, but it's the new titles that provide the zing. Predicting the literary successes of the future is a mysterious process that involves learned instinct and a certain amount of flying-by-the-seat-of-your-pantsedness.

If imagination fuels writing, an ability to spot the as yet unrecognized gems of the forthcoming season from nothing more than a blurb and a dust jacket is one of the most rewarding aspects of bookselling. Where's the fun in pushing generic rewrites of last year's bestseller? It's puzzling how some publishers spend so much time and money trying to duplicate and repackage last season's success story. People have already read *The Edible Woman*; they've read *The Name of the Rose*. Are they really in search of inferior imitations?

When Marilyn Robinson's first novel *Housekeeping* came out in 1981, my then partner and I loved it so much we ordered 50 copies, and proceeded to tell our customers about it. We hand-sold it to friends, to members of book clubs, and to every fourth customer who came in asking for a good novel. Those customers in turn read the book and told others about it, and before long we were reordering copies every couple of weeks. I suspect this same scenario repeated itself in hundreds of independent bookstores across the continent.

Likewise, when Joy Kogawa's *Obasan* came out in the fall of that same year, my partner and I were excited enough to order 125 copies, which at the time was a huge quantity for a hardcover first novel. But we were confident we had a winner. Not only was *Obasan* beautifully written, it was groundbreaking in its depiction of the Japanese-Canadian experience of the Second World War. We arranged an autographing session for Joy, who was being sent on tour by her equally enthusiastic publisher.

Total number of persons who showed up for the autographing: one. Total number of copies of *Obasan* sold by the end of day: one.

Joy continued on her tour, concerned that we would be "stuck" with the 124 books we still had on hand. She called from southern Alberta to tell us that she had come across a bookstore that was willing to take five or six copies off our hands. "No thanks," we said, "we're going to need every one of those copies before the season is out." She called again from B.C.: another bookstore promising to take some. "No thanks," we said again, laughing. We were certain that once word got out, people would be lining up for copies of her book.

*Obasan*, of course, did become a bestseller and is now a staple backlist title in all good bookshops. As for those 125 copies, not only did we sell them all, but the last six were resold to the publisher who had run out and needed copies for the judges of one of the various awards the book had been nominated for.

Thirteen years after the advent of *Obasan*, Orlando Books was set to open its doors, and the days of a small bookshop pre-ordering 125 copies of a first novel were gone. Should such a novel do poorly, the ensuing returns would eat up any profits; should the novel take off, the big box bookstores would be quick to jump on the bandwagon and discount the book, leaching away customers and leaving a small independent with the cost of heavy returns.

If my bookstore would be unable to match the discounts offered by the big box stores and internet giants, it would still be able to offer something they couldn't: an intimate and caring environment, face-to-face exchanges with the customers, real conversation — and gossip. Writers and booksellers thrive on gossip: it feeds our work.

Initially, Orlando Books held its own. During its nine years it evolved into a space that hosted more than 500 readings by writers from across the country. It provided a venue for emerging playwrights to stage workshops and singer/songwriters to compare notes, a venue where a monthly "tertulia" gathered, a "tertulia" being a sort of Spanish-speaking literary salon. And in conservative Alberta, the bookshop provided a place where political activists could meet and strategize.

Four years into the lease, however, gentrification of the Avenue pushed the bookshop into a choice between closure and a move to a poorer location across the tracks. I chose the move. In the end the bookshop in its new location proved to be a financial drain and was forced to shut down in October of 2002, leaving me with a large personal loan that I could not imagine ever being able to pay back.

The response from the community was overwhelming. Donations started coming in the day after I shut the doors. Friends of the bookstore organized a fundraiser to help pay down the bank loan. A neighbourhood cinema offered up its space for the afternoon, and local writers and musicians performed gratis. Neighbourhood businesses and individuals donated prizes for a silent auction; local restaurants sent food and refreshments. A group of poets brought tears to my eyes when they took up a collection and delivered an envelope stuffed with tens and twenties to my home — via bicycle. It felt as if the bookstore had belonged to everyone, with me as its privileged steward.

Like many before, the bookstore had been a financial struggle from the beginning, but never because enough people didn't care. The generous people who rallied round after its closure proved that creative endeavours should never be measured by commercial success, or the lack of it. But something was lost when it closed.

I lament the loss of so many independents over the last decade, along with their mixture of passion and expertise. I suspect that if Leonard and Virginia Woolf were publishing today, they would reach their audience mainly through a web site on the internet. But coming across a book on a web site is not the same as discovering it on a bookshelf next to other remarkable books, and then being free to thumb through it and discuss it around the coffee machine with another casual browser.

Most independent booksellers would probably be astute enough to recognize Virginia Woolf's genius. But are there enough of them left? I'm not sure.

# JANET CALCATERRA

Janet Calcaterra moved with her mother and siblings from Saskatoon, Saskatchewan to Toronto in 1954. Although educated in Toronto, Kingston, and Ottawa, her steepest learning curve occurred in 1972 when she home-steaded on 160 acres near New Liskeard, ON. There she acquired life-long passions for gardening, storytelling, and solitude. She has worked as a teacher, archivist, and curator, and published fiction, travel, and gardening pieces. Currently, she writes and teaches English part-time at Canadore College, North Bay.

## DO MY IMPULSES TO WRITE AND GARDEN COMPARE?

Why do I think of my computer as a toy? It can't be ridden, and it doesn't race quick-ly. If I struck it with a racket or bat, it might stop. And, it doesn't have any games...no, not even Solitaire! So, why do I sit, without promise of compensation, and plan for, research, and produce writings on it, for which I must find a publisher? The same ques-tions apply to my gardening. Why do I place shriveled seeds into an odorous mix of manure and peat moss and hope, without assurance, that they bloom, mauve and white, as stately Lavatera across the front of my porch? Their buds don't even open until mid-August. And yet, my children call what I do in the yard, "playing in the sand box." If gardening looks like playing to them, it must mean the same to me. Thus, writing and gardening are both creative and pleasurable. But, from where do the impulses to work at them come?

For as long as I can remember, to when I was three or four, I have loved books. I loved looking at them, touching their paper, hearing them read, being held while read to, and experiencing their stories. I still remember when Mrs. Bowerman, my grade two teacher at Etobicoke's Norseman Public School, read Gertrude Chandler Warner's first book, *The Boxcar Children*, to the class after lunch. I was transported to the hard-scrabble world of the novel's runaway children. Later, I would lie on the couch reading Lucy Maud Montgomery's *Anne* novels, believing for those moments that I was on P.E.I. with orphaned Anne and her Avonlea world. I could place myself in France or New Orleans when, as a teenager, I rode the T.T.C. for work at Eaton's and devoured Frances Parkinson Keyes' novels. On the subway, I would let my imagination delight me and take a much-anticipated vacation to somewhere exotic.

But, how are writing down words and reading them related, and what about gar-dening? When did my interest in blossoms emerge? My first gardening experiences were digging up dandelions from my mother's lawn or deadheading her flowers to relieve my boredom during hot Toronto summers. I didn't think of those chores in the same way I did reading. However, her requests for help soon became more interesting. She let me plant spring annuals or dig fall tubers, and those jobs so absorbed me that I had to be called in for dinner. Perhaps it was the unspoken permission to get dirty.

About the time of Mrs. Bowerman, when I learned to write paragraphs, then pages, I began to think I could write stories. Why would I want to do such a thing? Perhaps, first of all, I needed to make sense of my environment. In the mid-fifties, growing up in a Canadian, suburban home with three siblings, I had no idea what the world had undergone in the past fifty years or would undergo in the next. And both reading the newspaper and writing about my environment helped make sense of the quietly-polite chaos surrounding me. In addition, writing pushed me into the same dream-like trance in which I found myself when reading or read to. When I wrote, I could suspend disbelief for the storyline, characters, or setting in the same way I could when read to or reading. I would fill with comfortable pleasure while exploring the writing idea. And, if I could write about topics that I and others cared about or that informed us, I could bring pleasure and education to myself and others. Gradually, I realized that writing was something useful I could do with my life.

I was born in 1948, just after the Second World War ended. Canadian men came home victorious, but some had fewer limbs, and many had damaged psyches. I was the daughter of a teacher who turned housewife because her marriage prohibited her from working, and an army-captain-doctor returned from the Second World War. When I was five, my father and mother separated. My father stayed in western Canada, and my mother, grandparents, siblings, and I moved to Toronto. No explanation was offered for the relocation or why my father didn't live with us, and I felt it would be too bold to ask. By the time he died, I was eleven and felt I had the right to question. My mother's answer to "Why didn't my father (it seemed too personal to call him 'Daddy') live with us?" was that he wasn't the same after the war. At that age, I asked myself and relatives (who, in the then WASP Toronto culture, were loath to discuss personal things) what "not the same" meant? As any answers I gleaned, which often included, "I can't talk about that," were unsatisfactory, I began to create my own scenarios. These answers included that the man my mother married had come home from the war as a different person, someone my mother didn't recognize. But, my parents' wedding pictures contained a man in a uniform looking much like my father did the last time I saw him. Remember! I was five. How, then, was he not the same? After much thought, I realized it must be in some way I could not see. By then, I was worldly enough to know that what went on in people's heads could change without their children knowing. So, outside my single-parent, fifties home, when asked why my father didn't live with us before he died, my answer was that his head had changed in a way with which my mother couldn't live. The idea, in the fifties, that a woman could decide she was no longer willing to live with a man was so revolutionary to my friends that they stopped asking. Because I was dependent for my well-being on my, by then, teacher mother, I put aside the fact that my father was changed by war and got on with my life.

Then, the sixties arrived.

It wasn't until the Vietnam War took me from a safe, university student to a concerned, elementary-school teacher in a Canada that harboured draft-evading, American men that I began to think again of "not the same." While still in university, I met a man who came to Canada from the United Sates to resist the draft and, thus, to boycott involvement in the Vietnam War. We married and, on a whim, moved to northern Ontario. I began to write stories to clarify for me how the world had, inexorably, changed. These stories were not, specifically, about the war. They didn't describe battles, weapons used, or conditions in which soldiers lived; they were about everyday people and how their day-to-day lives were affected by this conflict. The writing of these stories made the concept that my father was changed by World War II very real. After all, those of us who observed the Vietnam War on television, were never the same as we'd, innocently, been before seeing. Thus, creating stories became, for me, how I clarified an increasingly, fractured world.

About the time I began writing stories, we finished building our wilderness home, and I began to grow vegetables for food. I also created a perennial flower border around our cabin to somehow civilize the backwoods where we lived. I even wrote about gardening in my stories, and an article of mine about rhubarb was published. In my life, gardening and writing converged as creative impulses on which I could act and which served to help me make meaning. Then, the public was flooded with documentaries, films, magazine articles, and books on the American involvement in Vietnam. Such classics as Francis Ford Coppola's film, *Apocalypse Now*, Oliver Stone's movie, *Born on the Fourth of July*, and Tim O'Brien's haunting books, *Going After Cacciato* and *The Things They Carried*, came to be, for me, the last words on the Vietnam War. Therefore, believing that my perceptions of the war were inadequate, I turned to other topics.

After our children started school, my husband and I decided they needed more activities, so we moved to North Bay, and I continued to write. I wrote travel articles, published in *The Globe and Mail* and *The Toronto Star*, and a few short stories, which met with rejection. Then, unable to find a teaching job and needing to save for my children's education, I trained for and got a position as an archivist for a northern-Ontario railway. This work taught me about historical research, and I realized that the trance-like state I occupied while reading, writing, or, for that matter, gardening, was the same state I occupied while searching for historical information.

This enjoyment made me think again of my father and where I could do research on World War II and, in particular, his involvement in it. It also made space in my creative brain for the original thought of what it meant that my father was never the same after the war. I started researching Canada's involvement in this war, and, in particular, I became fascinated by the little-noticed Italian Campaign, the theatre in which my father had participated. I read books including Farley Mowat's, *And No Birds Sang*, Bill McAndrew's, *Canadians and the Italian Campaign, 1943-1945,* J.L. Granatstein's and Desmond Morton's, *A Nation Forged in Fire, Canadians and the Second World War 1939-1945*, and Terry Copp's and Bill McAndrew's, *Battle Exhaustion, Soldiers, and Psychiatrists in the Canadian Army, 1939-1945*, along with many more. This reading was accompanied by the expected, trance-like state. In particular, the horrendous Battle of Ortona, which the Canadians fought at Christmas, 1943, fascinated me. I decided to write a novel manuscript about someone who'd participated in this battle and his family. I knew that such a large project would provide many opportunities to be in that pleasurable trance. About that time, my job was abolished, and with only part-time work teaching business English at North Bay's Canadore College, I was able to devote more time to writing.

And what of gardening? By then, my family had moved to a North Bay home with a treeless yard in need of a perennial border. This included growing purple clematis, orange honeysuckle, and red roses that would climb lattices. Every spring and summer I attacked this job and found that I had to be called, nightly, to come in for dinner. I was enjoying and still enjoy inhabiting the trance that playing in the sandbox called my garden provides.

Unlike the ongoing job of maintaining a flower bed, it took me ten years of thought, research, and writing to finish a manuscript that would bring me remotely close to understanding the horror of World War II. Along with comprehending a participant's horror, I gained empathy for the mothers and wives of soldiers who'd participated. At times, the research was emotionally painful, especially when reading the above-mentioned books, but these still put me into the trance-like state I desired. I had the fun of meeting my daughter, by this time at university in Montreal, for weekends in Ottawa, staying with her at a B & B, and reading War Diaries at the National Archives to understand what a soldier's life in the Italian Campaign entailed. After I had finished the manuscript's first draft, I felt closer to the experience my father must have had, and thus, writing it helped me understand my childhood. When I'd finished several drafts, my older daughter, by then a graduate in English, read the latest draft and gave me suggestions. We enjoyed tea and cookies while discussing changes she felt I should make. These pleasure-filled experiences are embodied in the trance-like state I occupied during the process. With the current war in Iraq becoming, for the United States and its troops, increasingly like the Vietnam War, I have felt emboldened to finish my stories and others about the effects of the Vietnam, Iraq and other recent wars on the everyday lives of Canadians.

By writing about Canada's involvement in the Italian Campaign of W. W. II and the effects modern-day conflicts have on Canadians, I believe that I'll not only bring trance-like pleasure to readers but also educate them on these events. How do I do that with gardening? Although many of my neighbours are more knowledgeable than I am about growing, I have often been awakened from my trance, while gardening, to help identify a weed. I've also divided perennials and given parts to friends who are fledgling gardeners. Thus, my creative urge to garden comes from a desire to bring others pleasure and to educate them on the joy of playing in a garden sandbox. If anyone cares to know why I, a teacher, who grows flowers and herbs passionately, also writes stories and novel manuscripts, it's to make sense of my world, enter a dream-like trance, and both entertain and educate my hoped-for readers and fellow gardeners. The worlds of writing and gardening are like giant sandboxes into which we can, happily, dig ourselves.

# JOE BLADES

Joe Blades lives the artist life with a twist. Often misidentified as just a poet or just a publisher, he is so much more and so much less. Blades exhibits bookworks, photographs, and *objets d'art* primarily in Canada and Europe. He is a community radio producer-host at CHSR 97.9 FM with the award-winning *Ashes, Paper & Beans: Fredericton's Writing & Art Show*. Blades was curator of *Videopoems: a screening* for the Tidal Wave Film Festival and he is the editor of ten books and chapbooks. His poetry and art have appeared in over fifty-five trade and chapbook anthologies, and in numerous periodicals. Blades has authored thirty poetry chapbooks and limited edition artist books, as well as four full-length poetry books. Two of his books have been translated and published in Serbian editions. He is also founder and publisher of the independent literary publishing house, Broken Jaw Press.

## BEARING WITNESS

My art, especially my poetry, is full of words. My journals, which I started to keep in 1983, are filled with words and images — what I needed to do on a given day, where I'd been, what I'd done, whom I'd met — plus artifacts and the detritus of my daily activities: stickers, ticket stubs, receipts, notes, posters, flyers, labels. I am rarely without pen, knife and glue stick. Journals hold my ongoing collecting of images, artifacts, observations and ideas, as well as their reworking, mixed media style, into whatever else.

Questions, and response to my art over the years, have caused me think about what I create and how I make it. Two things evident are, (1) much of my work seems to be contextual, and (2) much of it is site-specific to a place, a moment, a situation.

I work with the obvious and the overlooked and weave them to tell layered stories. Everything goes into my journal collage and related work. Central to my witnessing and transforming life into art, the journals are both reference works and artworks of themselves. Strangers, seeing one of my journals for the first time, want to look inside.

Similarly, when I write poems during a public artist residency I incorporate elements from everything around at that moment mixed with whatever it draws from my mind. Posting them on my brokenjoe.blogspot.com immediately and/or hanging the raw poems on a wall for anyone to read is a nervier act than most writers will undertake but my artist life is, ultimately, performance art.

casemate poems (coda) 2

absinthe refined with traditional spoon
vincent too his own ear after original

watching water over sugar cube green
into the glass below licorice scent rising

corner of york and george streets between
12 and 5 *ideal for gallery space* in window

sometimes choice is not subject but form
a means in a situation of art making

crammed into acadian bus window seat
my laptop open on lap playing music in earbuds

buddy student with laptop in seat beside watches
jimmy stewart kim novak artist movie colourised

homework while i handhold open sketchbook
journal above my laptop and write longhand

had enough of writing the blog i can't post
wireless without not-possessed satellite phone

not war correspondent but stand-up poet
coming off the road and prepping for next

only one trek visitor so far: co-ordinator
mary ann on saturafternoon promising rain

IMAGINATION *in* ACTION

crow caws night turning grey morning
almost time for *painting for sale*

i am my own staff my only staff in art
no apprentice no assistant no acolyte

ornament fiddle missing its bridge
sculpture collection of broken eyeglasses

i propose these works bearing witness
plexiglas file box filled with journals

white leather dallas cowgirl stiletto
heel boots on chinese student baptist

no that's not one of my proposed artworks
just an apré church york house sighting

kitchen wall instant photo shoot studio
one-hour processing monday morning do

trapped by promised transparent art making
studio open same hours as sunday shopping

text paintings catch passing eyes earn
smiles without visitors at artment door

how much space might i desire to need
if someone wants us seen? if we produce?

# JULIA STEINECKE

Julia Steinecke has been exploring her surroundings and writing about them for over twenty years. Her poetry, prose, and travel writing have appeared in *Descant, Canadian Geographic, Prairie Fire, The Writing Space Journal, The Toronto Star* and many other publications. Julia leads writing retreats in Cuba and on the Toronto Islands. She works out of her home office in Toronto and her cabin in Maple Leaf, Ontario. She can also be found at www.JuliaSt.net.

## DOING IT MY WAY

I pop in the DVD and the background music begins to play. Cheesy violins and flutes build up the intro for Frank Sinatra's hit song. Scenes of towering mountains and rushing rivers flash on the screen, canned landscaping captioned with song lyrics. I pick up the microphone and begin to sing.

What's a nice, intelligent writer like me doing, alone in my living room in the middle of the day, singing into a karaoke machine?

At this point in my life, writing doesn't completely satisfy me. Like a polyamourous bisexual, I seek pleasure from more than one medium of expression. Lately there's been poetry, travel writing, photography and karaoke. Each one has given voice to some part of me, satisfied some obvious or obscure need.

I've been writing stories since I could hold a pen; making them up even before that. When my friend and I used to camp in the backyard pup tent, we'd play a game where each of us would secretly make up half of a two-sentence story. I'd think of an opening sentence, like, "Once upon a time there was a girl who found a giant frog the size of a house." I'd turn to my friend who was quietly plotting her ending.

"Ready?" I'd ask.

"Ready."

Excitedly, I'd deliver my sentence, not knowing where it would go from there. My friend would roll over, laughing.

"What? What's the ending?" This is where I had to trust my friend not to tamper with her part, not to make it tidy.

"And the door slammed in her face and everyone died." The whole tent would shake with our giggles.

Now that I'm writing newspaper articles, for money, I miss those days when I could start a story and not worry about where it was going. Those pup-tent tales didn't have to be sophisticated and sensible. They had length limitations, for sure, but they didn't have to succinctly explain a point or convince someone of my opinion.

These days, I write a monthly column on gay and lesbian travel for a mainstream newspaper. I have a monthly deadline, a 750 word limit, and the requirement that I be witty, original, yet inoffensive to straight people; palatable, yet fresh. It's a fun challenge and I get to travel and create word imagery. Sometimes I can fool myself into thinking I'm writing a poem about a place and its people.

Still I love to flee into the arms of my mistress, Karaoke, with whom I can be crass, corny, and politically incorrect. Not to mention, mediocre and loud. These aren't the only benefits. Singing is a physical, tangible expression. I learn to breathe and I feel my voice moving from my abdomen, through my throat, and out to the world. It makes me feel, deep down, that I have a voice, in a way that words on paper never could. It cures my aches and depression, rewires my brain, and makes me laugh, on days when my head is fuzzy and my writing is blocked.

My interest in photography came early in life, before the pup-tent days, when I inherited my brother's Kodak Instamatic with a roll of black-and-white film. I went out with my dad, who was also into photography, and took pictures of the fluffy snow that piled four feet deep in our northern town. Indoors, I took a picture of my sister balancing a budgie on her finger in front of a mirror. I documented my world, all the things that were important to me. I've always liked the immediacy. Choose the right moment, and, *snap*, it's finished; no polishing, no revising. It either works or it doesn't.

I dropped photography and picked it up again when I got into travel writing. It's exciting to photograph the places I visit, though I get frustrated at how the act of snapping a picture separates me from the experience and the people. Everything is mediated by the lens while it's still happening. One way I cope with this is to leave my camera tucked away when I'm sightseeing for the first time, meeting people, making direct contact. This is when I can absorb the place into my bloodstream. I'll return the next day to frame it, to capture colour, texture and angles with my camera.

Each creative medium has its advantages and drawbacks; except Karaoke, which is fun, fun, fun.

# KATHRYN COLLINS

Kathryn Collins hails from Barrie, Ontario. She worked in England at an art magazine, *Studio International*, before graduating from the University of Toronto in 1970. Later, she studied at the Woolfitt School of Contemporary Painting in Toronto, and coordinated art shows at Vivaxis, a restaurant/gallery, subsequently called Les Pleiades, on Dupont Street. She was a senior editor at Harlequin Enterprises Ltd. in charge of the romantic suspense line, Mystique Books, and has published articles and genre novels, taught seminars in writing and participated in art shows. In 1989 she moved to Vancouver, B.C., and later to Victoria, where she writes for the provincial government. She volunteers at the Victoria School of Writing as a past Board member, and is currently completing a children's novel and working on short stories.

## WRITING AND ART

I started writing when I was eight years old, and painting soon after. It all happened naturally, because it was what I was interested in doing. I suspect it is like that for most people…we are born interested in certain things that we eventually discover and take up, if the circumstances allow.

At age thirteen I announced to my mother that I wanted to be a writer. Her response was ambiguous: "That will make your father very happy." My Irish father had always written stories and articles, which I am certain influenced me in that direction. After the war, he had a day job supervising the cleaning staff in the army section of Camp Borden, now called Base Borden, in southern Ontario. Later he became one of the managers of Pearson International Airport in Toronto, but in those early days he was still struggling to publish, and taking his high school diploma by correspondence courses. He completed a BA in sociology later in life and was able to write full time when he retired. He continued to publish stories and articles into his eighties.

My mother had also wanted to be a writer and named me after the first two parts of the pseudonym she had long ago chosen for herself, *Kathryn Maureen O'Brien*. But when she casually told me one day that she had given up writing shortly after marrying my father, it seemed inexplicable, even a little tragic. She had not been allowed to go past grade ten in school, and the Depression years had been hard. Later, in her fifties, she would get a degree in English Literature, and be commissioned to write a book about the literacy movement after years of volunteer work as the Canadian President of Laubach Literacy, a grassroots literacy movement founded by American Frank Laubach, whose inspirational motto was, "Each one, teach one."

So in a sense I inherited my parents' early dreams of writing, although it was clearly also my own. Concurrent with my youthful career announcement, I started keeping a writer's journal, influenced by L. M. Montgomery's chief character in *Emily of New Moon*, who kept "Jimmy-books." After some thought I called my first one "Reflections on Life." At the great age of thirteen, I felt I had a lot to reflect on.

I wrote a lot of poems throughout high school and dreamed of becoming a second Emily Dickinson, (another of my favourite Emilys). Afterward I earned a degree in English Literature with History of Fine Arts as my favourite minor, managed to escape teaching, and worked as a "Girl Friday" in London, England, for an art magazine called *Studio International*, while taking life drawing at St. Martin-in-the-Fields. I was impressed that Aubrey Beardsley had done the magazine's first cover in 1898, when it was called *The Studio*. An exhibition at the Victoria and Albert Museum of lino prints by Picasso, Matisse and other twentieth-century artists was my impetus to begin a passionate foray into printmaking in the tiny top floor flat I rented in the Earl's Court area of London. Later, back in Toronto, I attended The Woolfitt School of Contemporary Painting at night and on the weekends for about five years while working full-time for a Toronto publishing house. I also showed local artists' work regularly at a beautiful restaurant/gallery on Dupont Street, hosting a new show opening every three weeks for over three years. During that time I was privileged to host a show of the visual works of well-known Canadian poet bp nichol, as well as other Toronto poets. It was a show that certainly married writing with art because most of the pieces were concrete poems, using words to build visual images.

Although I cannot clearly say that my art work and writing have influenced each other, I recognize that visual images play a strong part in both of them. As well, I like to name paintings as a comment on the work, adding a verbal dimension, and have sometimes created art pieces that contain both words and images. Yet I think of art and writing as separate modes of expression. In a sense they meet only in my journals, where I scribble thoughts about the art pieces I am working on, or the stories or poems in process. Admittedly, I have fallen into the habit of buying thick, acid-free sketchbooks for my journals so I can draw and sketch in them as well as write. At the most, I would say there's never any conflict between my art and writing; instead, a degree of integration, a peaceful parallelism.

There is of course a very general influence, in the way that any creative process helps other creative processes. They put one in the zone, so to speak, although the games might be at opposite ends of the field.

I was once interviewed on TV about my books, and they asked me if I thought of an audience when writing. This question caught me off guard. I remember replying, "No, I just write what I like to write, and hope that if I like it someone else will." That's pretty much it. It would be too distracting to think about an audience when creating...that's the outer world, whereas creativity takes one to inner worlds, created by the imagination. My experience of writing fiction and painting is of deliberately entering a kind of dream world while working things out, a very intense space that focuses inward.

This may sound strange, when I have published three genre books, romance novels, in fact. Isn't one supposed to think of one's audience? Yes and no. I had worked as an editor for several years at Harlequin Enterprises and thought it would be fun to write some of their longer "Superromances" after I left, and to make some money doing it. It was, and I did. There are guidelines that defer to an expected audience, but they are very general: a man and woman meet, complications set in, a happy ending. The process of imagining any piece of fiction, light-hearted or serious, is similar in my experience, although when writing the latter one sets sail on uncharted waters.

People who consider themselves "not creative" are always asking where ideas come from. Essentially, they are asking about the genesis of creative works. "Ideas are everywhere," I always want to say. And they are, if you have your antennae up. But the ones that we choose to follow often turn up in mysterious ways. There's an inner seeing, hearing or sensing, possibly akin to, but not the same as, what psychic folks experience. Ideas come in those kinds of ways, through the portal of the mind. Receptivity is certainly necessary, but most writers and artists are naturally receptive, born that way. You can work at receptivity, prime the pump as it were, but mechanical methods seem to me inferior to true inspiration. Creative friends I've talked to have all had periods when ideas seem to crowd the air they breathe. And periods when ideas are nowhere to be found.

Although my printmaking days begun in England were inspired by hypnagogic images that appeared when I closed my eyes at night, and most of my later art work began as an inner image or intuitive impulse, the reason I finally decided to go to art school came about in an unexpected way. In my twenty-ninth year two words that happened to be in French kept running through my mind, *bleu foncé*. They just wafted in, from time to time, with a peculiar insistency, accompanied by a *frisson* that felt electric, alive.

I sensed that behind the words were paintings, waiting. I could feel them but not see them. It was this that eventually compelled me to find an art school at age thirty, and to begin a series of abstract landscape paintings. I moved on to work with various media such as chalk and ink, and later silk and feathers and other materials. This was a magical period of my life. All of the art seemed to flow from a secret source, a hidden spring. I worked from impulse, inner images, gesture mixed with emotion and intuition, and an attraction to certain colours; it all felt very headlong. I was also studying and looking at the work of many great artists; among my favourites, Jan Vermeer, Hans Hofmann, Georgia O'Keefe, Paul Klee, Paul Cezanne, Henri Matisse and others. Trips to New York with my art school or on my own to paint and visit the galleries were thrilling, especially when I met Helen Frankenthaler, whose work I very much admired.

More mysterious still, I realized a few months ago that behind those two initiatory words, *bleu foncé*, lie still more paintings, softly waiting. There is a much longer series than I first supposed. Why did it take an interval of twenty-some years for that realization to emerge? One day I just knew that the "electricity" behind the words is still there…the words retain their potency. They are a pathway to more work, that I can choose to take or not.

How does a writing idea arrive? Often I hear the opening line of a story or poem in my head, or sometimes a character talking. Of course, ideas come from the outside, too. Sometimes an urgent need to write about something wells up, such as after a hospital visit to a friend's dying mother, or to untangle the criss-crossed pattern of a friendship between three very different women. There has to be a certain level of intensity for the imagination to fire.

I am currently revising for the umpteenth time a comic children's novel I've written for the 8-12 age group. It began as a single phrase that rattled around in my mind for days; I thought it was the beginning of a poem and sat down to write one, but nothing came out right. I slept on it and woke up to realize it was really a short story, and that a little girl of ten or eleven was speaking. I wrote the story. It wasn't until a few years later that I workshopped it in a class with West Coast writer Julie Lawson at the Victoria School of Writing, and was surprised to hear her exclaim, "It cries out for a novel. I want to know more about this little girl." Inspired by her, I went home and spent four months writing a novel to wrap around the short story, which I ended up weaving into the longer tale. Writing the book was pure unexpected joy, and my first serious venture into children's writing. While still revising it, I have started another children's novel for the same age group, which also began as a little girl's voice speaking in my head. That little girl, like the first, compels my attention.

Other ideas come in more ordinary ways. A friend tells me about something, and one quiet little snippet, a seemingly innocuous detail, makes the hair at the nape of my neck stand on end…always a signal that there's a pathway that can open. Or I read something in the newspaper…perhaps someone has shipped the wrong body in a coffin to a funeral home and the relatives find out too late, all darkly hilarious to my Irish-Canadian sensibility. I often write down ideas on little yellow stickies that alight all over my house like cabbage butterflies. But only some ideas are vital enough to materialize. It's the intensity quotient that counts; an idea has to have the strength to make it all the way to the top of that carnival contraption when the hammer hits the ball—it has to make that bell ring. Then the discipline factor has to kick in; apply seat of pants to chair and get cracking: the hard part. Mostly I don't seem to decide on a subject; the subject clamps me in its jaws and hangs on. It has to, because I am very hard to start, although equally hard to stop once I'm going. My job is to decide if I'm going to work at the idea or give the character life, and carry the inspiration through to completion.

I've recently started a science fiction fantasy novel that also began as a character "talking" in my head, in fact at widely-separated intervals over the last thirty years. I captured her wild observations on yellow stickies, stowed them in envelopes and my journals, her conversation scattered all over the place, and then one day I finally sat down and began to tell her story, which is going in a shockingly different direction that I ever expected. I didn't even know it was SF fantasy until a friend who writes SF told me so when she read the first chapter. Currently, I've been making a map of the character's world, which is omnipotent fun. Now I wish I'd been making maps of fantasy worlds all my life. The whole thing just buzzes with "pathways."

Although I have at times yearned to be a writer-illustrator, I don't normally write and paint about the same things. They are simply as different as cats and dogs. My stories are narratives: my paintings and sculptures, images. However, I do think that poetry and painting are closer in nature that stories and paintings. Although some painters are definitely telling stories in their work, for instance, Bruegel the Elder, William Kurelek or Henri Rousseau. Some paintings have an implicit narrative line, like Picasso's *Guernica*; some stories and shorter novels have a colour-field quality, a purity of hue. Many poems just hang there, akin to visual art, "Beautiful as an Iroquois," as Toni Morrison says in *Jazz*. In the making of art or a poem or a story, the human mind and human gesture meet; we can't create without both.

I haven't read much on the theories of creativity, but there's one thing I do believe: that best creativity happens in an altered state, just a little left of wide-awake. I discovered long ago that I could induce this state by looking out the window at the wind in the trees, at clouds, or listening to music. My characters start talking in these alpha states, and I hastily write it all down in my notebook, even though I don't know where or even whether it will be included in the story as it unfolds. Yet it's all grist for the mill. I think everyone finds their own gateways to their material, to enter the flow.

I also believe that everyone is a creator in one way or another, and that we're always creating, whether it's a painting or dance, a perfect café latte, an amazing ski run or a bad hair day. Our thoughts go before us and bend life as it happens. Mostly we create half consciously. We think, I want a coffee, and if we're at home we get out the ingredients, make a pot and then drink it. It's no different with any kind of art. We're visited by an idea or desire to make something, we get out our tools and make a picture, a poem or a story, a dance or musical composition, or a modern-day cathedral called a bank tower. If all goes well and the work gets done, the world drinks it in.

Unexpected things influence creation. For Delacroix, the colour of the sunlight in North Africa profoundly affected his art. For Proust and Matisse, sickness was an entrance to writing and art. Perhaps it altered their brainwaves, allowing a receptivity that would not have been there otherwise. Madness and creativity have intrigued mankind for decades, in Virginia Woolf and other artists. There are edges we all have to dance on, and for some, on either side lies the abyss. I am grateful for their courage, and that many have danced so brilliantly under painful circumstances.

For most of us, the things that hinder us are as mundane as the need to make a living and the difficulty of finding a way in a frantic world to conserve our inner resources for creating. It's never easy, and much time can be lost. Carving out the time and energy from a busy work life to follow our dreams is essential. The most important thing is to keep on working at the things we love.

Why do we want to create? For those of us who remember late twentieth-century ads, the mystery is as great as how they get the caramel into those Cadbury chocolate bars. Honestly, I have no idea why we create, other than it's a built-in feature of humanity. I am, in fact, afraid to know; it might jinx the mix. I'm just glad to be able to keep on doing work that always feels like play.

# K.D.MILLER

K.D. Miller was born in Hamilton, Ontario in 1951. In 1973 she graduated with an Honours Bachelor of Arts degree in Drama and English from the University of Guelph. In 1978, she graduated from the University of British Columbia with a Master of Fine Arts degree in directing. K.D. Miller's first collection of short stories, *A Litany in Time of Plague*, was published in 1994. Her second collection, *Give Me Your Answer*, published in 1999, was shortlisted for the inaugural Upper Canada Brewing Company's Writer's Craft Award. *Holy Writ*, a series of personal essays which explore the link between creativity and spirituality, was published in 2001. K.D. Miller lives in Toronto, and is working on a third collection of short stories.

## THE SUM OF MY PARTS

I was stage-struck when I was eleven. That sounds like being bonked on the head by something. It was more like waking up in the early dark and watching the light pick out shapes in the room. Things that had been puzzling me started to make sense. That odd restlessness I felt sometimes while watching old movies on TV, for instance. If the heroine was somebody like Anne Frank or Joan of Arc, I would run upstairs to my room during commercial breaks and pace back and forth, gesticulating and mouthing lines. Now I knew why. And I knew where my destiny lay. Chubby, bespectacled bookworm though I might be, I was going to metamorphose into Katharine Hepburn.

Well, I had a lot of fun trying. I did two degrees in theatre, got paid a few times for stage and voice work and was married to an actor. Though the last play I was in closed decades ago, I still think of myself as an actor who writes. It was good for me to step out into the stage lights and perform. It was the most audacious, outrageous thing I've ever done, and it's served me well. Many writers dread doing readings and interviews and other promotional gigs, but I'm a ham. I love the electric *zzzt!* of connecting with a live audience. And to this day, while sitting in the dark watching a play or a movie, I still sometimes feel that old restlessness. That, *Let me in! Let me do what you're doing!*

But then I go home and write something.

\*\*\*

Why do we do this? Write or act or paint or dance? Nobody needs what we produce, at least not in the way they need food or coffins or shoes. Oscar Wilde cheerfully admitted that all art was essentially useless. But he also said, "It is through art, and through art only, that we can realize our perfection; through art and art only that we can shield ourselves from the sordid perils of actual existence." [1]

Well, I think I agree with most of that. I wouldn't use the word *shield,* however. I prefer my art to *engage* the sordid perils of actual existence. But I'm not sure even that's what I had in mind when I used to pace during commercials.

There is a common belief that actors act because they crave attention and love. The sweet sound of applause is supposed to make up for a hideous childhood or heal a perpetually broken heart or something. Makes me wonder how all the computer programmers and retail workers in the world heal *their* broken hearts.

As for writers, the sand-in-the-oyster theory is a popular one, especially if they write autobiographically. They take whatever's itching their psyche and coat it with nice metaphors and images and other goop in order to form it into a literary pearl. Sometimes, they make it into something darkly baroque in order to enact revenge.

So is art some kind of buffer, or salve? A kiss-make-better that the artist plants on his own wounded self? Ick.

I think I prefer the love theory. Actors are without doubt adored. Oscar Night is awash in tearful declarations of love for the relatives and deities who made it all possible. In the literary world, being accepted by a publisher can feel like being loved. Even huge international book prizes are about more than money. They convey honour, recognition, appreciation, respect — all necessary ingredients of genuine love.

But is that why we do it? To be loved? To get something we feel we've missed out on and can't get in the more usual way?

I can only speak for myself. The brief bits of applause I've heard have indeed sounded like love. For about thirty seconds. But I think an actor would have to be awfully thick not to realize that the love, such as it is, is directed not at herself but at the character she has just portrayed — at whatever noble or funny or deliciously evil thing the script has allowed her to do for a couple of hours. As a writer, I've won a couple of prizes and been nominated for a few others. I like to joke about the tens of thousands of dollars I've "lost" through not winning. And I've learned that it's best to put a nomination out of my mind. The one time I obsessed about winning, I almost made myself sick. Lovesick, you might say.

The pathological explanations for why artists do what they do don't convince me. They're petty. I do believe that love is involved. But in any creative endeavour, what drives the creator is surely more about loving than it is about being loved.

***

Not too long ago, I made a mask. It was the Christmas holidays and I had some kind of bug that left me sick enough to be housebound but well enough to be climbing the walls. So I gathered up a bunch of stuff I had been collecting, covered the dining room table with newspaper and went to work.

I had forgotten how much fun it is to make something by hand. My finished mask is dear to me because I know exactly what went into it — paper and paste and yarn and paint and swearing and sweat. Plus a bit of blood from where I poked myself with the yarn needle. That mask and I have a relationship — one that puts me in mind of a favourite psalm: "You it was who fashioned my inward parts; you knitted me together in my mother's womb... You know me through and through: my body was no mystery to you, when I was formed in secret, woven in the depths of the earth."[2]

The words "knitted" and "woven" capture the made-ness of the made thing. The time and patience that go into creation. "Formed in secret," though, captures something else — something that I can't see or touch or even name. But I know it's there.

Sometimes, when I come upon my mask unawares — glance up from my book, say, and see it hanging on the wall — I fail to recognize it. For just a second, it's completely strange to me. I know I put it together with my own hands, but I swear I've never seen it before. It's not the greatest mask. Up close, it's crude and obviously homemade. But when I do manage to perceive this strangeness, this alien otherness, I'm actually humbled by my own creation. Somehow, in spite of my clumsy efforts, my mask has managed to become greater than the sum of its parts.

There. That's more like what got me pacing when I was eleven. What still gets me out of bed every morning and makes me head to my desk, now that I'm fifty-five. I want to "make" something. Something that can only be made by me, yet will somehow end up bigger and better and wiser and stranger than me. Greater, in other words, than the sum of my parts.

***

This is not to dismiss those parts, or the sum they add up to. A made thing, be it a mask or a play or a novel or a human being, is first and foremost a thing. A theatre production, for example, is built from the ground up — lumber sawn, canvas painted, costumes fitted, lights hung, props hunted down. Putting a play together is a labour-intensive, nuts-and-bolts affair, and I'll never forget the joyful racket of it. As a theatre student, I didn't just muse on the motivations of Hamlet. I fetched and carried and drilled and glue-gunned. Once I was part of a human chain conveying big, awkward set pieces down a rickety fire escape in the freezing rain — risking my neck and loving it. There were times in rehearsal when I had to project above the pounding of hammers and the whine of saws. I was expected to stay in character, to live in the world of the play, while that same world was being created, loudly, all around me.

How silent and solitary writing is, by comparison. And how isolated from the physical creation of the end product. As I write this, a magazine containing an article with my name on it is in production. The next time I see that piece of writing, it will be tucked between glossy covers and displayed on racks in stores. How it got there, the step-by-step making of it as a published work, is completely out of my hands.

Not that I'm complaining. It's just the nature of the beast. Some writers bemoan what they call the loneliness of writing and the writing life. I think they're missing the point. Solitude is absolutely essential to getting anything written. And I actually cherish the solitude of writing. I start every day with it — a bit of sacred time alone, without which the rest of the day would be unbearable or even meaningless.

Besides, writers are as likely as any other odd breed to form associations, attend conferences and invent reasons to bump into each other. For eleven years, I belonged to a writing group that met every month without fail. Three of us from the original bunch got back together recently and formed a spin-off that seems to be doubling in size every time it meets.

But the fact that I can even separate *writing* from *the writing life* says something. I may benefit from courses and support groups and bull sessions with other writers, but at the end of the day (or in my case at the start of it) it's between me and the blank page.

For an actor, there is no such differentiation. Acting *is* the acting life. In order to practice her art, an actor must be part of a community, however ephemeral. First, she has to get cast in something. Then, even if it's a one-woman show, she's never really alone. Her performance might look like a single thread, but it is in fact a tight weave of relationships — with the playwright via the script, with the director who scrutinizes her every move, with the technical crew who support her, and, most important, with the audience.

That last is where acting and writing once again join hands. Perhaps I should add, "in my opinion," since there's a bit of controversy here. No one will dispute that I write "by" myself. And I'm comfortable with the popular notion of writing "for" myself. But I refuse to add the word "alone" to that. Again, I am an actor who writes. And even though acting requires such complete concentration on the character and the world of the play that the audience imaginatively ceases to be, nevertheless connecting with that audience is what the actor is there to do.

I remember years ago, a woman I hardly knew looking into my eyes and saying, "I've just finished reading one of your stories. You and I had the same mother." I'll never forget that moment of connection. I was pleased and proud, yes, but also humbled by her reaction. My story was no longer just mine. It had grown up and away from me, and now, for all I had chosen its every word, it was a little strange. Alien. Other. Somehow, it had managed to become greater than the sum of its parts.

*\*\*\**

So what does this "greater" consist of, and how does it come about?

When actors do the initial read-through of a new script, they do not emote or declaim. Quite the opposite. They savour their lines, taking their time and listening to each other. They are waiting in readiness, keeping themselves open to something I can only call a "quickening."

I have never borne a child, but I suspect that the first time a woman feels a fetus moving inside her might be comparable to what I'm trying to describe. All at once, an actor is seized by something in the script. It's not necessarily the big climactic scene. It might be a single phrase of dialogue, or a silent bit of business. But a cold finger will go down his spine, or a tear will well into his eye. Actors are trained to recognize and respect this moment of quickening. It is the beginning of a journey that they and their character will take toward each other.

Any story I have written has begun with such a moment. I overhear something or see something or remember something. Whatever it is, it "beckons" to me. I could never mistake this beckoning for anything else. On my desk blotter there's an inch of newsprint I cut out of the paper years ago. It's brown with age now, but every time I catch sight of it, it's as if I'm reading the words on it for the first time: "The place God calls you is the place where your deep gladness and the world's deep hunger meet." There. I can't do any better than that. When a story beckons to me, I am aware of both of those things — a deep gladness and a deep hunger. And I simply have to go where I'm being called.

***

Well. Going is one thing, but getting there is another. Both writing a story and playing a character are journeys of discovery. And both journeys are marked by false starts, missteps, shortcuts that turn out to be dead ends and the all too rare, serendipitous detour. There is a side of the creative process that is downright tedious. In rehearsal, entire days can be spent on a single line of dialogue or a tiny bit of business. A writer can polish and perfect one paragraph for weeks, only to have to cross it out at last and try to forget about it.

Yet none of that time and effort is wasted. It's all part of seeking out whatever quickened within the actor or beckoned to the writer. The discovery — more like the rediscovery — of that first impulse has about it an unmistakable feeling of inevitability. The lines a character is given to speak, the actions he is made to perform, become for the actor the "only possible" lines he could come out with, and the "only possible" things he could do. For the writer, the words that are allowed to remain on the page are the "only" words that could "possibly" appear there.

It has been a labour of love. I love the books I've written, flawed as they are. I love whatever I'm writing at the moment. I may not *like* it very much. At times I may even hate it. But I still pay attention to it, fuss over it, fight with it, make up with it, despair of it, then decide to believe in it all over again. And if that's not love, I don't know what is.

***

The most poignant thing about writing or acting or any other creative endeavour is that whatever you're working on gets finished. A book is published. A production closes. I know Goethe said art is long, but try telling that to an out-of-work actor. A show, for all its nuts and bolts and noise, survives only in memory. After closing night, the lights are taken down, the set pieces dismantled and the costumes bundled away to be torn apart and remade as something else. And the actor, if she's to survive as such, must move on to a new role. If she can get one.

It's the same with writing. Granted, a published book or magazine is a tangible thing that can last for centuries. But writing itself, from the writer's standpoint, is constantly moving and changing, like water. I no sooner finish one story than I'm praying for another to catch me like a current and pull me along. Please.

Well, maybe Oscar Wilde was right about needing to be shielded from — what was it — the sordid perils of actual existence. For me, it's a need to be reassured over and over that things don't have to be as small and limited and petty as they can seem when I'm "between stories." (Or "reading scripts" as the actor's euphemism goes.)

I am as excited and gratified by a great performance as I am by a great book. Both can convince me that the world is somehow bigger than I thought it was, and better and wiser and more humourous and beautiful and strange.

I'm running out of words here.

"Greater than the sum of its parts" really is the best I can do.

[1] Wilde, Oscar. *The Critic As Artist*, 1891.
[2] Psalm 139, vv 13-15.

# KEN STANGE

Ken Stange is a writer, visual artist, and occasional scientific researcher. His works include books of poetry and fiction, arts journalism, scientific papers, computer programs, philosophical essays, and visual art. He pays the bills as a university lecturer at Nipissing University in North Bay Ontario, where one of his courses is on the psychology of art and creativity. He has a wife who teaches philosophy, a daughter who is a theoretical mathematician, and a son who is website designer. He also has two dogs and no time.

## THE SECRET AGENTS: CREATIVITY IN THE ARTS AND THE SCIENCES

*What follows are two excerpts from a large work-in-progress, entitled* The Secret Agents, *a book that deals with the theme of creativity in the arts and in the sciences—both the profound similarities and the profound differences.*

~~~~

from the... "PROLOGUE: THE MYSTERY PLAY; THE MYSTERY OF PLAY"

> *"Beauty is truth, truth beauty."*
> — John Keats ("Ode On A Grecian Urn")

We are moved to tears. Transported. By certain passages of music, perhaps a Bach concerto wherein sensuously intertwined strands of melody entangle us in their intricate mathematical interstices and make of us glad captives, happily trapped in a contrapuntal web. Or by an old and—more often than not—saccharine pop-tune that triggers vivid memories of our first exploration of the slopes and planes of a young lover's body. By the glistening perfection of an autumnal forest after rain, where the late afternoon light invents a new colour spectrum to display on its canvas of dappled leaves. Or by the sight of a patch of dirty weeds which suddenly brings back the empty lot where as children we imagined ourselves daring, pith-helmeted jungle explorers. By the dramatic pathos of a prideful old man orchestrating his own madness by not recognising his daughter, Cordelia, as being his one offspring loving enough to be honest. Or by the silly lines of a bad poem we loved and memorized in Grade Six before we learned, like King Lear did too late, to distinguish gush from gumption.

IMAGINATION *in* ACTION

We are moved, moved to the highest emotional plane, not so often by life events, by visceral satisfactions or physical suffering, but rather by the contemplation of the world about us, by deeply apprehending Nature's and Humanity's creations: perceptions and memories of perceptions. It is in creation, recreation, play—that is where the mystery of human emotion resides. It is from the closing of the eyes that the medieval mystery plays took their name; it is from the opening of the eyes that the play of art and science invoke our deepest emotions. It is reasonable to assume that we share with many other creatures such fundamental emotions as pleasure in being fed when hungry and pain in being physically injured, but it is hard to imagine any other species experiencing far stronger emotions than these *from merely observing*. We are special in that we feel most deeply in contemplation of perceptions and the ideas they invoke, not in the response to the vicissitudes of mundane physical experience. A sunset can cause even a young child to weep; sunburn can only make him cry.

It is an assumption of this book that this uniquely human experience, which I will call—for lack of a more felicitous term—the "aesthetic experience," lies at the heart of our humanity, is the foundation on which human civilisation is built. It is a further assumption that this aesthetic experience is as essential to science as it is to art. These assumptions point to a deep mystery that has always concerned mankind—the mystery of creation. It is most natural that we speculate about from where originates this magic in ideas and images and sounds that so moves us. Whence beauty?

We know how some of the things that touch our souls came into existence. Human beings made them. We, *Homo sapiens*, created them.

~~~~

*To understand the nature of creativity in the different domains of art and science, it is essential to clearly delineate our different apprehensions of world. The following early chapter from the book attempts to do that.*

~~~~

# from... THE PARTING OF THE WATERS

*"Water, water, everywhere,*
*Nor any drop to drink."*

— Samuel Coleridge (*The Ancient Mariner*)

*"Between the idea*
*And the reality*
*Between the motion*
*And the act*
*Falls the Shadow"*

— T.S. Eliot (*Four Quartets*)

Thales, often considered the first Greek philosopher, postulated that the world was made of water. At first encounter this seems a strange and naive idea; but if water is compared to the three other ancient elements, there is a certain compelling logic to its selection as the ultimate element. Fire is a rare thing and rarefied. Air just does not seem substantial enough to be considered the ultimate building block of material existence. And earth, while certainly substantial, probably did not appear as limitless as the sea must have seemed to this Milesian philosopher as he contemplated a sunset over the Aegean. Indeed we now know what Thales might have suspected: two-thirds of our planet's surface is covered by water. So Earth is very little earth: its surface far more water than land. Actually it is the thin skin of 'earth' on a mere third of our large wet rock that is the anomaly, an anomaly that only surfaced relatively recently in the history of our planet.

Yes: water, water, everywhere. Deep water. And much of it undrinkable. Not because it is salt water. But because it is not the water used to quench mundane thirst. It is the water of appreciation and explanation: the water of art and the water of science.

## WHAT IS WATER?

Water is many things.

There is the water of art. It is the doldrums water of the Sargasso Sea in Coleridge's *Ancient Mariner* and it is the magical, watery highway of Kenneth Graham's *Wind In The Willows*. It is the churning, oily water in a Turner seascape and it is the placid Venetian canal water in a Tintoretto. It is the melodic, aural water of Debussy's haunting tone poem *La Mer* and it is the bubbling brook water of Schubert's *Trout Quintet*. It is the water of literature and painting and music. It is water that is not water, composed of substances fluid in a different way: words, paint and musical notes. But nevertheless these waters are deep, intensely real, and capable of quenching a very different kind of thirst.

.

And then there is the water of science: a tiny molecule composed of two gases! (Ironically Thales' 'ultimate' element is actually made of 'air'!) Water as two parts hydrogen and one part oxygen. As if this is not bizarre enough, science informs us that these elemental gases are themselves composed of unimaginably tiny electrons, neutrons and protons, and furthermore and further down even these subatomic particles are really no more than probability waves in the Wonderland World of quantum physics. Water as abstraction, as mathematical formulae, but nevertheless deeply, intensely real. Just as the thirst for knowledge is real.

.

And finally there is sensate water. The water of our experience, from womb to suburban swimming pool. The water we actually drink when thirst isn't just a metaphor.

.

So which of these waters is *most* real? The magical, metaphoric water of art? Or the abstract water of science. Or the water of direct sensory experience?

.

Probably the commonest response would be that what we perceive, through our complex perceptual apparatus, is the ultimate reality. Most of us, no matter how hard-nosed and rational we fancy ourselves, credit our direct sensory experience more than anything else. Everything else, it is tempting to think, can be relegated to a mere attempt at explanation (if science) or at simulation (if art).

.

.

SENSATE WATER

.

It is a brutally hot summer day. Surely the feel of silky coolness on your sunburned skin as you dive into a northern lake or the crisp taste of spring water on your parched palate or the image of whitecaps glistening in the sun is the definitive *reality* of water!

.

Of course I just stacked the cards in that last paragraph by trying to inspire recollections of *intense* experiences of water. Now consider instead those many tepid times when water was nothing. For example, you are washing dishes while engaged in a heated discussion with your spouse. Or you are sipping a glass of water while engrossed in a book. If you compare your experience of water at times such as these, times when water was something scarcely noticed because your attention was elsewhere, then sensate water is something far, far less experientially intense than what you felt the first time you read *The Ancient Mariner* or *Moby Dick* or *Huckleberry Finn*.

.

Consider, too, what physiologists and psychologists say is *really* happening when you perceive water, the cold hard facts about what is actually happening when on a summer day you dip your hand in a cool brook. Neural receptors located in your dermis are triggered by the temperature *change*. This results in a flow of sodium ions through the membrane of an afferent (or sensory) neuron, which in turn causes a voltage differential (in the area of 40 microvolts) to travel along the membrane of this nerve cell. When this charge arrives at the axon terminal of the cell it stimulates cellular vesicles (little bubbles full of organic chemicals) to dump a stew of neuro-transmitters into the synaptic space. If enough of these neuro-transmitters (arriving from different afferent neurons with receptors in the same vicinity of the dermis) happen to be splashing around in a synaptic space by the dendritic end of another connector neuron, the whole process will be repeated—and the next neuron in the chain will carry the 'message' along. If all goes well the process will continue up your spine to your brain where that midbrain switching station called the thalamus will route the information up to the association neurons of the particular area of the sensory cortex that is dedicated to how you feel. (It is reassuring to know something cares about how you feel!) Then somehow, miraculously, the stimulation of these neurons, the actions of the tiny sodium ions leaking through the cell membranes, generates the *experience* of coolness on your skin.

.

So how dare we anthropocentrically claim that our particular experience of water, an experience that is demonstrably different from that of amoeba or paramecium (who have no neurons) or that of electric eels or whales (who have specialized receptors capable of detecting attributes of water not even dreamt of in our philosophy), is the ultimate reality of water?! Even without having to resort to sobering science, epistemologists have repeatedly warned of the danger of confusing perception with underlying reality, what Immanuel Kant called, respectively, phenomenon and noumenon.

.

So let us resign ourselves to the fact that Water is not the specific water of our sensory experience. The hardwired circuitry of our nervous systems creates the water of sensate experience. It is not ultimate Water. So where then do we look for *real* water?

.

.

IMAGINATION *in* ACTION

# SCIENTIFIC WATER

Is the water of science, $H_2O$, more real? Since it is science that explains what is *really* happening (or at least so most educated people in industrialized nations believe) when you feel, taste or see water, does it not make sense to look to scientists for the truth about water—instead of naively assuming our quirky, neurologically-determined and anthropocentric 'experience' of water is what water is *really* about. The water of modern science may be abstract, even arcane, but scientific abstractions which we may not understand have significant effects which we observe daily, everything from television to medicine.

Those who are not scientists (or not very good scientists) put a great deal of faith in science as the only true path to reality. But those who actually do science at the cutting edge of philosophy are far more circumspect. Consider physicists.

The overwhelming majority of contemporary physicists endorse what is called the Copenhagen Interpretation,[1] a dictum usually attributed to Neils Bohr, Nobel laureate, the originator of modern atomic theory, and founder of The Copenhagen Institute for advanced studies in physics. This dictum is bipartite.

The first part of the Copenhagen Interpretation is the startling claim that *there is no deep reality*, that all there *really is*—is appearance.[2] What the philosopher Immanuel Kant called the *ding an sich* (literally "thing-in-itself") just plain does not exist. To use Kant's terms, there are no noumena (underlying realities); there are only phenomena (observations). Plato maintained that what we saw and thought to be reality was only shadows on the wall of a cave. Modern physicists would not only agree, but would go much, much further: they would argue that *there are no objects with distinct shapes casting those shadows*. We draw the shadows ourselves by the act of looking at them.

The second part of the Copenhagen Interpretation seems even more outlandish. It states that *reality is created by observation*. Nothing, or more accurately no dynamic attributes of anything, exists in the absence of observation.[3] Some physicists would even insist that a conscious, sentient being is prerequisite to the existence of anything. At first this sounds like crazy talk at the Mad Hatter's tea party, but there are some very eminent, very sober people at this party. In fact, John von Neumann, often said to be the clearest thinker and greatest mathematician of this century,[4] the author of what is called the Bible of Quantum Mechanics (*Die Mathematische Grundlagen der Quantenmechanik*), is usually credited with originating the idea that "physical objects would have no attributes...if a conscious observer were not watching them."[5]

Imagine a lake, hidden deep in a virgin forest of the North. Imagine the attributes of that lake: isolation, water as pure as polar ice, blue as cobalt. Sorry, the most scientific of scientists would say, but such a lake *does not exist* until a human being, seeking after ultimate wilderness, reaches the light at the end of a long portage and gazes upon it. And then, of course, it loses that first mentioned attribute: it is no longer truly isolated. Or, to change the metaphor: for a physicist, there can be no virgins until they have been deflowered.

ARTISTIC WATER

So if science, by its own admission, fails to serve up objective reality, then where oh where can we turn—but to art. Undoubtedly there is a special understanding to be had in art. I have seen the sea, have swum in it, even canoed on it. I have read scientific works dealing with the sea. But, personally, my strongest impression—and what feels like my deepest *understanding* and profoundest experience of it—comes from Melville and Coleridge and Conrad.

I think that to view art as imitation or simulation is anachronistic, naive. I will address this issue later, but for now assume that art is not imitation but creation, that Conrad's sea (or Turner's or Debussy's) is not a representation or explanation of water, but rather a reinvention of it. If in physics, the nature of water does not exist until observation creates it, in art the nature of water does not exist until the artist creates it.

ARE ALL OASES MIRAGES?

So where does this leave us? Water, water, everywhere, and not a drop that's real. Yet the Grand Canyon is there—because (or so we all believe) the rushing waters of the Colorado River have, over eons, *created* it.

And yet water, that original element, that daily experience, that component of our body that accounts for 65% of each of us—is not something real. It is created by us, by our bodies or our minds. And it is created again and again, each and every time in profoundly different guises.

To review the options:

~~ There is the water of sensation or experience: our bodies, our nervous system create this water of subjective experience.

~~ There is the water of science: scientists create formal, abstract structures from numbers and symbols and logical relationships they claim define water.

~~ There is the water of art: artists create a water from unwatery things (words, paint, musical notes) capable of seeming deeper than the deepest pools of direct experience.

The important thing to note is that in all of these cases there is creation. This is not to maintain, in pure Idealist fashion, that there is absolutely no external reality. But it *is* to maintain that the *attributes* of this reality are created by us.[6]

In the first case (i.e., sensate reality) what is created is created not by our minds, but rather by our bodies. The creation of this reality is by our perceptual apparatus and neural circuits, and does not contribute to the collective human enterprise. Although some hedonists have tried to raise sensuality to the level of an art or science, no one receives a Nobel Prize for feeling good or intensely.

It is only in the other two cases that the thing created is not merely physiological, personal, and ultimately trivial. For any person whose teleology is not naively based on the God Myth, but who nevertheless does believe that if human life can be said to have any ultimate purpose, that ultimate *raison d'être* must be the invention of the world through art and science.

And *this* is what creativity is all about: the invention of the world. The secret is out: science and art (too often irrationally at odds since the Romantic Period) are really agents working toward the same goal—just taking different approaches. From the very beginning of this noble enterprise, they have worked together, offering each other new tools to proceed. Their historically brief estrangement is coming to an end as both come to appreciate again what the other has to offer.

Both are diving deeper than ever before into what once were purely philosophical waters, but they are no longer going it alone. I believe that because of their collaboration they will undoubtedly return with wondrous images never dreamt of in anyone's philosophy. This book is about their methods.

[1] There are some notable exceptions, including Einstein.

[2] My wording and explanation of the Copenhagen Interpretation is largely based on Nick Herbert's *Quantum Reality: Beyond The New Physics*. However, his description matches well with numerous other explicators of quantum mechanics.

[3] Physicists do not go quite as far as the philosopher Berkeley: they do not deny the ultimate existence of, for example, electrons, but they do maintain that electrons do not have, for example, any *real precise* position in space until they are observed.

[4] John Allen Paulos in *Beyond Numeracy* goes even further: "referred to by some as the smartest person who ever lived." Von Neumann will be discussed in some detail in a later chapter.

[5] This is Nick Herbert's paraphrase (in his *Quantum Reality*) of Von Neumann's position.

[6] As already remarked, few physicists would agree with the first and most radical Idealist, Bishop Berkeley, that there is no external reality at all, only mind. What the majority of physicists will say, however, is that dynamic attributes (variables) do not exist until observation: an electron, all electrons, have a given, real atomic weight (the same for all), but no electron has a particular, distinguishing position or momentum until the moment of observation. Similarly, the artist does not invent the sea, but a particular sea, and what you feel or don't feel when you dive into a lake depends on your individual physiology.

# KENT L. BOWMAN

Kent Bowman has been involved with music and songwriting most of his life. His father, a professional trombonist, played with Artie Shaw and other prominent swing bands. Kent's first instrument was the piano. He then took up trombone, played upright bass and guitar, later studied voice and piano for a year at San Francisco State College. As half of a folk duo called *The Dusty Road Singers*, he came to Toronto from Vancouver in 1970. Ted Plantos encouraged him to write poetry, and he became one of the original House Poets, performing occasionally at the Gerrard Street Library House. Besides an anthology of the House Poets, he has been published in several chapbooks and has a collection of poems entitled *Glasseater's Banquet*. He has played trombone and guitar throughout Ontario with various groups (York Jazz Ensemble, Edge of Dixie, and Upper Canada Brass Quintet).

## THE CREATIVE PROCESS (SONGWRITING, COMPOSING, POETRY)

I am a jazz musician, composer, songwriter and poet. As a jazz player I have always improvised, which basically means, interpreted the melody, chords and lyrics of a tune; creating alternate phrases based on these elements. Needless to say, improvisation can be considered to be a type of composition in that it is an immediate composing of phrases related to a specific melody and chord structure that becomes alternate melodies themselves (e.g., Bunny Berigan's trumpet solo on "I Can't Get Started With You" or Ziggy Elman's trumpet solo on "When the Angels Sing."

Regarding songwriting, in my opinion, it all depends on how you write and with whom (because other writers influence your writing—Lennon and McCartney, Rodgers and Hart, Rodgers and Hammerstein). As an example, if a lyricist gave me a set of lyrics, I would concentrate on the style of the song (i.e., jazz, country, rock, classical, latin, etc.), meaning of the lyrics, "feel" of the song, mood it seems to establish, preferred tempo, time and key signatures. When I am writing alone (my preference), melody or lyrics may come first or together. How long it takes seems to depend upon how long my unconscious has been working on it and when it is ready to produce the work. (One of my better songs was written in twenty minutes; another song took closer to twenty years of revisions before I was satisfied.)

My general comments on composition include the need to write regularly which seems to be as necessary as regular instrumental practice to maintain writing "chops." I do not advance without practice and influences (many types of music and ongoing music studies). In this way, I believe music to be similar to what I can only imagine happens in visual arts in that you need to develop a "palette" of sounds as well as a style to have interest and meaning in your work. In my experience, both composing and arranging of music seem to work along similar lines.

As a poet, I find the creative process to be similar, but it seems to be closer to the freedom found in composing instrumental music where the concern for form can be much freer. Rhythm, rhyme, colour can all be used with greater ease in poetry as compared to the normally more rigid forms found in songwriting. In my experience, these conventions normally apply, but there are always exceptions, made by exceptional artists, who contravene rules, but still create artistic, poetic/musical masterworks. (P. Picasso, e. e. cummings, B. Dylan, T. Monk, C. Ives, I. Stravinsky.)

# KRISTIN ANDRYCHUK

Kingston writer Kristin Andrychuk was born in Northern Ontario, but raised in Ridgeway/Crystal Beach a few miles from the U.S. border, an area that combined a conservative village, a wild summer resort, and the seething American city of Buffalo. This was an inspiring environment for someone who would grow up to be a writer, though she didn't realize it at the time. After graduation from Queen's University she taught school in Thunder Bay, where she met her husband Don. They raised their four children on a farm near Kingston. She writes poetry and short stories, and has published two novels with Oberon Press, *The Swing Tree*, and *Riding the Comet*. She is currently writing a novel for teenagers.

## THOUGH WE CAN'T CREATE PARADISE

My mother was a powerful influence in my life. In the fifties we often went on Sunday afternoon drives — a common practice then. We lived in the area where she was raised.

She was a great storyteller. Her foster mother forced her to quit school after senior fourth to work on the farm. She took that life of drudgery and made it something else. She quoted Tennyson to the cows as she herded them back to the barn. A book of his poems had been a parting gift from her teacher. Each night she read till her lamp was out of oil. When she was an old woman she could still quote those poems from memory.

Every farm we passed, every little house had a story. Some were glorious, like the woman who danced naked on a picnic table. Most were gruesome. "There's the house where the meanest man in the county lived. He beat his horses so badly, no farmer would sell him one."

When I was a teenager she told me more. His fifteen-year-old daughter jumped in the well with her new baby. Her father dragged them out, but the baby was dead. Many years later this same daughter hung herself in the barn.

What intrigues me about writing is how the story expands. I start out to write a simple story of star-crossed lovers, of letters not delivered, a story my mother told me about her landlady. The story refuses to stay a simple love story.

I think about the place my young heroine, Clara, lives. What comes to mind is a blackened never-painted house. The image is so clear I think I must have seen this house and then realize I have. On one of those long ago Sunday afternoon drives we passed this place. I only saw it for a few seconds, but it stayed. A standard farmhouse with at least four bedrooms upstairs. Most old unpainted houses have turned a silvery grey. I have no idea why this one was nearly black. Trees and shrubs grew up around it. It had a blank, unlived-in look, though Mother told me the name of the elderly couple who lived there and still farmed the seventy-five acres.

This house becomes Clara's house. In writing it into my story it becomes, not the house I glimpsed, but a composite of many old houses I've experienced. Clara, canning tomatoes, longs to sink through the linoleum, through the wood floor to the limestone cellar, to curl up on the cold stone floor. Our farmhouse had a floor like that.

The elderly couple become her guardians. Those stern grandparents, whom I have created simply as a foil for Clara's love affair, become themselves, with their own griefs, their own stories. The bitter grandfather, who drowns kittens and growls at his granddaughter, has a story he demands be told.

I am fascinated by how one story evolves into another. The first time I wrote about Clara, about twenty years ago, I made her an old woman telling her life.

The story is always incomplete. Last year I reread this story and began writing Clara as a child. I wrote about her being forced to quit school and slave on that farm — shades of my mother. I wrote about her stealing a half hour for reading, by sitting on the warmed grass where the cow had lain. She would tell her grandfather she had to hunt for the cows back in the bush. The story expands.

Stories change. When I first heard the story of the young girl, the new baby and the well, I was a teenager myself. My reaction was — such a sad story, yet she would've known some happiness because she must have had a boyfriend. In those days boyfriends were on my mind.

Many years later when I thought about that shy girl, who refused to tell who the father was, it occurred to me, that her father could well also have been the baby's. Why was he known as the meanest man in the county? Why, when the hospital said she could come home (she'd spent a year in a mental hospital), wouldn't her father have her back? Said, he wouldn't have a murderess in his house. Was he afraid the truth would out?

I wrote some of the possibilities of that story into my first novel *The Swing Tree*.

Creativity is not just in the writing. My mother's creativity was not expressed in print, but in the stories she told, and in how she lived her life. When she quoted Tennyson to those cows, she made her life of drudgery into something wonderful.

She was able to take the ordinary and make it something more. When I was a child I complained about having to wear a hand-me-down bathing suit from my sister.

We always had a rest after lunch before walking out to the beach. I lay on the porch swing, feeling sorry for myself. When I woke up, there on top of the faded suit, lay a little short skirt, bright yellow with sunflowers. How could she make it so fast? I thought she had magical powers. For a long time I thought that. Perhaps she did.

I watched her setting out tomato plants. How carefully she tucked the soil around each one. She cared about them. Her garden produced bushels of tomatoes.

IMAGINATION *in* ACTION

Making things. There's satisfaction there, whether it's a story, a garden or a toy. We take the given, make it into something else, give it meaning.

When my daughter was a small child I made her an Inuit doll. An old sock became a little rag doll. From fleece scraps I made a parka and pants. Decorated them with beads and rickrack.

I looked at my little Inuit woman. She wouldn't be comfortable in just parka and pants. I sewed her a cotton dress and underwear. I gave her a baby made from an infant's sock. I tacked straps to a tiny piece of plywood and glued on a decorated fleece sack. I made the baby terrycloth sleepers and a flannel diaper. Placed him in the carrier. I smiled at my mother and baby. My ideas in material form.

My dolls are different from those mass-produced ones in the souvenir shop. What makes sewing creative? Perhaps it's motive. The motive behind a mass-produced souvenir is money. There is little care taken with the product, because it's the profit that's important.

My Inuit doll is an expression of my delight in making something. It is a part of a larger making, my child. As she plays with this doll, makes up her stories, I delight in her. The souvenir baby is glued in. The mother doll has neither dress nor underwear. Those dolls would disappoint a child.

My daughter said they come alive when you give them eyes. She played endless stories of their daily lives in the North.

Children are naturally creative. They hear music, they dance. A kindergarten table and a blanket become a hideout where the lion and my grandson live. When my son was four, after seeing giant trees that had become driftwood, he told us that long, long, long ago seeds floated through space from birdland. They grew into the first trees, the great, great, great grandfathers of the driftwood trees.

We create our lives out of what we are given. There was a popular song in the sixties, "Little Boxes." The song annoyed me. "Little boxes made out of ticky tacky, little boxes all in a row." I felt the song belittled the lives in those little boxes, assumed they were dull, meaningless.

The first house my husband and I bought was a little box house. We ate in a sunny kitchen and slept in clustered small rooms. I sat on the lawn swing, rocking my unborn baby, while watching my husband and the children turn a lilac bush and a few boards into a tree house complete with ladders and lookouts. Marveled how we had charmed the earth and made it ours, in a little box house created paradise.

We create homes not only for our fictional characters, but for ourselves. How egotistical of me to think we could create paradise. When I sat on that lawn swing I was not prepared for when I would lie in a darkened room and stare at a splinter of light between the drapes. I saw the new blue glider carrying my children, their hair kitten soft. I wished to be a god who could stop the world and make this stay. I couldn't stop the bleeding. Felt us all flowing away in my baby becoming blood on a bed.

Though I couldn't create paradise, I could write a poem about the miscarriage. We create meaning. Almost making something out of nothing.

Our lives are full of making. My mother in telling her stories was creating the writer I would become. Our creativity is in anything we do, with caring.

# MARJORY SMART

Marjory Smart was mainly self-taught. She began painting in 1940, and writing in 1980, so the paintings came first, and she used some of those paintings as a starting point for poetry. She stopped painting for fifteen years, but even during that time felt that "my mind painted and was drawn by great admiration for abstract nature as a great force, great space." She said she was occupied with it every day, and then began painting again. "I start with nature, dramatizing, exaggerating, abstracting a great central force." She published two books of poetry, *Empty Sky Go On Unending*, and, *All on a Litmus Day*. Marjory was beautiful in appearance and spirit. She died in 1999, leaving an absence others cannot fill.

## LEAVING OUT THE NON-ESSENTIALS: EXCERPTS FROM A 1991 INTERVIEW

ON SIMILARITIES BETWEEN PAINTING AND WRITING: There are great similarities and great differences. They help each other.

Each has one centre of interest, chief character. You learn how to emphasize, dramatize. You don't cloud by introducing the irrelevant. You use best colours or best words to make it vivid, interesting, and create mood.

Both should grow to something bigger. I am striving for force in both. I think anything I did would be strong, fairly strong. I'm not weak-minded.

The main thought has got to be sharpened. If you're writing a very long novel, you've room to embroider it a little bit, but if you're writing in a short form, like a short story or poetry, you keep pretty much to just what builds up to the strength of that main point. Nothing's brought in at the first that isn't clear, has some purpose. I think that's true. And the same in painting. You see the old masters' paintings on triangles, the letter S, and circles, about seven different designs which were combined and altered, and today they're still there, but they're not obvious.

I kind of pride myself on being present-day, and I think I try to catch the spirit of creative work, whether it's in writing or in watercolour, or in oil. I'd never go back to the same way I did it years ago, although mine didn't seem to date, particularly. Now I've been away from painting for fifteen years, but my mind's been active and I've been thinking along abstract lines, and whatever I do will be fairly abstract. But then when you come to writing, you take that one about the barn doors, I painted that twenty, thirty years ago, and it was only done on newspaper because it was just a trial print, and I love black and white. But the idea of great doors opening and closing up opportunities, that didn't come to me until thirty years later, but that's all I used out of the sketch. It was only the idea. It wasn't anything to do with what was there.

ON PAINTING: My father painted, and his mother painted. A little bit. Everybody painted a fine scene or sewed a fine seam. Or played the piano.

I studied classical music for years. I can't play now. I had a half-inch cut off that finger. And then you see, these fingers, (arthritic), they all play a note off. They don't hit the right notes. I could memorize like a fiend in music, and I got to where I was either going to be a musician or get out. I didn't want to be a concert pianist. I have all my exams with honours.

I guess I must have always loved painting. I think I'd always been conscious of art because my grandparents had paintings in their home which I haven't kept. My mother had an artist friend. Mother died at ninety-nine, so that was quite a while ago. And her artist friend in Oshawa was always ahead of her time. She rode horseback. She painted. All her friends questioned this young woman having such a revolutionary life for the women of the time.

I was married with a child before I ever started painting.

I think what kept me going was I found a group of friends who were keen about painting. Three of them were graduates of the college, but I knew nothing about it, except maybe a week twice at a landscape school. But it was fun being with these artists, that is, before you started painting, because once you painted you scattered like grains of sand. You never spoke for two hours, nor saw them. Woe betide them if they came along and interrupted you when you were coming to your final decisions, putting in your accents.

We went down to Cape Cod five times, in the summer. We sat up all night to go, we hadn't the money to put on the train. And we'd get there, we'd get a flat, and one would cook, and we'd paint morning, afternoon and evening. We'd paint three to five paintings a day. Once it's dry you can brush the dead flies and insects off. And you could carry your watercolours home, but you couldn't get home with wet oils. You couldn't pack them together on the train.

You're on your way. If you're going up to Algonquin, you have a hilarious time, exciting. When you get there you're all stimulated. Everyone scatters and finds a subject. And you take your own meal, a chunk of cheese or a banana. Have a lunch outside, continue painting in the afternoon.

You don't want anyone to talk nor be with you when you paint, that's for sure. I got left out in the marsh two summers ago. When the wind blew my paper, a watercolour, into the stream, and I had to wade in and catch it before it disappeared, I suddenly realized that there wasn't anyone around. I hadn't seen anyone for two or three hours. I hadn't been with anyone, but I had been able to hear them off in the distance.

IMAGINATION *in* ACTION

Some people paint together. Those three did. But they were all gone. Here I was, miles out in a rough terrain and wilderness, and petrified. So then we arranged they would blow the horn when they were leaving.

You paint alone. You don't paint the same subject very often. You hope not to, and if you did it wouldn't look the same anyway. No two people see the same things, nor have the same colour sense nor love of mood.

I practically always paint from nature. For a period of fifteen years I stopped painting, but feel my mind painted and was drawn by great admiration for abstract nature as a great force, great space. I am now painting again. I start with nature, dramatizing, exaggerating, abstracting, a great central force.

I feel I paint largely by instinct. I have had very little instruction, and seem to have a sense of balance, mood, and colour. I feel abstraction enters all strong painting. All good painting has a touch of the abstract in it.

The whole picture is stated. It means a different thing to viewers according to their lives, and probably relates to something bigger.

In painting you try everything and never know if it will succeed or work. It can't be changed like writing.

I never paint inside, except to deal with what I've already painted outside.

You're working with the light on the earth, or your scene, whatever it is. And it's something that catches your mind, your imagination, something fleeting. You're working to get something that's passing away.

The shadows are changing, and the sun may be gone. It might be a grey day and the sun comes out. Well, the whole thing's changed. That is referring in a sense to representational painting. Something that actually exists. Unless you've caught it in your mind, a sort of gleam, on a bigger topic, like a force, a force in nature that is revealed by the light, or the mood. Mood is one of the big things in painting.

Watercolour's a lovely fresh thing. In the old days pure watercolour required a mastery, and I think one reason I progressed a bit was I never permitted myself to make a mistake or else I threw it away. I never corrected a thing for a matter of twenty, thirty years, and so you made your decision, every brush stroke being different because of the way the light falls on it, on a different angle. Every stroke you put down you mixed, more or less.

In watercolour, white paper is left. The viewer can think. Space allows for thinking, for layers of meaning, clarity of thought

Watercolours are supposed to bleed. That's part of the technique. But there are controls that can guide you. You can leave a little strip of dry paper. You generally immerse your paper and let the gloss go, or else you sprinkle it with water. Some places you want it to merge, and other places you leave white paper showing through. That gives the vitality, the sparkle. It's the white paper, not white paint. And some claim as much as seventy-five percent of the page can be left empty, white paper. And the only thing I can think of in writing that's similar is a haiku. It depends largely on the white page being left.

The last really beautiful watercolour show was in the Macdonald Building, a fine showplace and a fine show. So different, lovely, flowing, wet, thin. It was a delight. Colours sparkling.

There's an absence of detail. You're painting in a certain abstract way, even though not completely. You're leaving out detail anyway. Often too far away to see it, fortunately. Then you've a strong statement. And it's just like haiku. You're leaving out all the non-essentials. You've got the quintessence. Not putting in detail. If you haven't got something bigger than the detail then you might better quit.

I started in 1940. Oils were the big thing in those days, and then suddenly watercolour was very popular again. Pure watercolour. And then pure watercolour turned into mixed media, and you could work forever over mixed media, but i was never attracted to mixed media. Thick paint. Impasto was the word for thick paint. Chalky paints.

You see, I always worked with Windsor Newton paint, and it's just like having your own musical instrument. You can pick up just exactly without hardly looking. Two, three colours. You never paint with one. Never in the old days, and I guess not ever. But you had this wonderful Windsor Newton paint, and then when I changed to watercolours I still painted Windsor Newton but it became too expensive for anyone to use. Students, I mean. It's like a ballet dancer with her ballet shoes, a violinist with his own violin. You have to have whatever you use.

In painting, you're painting something about what's there and something that's in your mind, or your feeling about it. But it's there, that moment on the canvas. You can't keep adding things too much. You've got to keep to a focal point or you'll lose it. The old masters, in Holland, they say the Dutch used to take their painting knife and take two inches off the canvas all the way around, to leave a strong focal point, a centre of interest, and let it fade away, as you do in photography. You focus in on a zoom lens and then the field fades away.

I do think I have an innate sense of balance. My painting's going to have balance. I think I have a moderately pleasant sense of colour. It's not garish, it's not Mexican. I'm not fond of those colours. I don't care how right they are for Mexico. They're not right for me.

I painted in the kitchen and did a still life, I can show it to you, sitting up on top of the fridge, Well, my husband said, "It's time we had supper." I had to leave it unfinished, and it was turning out to be something good. But it saved the day. If I'd gone on any further I probably would have spoiled it.

It's gone, you see. There's this about the difference in painting and writing. Painting, it succeeds or it doesn't. I never permit myself to alter any painting.

IMAGINATION *in* ACTION

I think with painting, that you're painting something that's fleeting, that you see, whether it's just the contrast of light and shadow. You can't paint all the stages. You're painting something that's in the present although sprung in the past. You're creating what's right before you. In writing you can add, ad infinitum.

In painting, you're painting the light that falls on it.

I never missed a show for thirty years. I used to go down to New York for two or three days or a weekend to go to the shows.

I went to the openings. The room looks like broadcloth, people standing up. You couldn't see anything on an opening night. We always went down, a bunch of us, five of us, we'd go for an hour or two and I think they were interested in how they were done, in technique. I just look from a distance, and most of them I pass by. I'm not interested. Once in a while you see something… You see, if your painting's just a display of technique, it's a technical thing.

It's whatever you have in your past or your life that helps you tie in, entering into the abstract painting. The person has trouble finding the way in, and then he sees the bruise-blue and the scarlet bleeding, and turns his mind, his thinking, into the social aspect of the day, then he sees this white light glaring, and he thinks, if he's a thinking person…

I could sculpt. I have sculpted. When I was up in summer cottage country, up in Georgian Bay, there were natural clay banks up there. I had neither the money to buy any paint. It was a real struggle. Not even brushes, hardly. My parents used to give me a little money. I think I could have done just fine, but you see I'm an artist at heart. That's what I say, in "the light that never was," *I'm caught in the quicksand of an artist's life.*

ON WRITING: I think that writing is a more solitary thing when you're actually writing. You get together in between, then you meet, but you never write with someone.

I think I have a dreamy poetical side, that one has to hone.

I feel my writing is also by instinct, as I have had very little supervision and rarely attend readings. I am now influenced by a general *dis*interest in nature. I try to interpret into bigger issues, and of course avoid rhyme and set lines as too passive.

I start with an idea, frequently, drawn from a painting done twenty or thirty years before, and a few lately done from recent paintings. Mostly from life experiences. The picture is a starting point only. I am not staying with the picture.

In writing you have several layers of meaning.

I've done a few short stories over the past, say, six or eight years. I've learned from the poems about having a theme, that you have to strengthen it, and build up to a climax or problem and settle it, and draw to a conclusion, whether it's a surprise, or winding back to the first. Writing grows to a climax, a surprise ending, or it circles, and also takes on a broader meaning. A long novel would allow for detail and a bit of embroidery, but not a short story. Not much. It's got to be very vivid, exact, and some-what startling. The surprise element.

When I read some good writing I think, My, I'll never get there. I don't know. I'm sure I'll never get there.


ON AN AUDIENCE: There's no use having your friends in to look at your work. In the first place, they don't know beans about it. You're doing it for yourself. I never give a thought to anyone while painting or writing.

Other people only matter if one is interested in being juried (hung) or published. Well, if you want to publish, yes, you have to think about it with writing. And the same if you want to hang your paintings. If you want to be published there's no use writing if you don't want to follow the modern way of no rhyme, and maybe the short line mixed in with the long one, and following something bigger than nature.

I didn't start writing ever thinking of publishing, but you can't, when you're adult, do anything from making a cake or a tea biscuit… It's got to be good enough to eat. It's got to be good enough to publish finally, and you want it to be that way. So you have to conform to the dictates of the time.

I think fine writing or fine painting, there's no difference. I'm not content to write poorly. And if it isn't good enough for acceptance I'm really not interested.

I was never influenced by anyone's painting, nor anyone's… Well I don't know, maybe I have been about writing. But I think they're my own.


ON BEING AN ART STUDENT: You start with drawing. I used to go down to night school at the Art School. The instructor would put his head in around the door. "Carry on," he'd say, and he'd never come in.

When we went down to Cape Cod, we would go to the German-American abstract artist, Hans Hofmann. He's the one that Harold Town sort of followed, and the Group of Eleven, when they got into abstract they were influenced by him. We'd go down to Cape Cod. We'd sit up all night, and we'd get there, and then we'd go over to Hans Hofmann's studio. He had this house all painted in psychedelic colours, every room was orange or purple, yellow, and so on, and he'd have this model. We'd say we're five Canadians, could we have permission to sit in on his class. He'd say, yes, that we could go in. We'd pay five dollars to go in and sit, and we didn't know one word he said. It was all German. He'd just "mmmmph," you know, I mean grunt, and you'd know the tension's this way or that way. He'd get through and have a round circle on the canvas, about all I could see. We didn't know a word he said. We could see him, hear him grunt, see him maybe gesture, but still it was fun being there.

IMAGINATION *in* ACTION

ON TEACHING ART: I think they were paying fifty cents, and I had to take all the material, carry it in from my car, take it up three floors to their auditorium, and since they were paying so little they didn't care whether they came or not. And it was killing. I had five dollars when I was through. I would have enough to buy a tube or two of paint. It was cheap in those days.

Still life. That's all I could teach in there, but I gave them the basics. I attempted to give them the basics so they could carry on.

# MARVYNE JENOFF

Marvyne Jenoff was born and educated in Winnipeg and has lived most of her adult life in Toronto. Her books are: *No Lingering Peace*, poetry, Fiddlehead Press, 1972; *Hollandsong*, poetry, Oberon Press, 1975; *The Orphan and the Stranger*, poetry, Wolsak and Wynn, 1985; *The Emperor's Body*, fiction, Ekstasis Editions, 1995. In 2006 she published four chapbooks with Twoffish Press. Though she considers her books to be her *oeuvre*, she has had parallel involvements in other creative fields at different times: teaching, storytelling, visual-tactile arts. In 2002 she had a solo watermedia show, *Dark Light*, at the Annex Art Centre in Toronto. See her listing at www.library.utoronto.ca/canpoetry.

## ALIVE, UNIQUE

Why do I create? Creativity is a natural process of my ever-active mind. I create for pleasure — when I am creating I feel most alive and unique. I create to identify with my own kind, other creators. To emulate creators I admire. To purify, beautify, complicate, and make humorous whatever bores me. Creativity is ultimate control: if not for my arts, my energy would take another form, such as meddling, and nothing would be safe.

As soon as I focused on the subject of creating, these ideas came quickly. Then the hard work began. Some ideas were discarded and reclaimed, some reworded in the hit-or-miss process of trying different possibilities until something felt right. The paragraph was restructured several times. If it now seems light and effortless, my work has been successful.

I create out of both internal and external motivation. These ideas might have just floated around and possibly found their way into conversation if it weren't for the strong external motivation for actually writing this essay: pleasure at being asked, the opportunity to be published, a launch party. External motivation usually presents the challenge of working to a prescribed length and deadline. All these considered, my primary source of any creative project is what comes from the well of inner motivation: the pure, direct, innocent, and spontaneous creativity from which all art comes, the aspects of childhood that stay with us.

My poetry stems from learning early rhymes and songs, which I'd repeat to myself for pleasure as I skipped down the sidewalk. If I couldn't remember all the words I'd make up some that fit. In the late 1950s at St. John's High School in Winnipeg, thanks to teachers who loved what they were doing, literature opened up for me. They helped me read in depth by providing historical background, reading parts of the work aloud, and pointing out the ironic, the complex, the morally uplifting. Literature was the world I wanted. My career choice at the time would have been King Lear's fool.

During less interesting classes my mind would drift and I would coax out poems of my own. Writing soon consumed me. At the University of Manitoba I majored in English literature and wrote poems in response to my concerns at the time, falling in love ("Song of a Thin Lover"), my surroundings ("New Snow in March"), and my studies:

> Poor Milton, canst thou ever see
> Thyself beneath this summer tree
>
> . . . . . . . . . . . . . . . . .
>
> And I will suntan past the knee
> And I'll be young long after thee,
> And I'll be young long after thee.

Encouraged by my professors, I submitted work to literary journals and lo, my poems appeared in *The Fiddlehead* and *The Canadian Forum*, among others. What a boon for a socially awkward girl with a tendency to rant! With suitcase and green portable typewriter I left home to seek my fortune.

How does my writing actually begin? First there is an underlying deep focus, a meditative state, and I notice my breathing slow down of its own accord. Then a poem might start with a few spontaneous phrases, a line or two, a twist of logic. Whether initiated by playfulness or darker emotion this process is the same, and I chuckle to myself as the poem builds in my mind with irony, with harmony of sound. A story starts similarly, though the idea more often comes out of character or situation. During this process I am open to whatever is around me: a neighbour mentions the wet weather and my character builds his home in the clouds. Or a poem starts, *climbing the rain*. And then there are everyday objects at hand, pencil-sharpeners appearing in several of my recent poems.

Quickly, for they are fleeting, I capture these ideas on bits of paper which I keep within easy reach. I type the ideas in the order they will likely occur in the final piece and call it Draft One. Then I work from a printout, adding, massaging. When there are so many pencilled changes on the printout that I can't read it clearly, I retype the piece into the computer and call it Draft Two. Early drafts are the opportunity for incorporating more ideas. There's a turning point at which I know, with relief and exhilaration, yes, this is the shape of the piece, and it will not significantly change direction — if a different direction suggests itself, that becomes another piece. And I know it's going to be completed. Subsequent drafts are then a matter of shaping and editing. A piece of writing, for me, can go through as few as two or three drafts or as many as forty.

Writing after a long break is usually motivated by strong emotion. At first I have to push myself to get back into the habit of creative thinking, but soon momentum builds up and then any trifle can start a new work. When I came to Toronto in the early 1960s I experienced such momentum. In a rented room of my own, in a city of my own, I was writing one short story and twenty poems per month.

At that time I had a day job at a company that produced catalogues. After work I often refused social invitations because I couldn't wait to get back to my writing. Forty years later it's a different matter, procrastination and its attendant anxiety often setting in. What is procrastination — fear? doubt? perversity? laziness? part of the creative process? Creating is scary. Perhaps I want to hang on to the excitement of an idea rather than risk spoiling it by working on it. Perhaps it's a lack of external motivation, since publication is never a sure thing.

Creativity can strike at any time. When ideas come as I'm falling asleep, unless they are complex and require the computer, I write them down in the dark. I hold a tablet of paper with my left thumb at the top and, by feel, start the first line there. I move the thumb down for each new line so that there is no overlap. I write large, only four or five lines to a page, to ensure legibility in the morning. When ideas come at awkward times, such as during physiotherapy or a haircut, I let them go. They, or other equally good ideas, may or may not come again later.

What stimulates my art? The art form itself, whichever one I am immersed in at the time. And my circumstances: the poems in my first book basically reflected young exuberance and were a collection of ten years' writing. My second book was a product of being in love and the eventual decline of that relationship. My third book came out of the deaths of my parents. These books have been infrequent. During the fallow years I change, and when I start writing again I enjoy seeing the differences in what comes out. Years after the publication of my poetry books I was active in the Toronto story-telling community, steeped in folktales, and my next writing came out as narrative.

Its early seeds emerged on public transit. It was rush hour, and I heard estimates that the bus would take ten minutes to get around the corner. As I half-dozed, a story, fuelled by the pain of lost love, betrayal, and injustice, formed in my mind. I could visualize it complete on one page, short enough to remember until I could get home and write it down. Over subsequent days a three-page story emerged in the same vein, and a five-page. With the eight-page story I realized I was writing a book, *The Emperor's Body*, and I bought my first computer.

Even in fiction, I use poetry technique: minute attention to the meaning, sound, and implication of every word, the rhythm of every sentence. *The Emperor's Body* is a dense book, tightly packed with innuendo and allusion. From the title story:

> *The Emperor of the High Peak, Emperor of the Sharp Peak, Emperor of Blood in the Snow. These were the fur-clad Emperors high on the mountain, surveying the distant*

*east, who planned defences of the territories they held and those they intended to hold. Over time, responsibility for outlying territories became burdensome and peace was seen in a favourable light. The Emperor of Clinging in the Wind moved the palace down the milder, west slope of the mountain, releasing the territories he could no longer see. In the time of the Emperor of the Cozy Crevice, the first to replace boots with slippers, the beginnings of a town gathered around the palace. Gradually the palace and its surrounding town moved right down the mountain to the edge of the sea. The citizens enjoyed the beach, and there flourished a long, uneventful dynasty characterized by reflection: The Emperor of One Toe in the Water, Emperor of Two Toes in the Water, Emperor of Three Toes in the Water, and so on, to the twin Emperors, Their Majesties of Infinity and Grain of Sand.*

Writing has its sensuous aspects, with rhythm, rhyme, and the feeling of words in my mouth whether or not spoken aloud. The visual-tactile arts are sensuous in a different way. There is the experience of colours and shapes, the smells of the materials, the physical freedom of spreading out and moving things around. Needles, scissors, brushes, pencils all handle in their own way; drafting tables, sewing machines, computers require specific postures.

The visual-tactile arts (and crafts — I see a continuum, rather than a strict division) have always been with me. As the first child in an extended family household, I was included in sewing sessions with my mother and aunts, and I loved to handle fabric even if we were only hemming dishtowels. When I would complain I had nothing to do, my mother would say, why don't you make something? I eagerly learned crafts at school and from children's magazines. I would follow directions, then invent other projects using the techniques in creative ways. Original intricate paper doilies and crêpe-paper flowers found their way into greeting cards and party decorations. I sewed whenever I could, and in my teens was allowed to make clothes, first for my younger sister, then for my young aunt, and finally, for my mother. For most of my working life as a teacher of English as a Second Language, an extremely verbal and involving experience, I found an enriching balance in the meditative pleasure of choosing patterns and fabrics and sewing my own clothes, including swimsuits and a winter coat. In the early 1970s at Sheridan College I studied fibre arts, which included weaving, fabric printing, and soft sculpture. I made velvet liturgical pieces for a religious institution, and a banner for storytelling events.

In recent years at the Toronto School of Art I've studied watermedia, that is, watercolour plus acrylic medium, watercolour pencils, and charcoal. In 2002 I had a show of watermedia pieces at the Annex Art Centre. Now I exhibit fairly regularly in the Arts & Letters Club group shows for members. I find the external stimulus of making something specifically for a themed show becomes a springboard for inner creativity.

For a self-portrait show I tried drawing myself in the mirror, but I couldn't get beyond the severe, concentrated expression of someone who is drawing. I made an attempt at a painting based on photographs, but found it tedious and my heart wasn't in it. Then I thought of using the photographs themselves and immediately felt relieved to be constructing something, still easier for me than painting. I photocopied them in black and white, greatly enlarged, and cropped them into sections, which I planned to paste onto dark-coloured paper. It was the middle of the night and I couldn't wait for the stores to open. I removed the poems from a dark green hanging folder, and there, with its metal hooks sticking out the ends, was my background. It was not intended to be permanent, but I realized how apt it was. The piece became "Self-portrait: Writer" and initiated my Office Series, which combines watercolour with envelopes, elastic bands, and staples. Now in a stationery store, as well as getting excited about writing, I get excited about visual-tactile arts, as I do in a fabric or art supply store.

When the Arts and Letters Club was planning a watercolour exhibition I wanted to do a straightforward watercolour painting. As a subject I chose Bosc pears, out of visual attraction. I have always liked the way the tops of these pears elongate and extend into the stem. I had in mind to use this line in mirror image, but the samples I sketched felt contrived. I painted samples in which the pears were too realistic and I had no idea what to do with the rest of the space. These were only ten inches square, so when one didn't work out I didn't feel I'd wasted much paper. This is also a convenient size for people to hang in their homes. I liked what I did with colour. The golden beige of the pears I fractured into the brighter colours that would make up that beige, and painted very loosely, so that the shapes of the pears were only suggested. After many failed attempts I completed a series of ten paintings. I knew what I was doing, deliberately moving the pears around on the page, experimenting with new brushes and emphasizing different colours in the same palate. Weeks later I became aware of an unconscious aspect. Two paintings in the middle of the series, with their sharper angles and stronger colours, seemed agitated. These had been done just before the arrival of a houseguest. I was both excited at having company and resentful at having to fold away my main art table to make room for the air mattress.

My commitment to my arts has sometimes created difficulties in living in the real world. I was once in a situation in which my partner at the time was very happy to be the subject of love poems. But when I was writing poems about my parents, my partner was not pleased. To be fair, while writing I am uncommunicative or, at best, distracted. Yet it seemed to me that he picked arguments based on trifles, and when the arguments escalated he finally left at my request. Any kind of adversarial relationship or forced emotional entanglement is an anathema to my creativity and I avoid such situations. In response to expressions of hostility I curb my impulse to repay in kind: being open, even gullible, rather than calculating, is essential to my ability to create. A large part of what I've wanted in life is simply to be left in peace to work on my arts.

Contrary to my expectations in my early twenties, earning my living through writing has turned out unrealistic. What I choose to write tends not to earn much, and money as serious external motivation rarely applies to me. Teaching and other activities that involve engaging with people use the same kind of creative energy as writing: feeling my way, responding, using words. I've enjoyed teaching and have found that a little teaching can stimulate writing. A lot of teaching exhausts me. Would a job with less mental involvement be better? I don't know from experience, and earning a reasonable income is of course a consideration. The stress of not being able to pay the rent would seriously hamper creativity. Now, early retirement has nicely freed up time for my arts in exchange for a more modest standard of living.

While I was writing *The Emperor's Body* I was able to take a year's unpaid leave from teaching. I was really able to focus on the book, and I would work on it for one or two three-hour sessions a day. This sometimes required discipline, but basically I was steeped in the writing and came back to it as eagerly as to an intimate companion. I would punctuate the flow of these sessions by getting up and stretching, making fresh tea or, alas, snacking. I would take printouts to restaurants and work on them before my lunch arrived. The minimal interaction with the wait staff would be my only human contact. I soon found I could go four days like this before becoming anxious and needing company, so I planned social activities in advance and the work proceeded nicely.

I find the solitude of writing easily disturbed. One intrusion is music or television, with its imposition of rhythm and emotional content, even when muted from a neighbouring apartment. Knowing that I have an appointment later in the day breaks up the ideal of uninterrupted time, even though much of it might not be spent in actual creating. I dislike having to consider whether to put aside my creative work in order to finish a library book coming due. Before the days of phone-answering systems, if I were creating and the phone rang I got enraged. The rage was even more frustrating when I was just about to start creating. Having to engage in real talk, having to meet new people and draw them out in conversation, or to be drawn out — these wrench me out of the world I am creating as I write. Once while I was immersed in writing I had to buy a gift for someone close. It would have been easier to buy gifts for my characters, with whom I was more intimately involved at the time.

That being said, friends are an important part of my creative process. When I take a piece of writing as far as I can, I show it to one or two friends for their feedback. Part of this is affirmation: it seems to me that writing, as all art, is a communicative act, which needs to be experienced by someone else before I feel it is complete. This reading by my friends also serves to check whether the piece is clear and gives the overall impression I intended, in short, whether I've succeeded.

These last few weeks, in addition to working on this essay, I've completed a skit for a satirical review and a poem. Now it's time for a few days of puttering, going for walks, seeing a movie, enjoying social life. Next is an art project for a show to be hung in three weeks. I'll be combining watercolour with the tiny black paper-clamps I love so much, and will have to make sure there are some black-and-white areas so that the clamps are integrated. I will likely use charcoal, which smudges richly when painted over. I'll be cutting out shapes so the clamps will have edges to fasten onto. I might use conventional paper clips, as well. At this point I have no idea what it will actually look like and am excited to find out.

# MARY McKENZIE

Mary McKenzie is a Toronto-based artist/writer. She received her Bachelor of Fine Arts from the University of Alberta. Her work has been shown in Toronto, North Bay, Montreal, Saint John, Edmonton, Vancouver, Norway, Austria and South Korea. She was short-listed for the Royal Bank New Painter Award for Central Canada, and received an Honourable Mention at the Millennium Show for the Arts & Letters Club. Her poetry and art books include: *Termination, Juicy Verbs, Love Turns on a Dime, Truth is a Version* and *Recon_figure. Friend is an F-Word* and *Continue* are works in progress. In addition she published the short-lived art-zine *Flack*.

## COLD WATER WORKS BEST

From washing machine to tumble dry is considered a weight-bearing exercise. The stretch, lift and bend of a week's struggle. A life baptized in the wash-rinse cycle prepares us for a fresh, hung-out-to-dry week. Each day a clean shirt faces a dittoed-day from the week before and the week before, and before that. Maybe it even gets an assigned day of the week. Perhaps we face the world in red on Monday. Tuesday's blue. Wednesday middle-of-the-week beige. Beige makes a neither-this-nor-that statement like low-impact aerobics. A beige day could come and go and who would notice? Wednesday is definitely beige. On second thought, though, Monday is at best a mauve. Red has nothing to say about Monday morning's post-weekend ritual, the forcing-of-feet-to-the-floor. Red gets in your face. Screams passion. And that could only be a Thursday. Thursday, with all the bloodletting of almost-Friday angst. Then again, stereotyping colour, like anything else, has the potential for false assumptions. Who's to say that on a beige day you won't attack the parking ticket attendant, run a light, or murder your boss. Beige has that overlooked advantage. No one would be the wiser. A cautious beige knows not to draw blood. But, if unavoidable, cold water works best. Doesn't set the stain, preserves the colour.

Despite all the thinking that goes into creating visual art or writing, the click that switches the whole thing on is the desire to do it in the first place. That gut feeling that something's not right if you don't.

Anyone can doodle. Even before I called myself an artist, I drew, cut things up and took things apart in an ongoing process of configuring and reconfiguring. It wasn't a conscious act. It was just part of being, or growing up, like playing baseball or watching TV. Writing on the other hand was about as unlikely as catching a bone tossed in the company of bigger dogs.

Why art? Well, think of art as this animated game of leap-frog. Where your brain is the pond and it's dusk and the whole place is zinging with mating-calls or ideas. Questions are the active ingredient. They rebound off each other in a vibrant cacophony of predators and victims. Far more ideas die, or become fodder for the next idea, than become potential solutions. And only a fraction of those get expressed in any of a variety of media. And despite the ad hoc mix of these various ideas they're often investigated concurrently, in separate series.

"What is a landscape?" started, while looking at an exhibition of traditional landscapes. In quick succession an ever-expanding list developed.

What if the horizon line was removed?

What if a landscape was just water and sky?

What if a landscape was the colours of the sky?

What if water and sky were eliminated?

What if a landscape was a place on a map?

What if a landscape could show seasons?

What if there were people?

What if a landscape was a neighborhood?

What if it was a postcard?

What if it was a place found on the internet?

Possible solutions started becoming actual objects or images that depicted just the colours of the sky or just a line. In one possible solution I Googled the words "Canadian landscapes," which brought up the Natural Resources Canada (NRC) website. Low-res jpegs and text at this site document many Canadian landforms and inspired the Googled series. It looks at the effects of arbitrary scale and colour-gamut changes with regard to signification of specific place. Places translated by camera, computer, printer, eyes and imagination.

Stenciled text appeared in my art work at about the same time that my compulsive list-making was harnessed for poetry. A harrowing hard-drive failure and a tenuous recovery, initiated the process of reviewing, discarding and re-writing these lists for back-up purposes. Dozens of lists distilled out into ten or so contractions of only a few lines each. These evolved into compact narratives, little fictions of exaggeration and distortion. I dared to call them poems.

The poems eventually, like doodling, evolved. Now art projects rarely begin with a doodle, and writing for the most part doesn't start from a list. My writing often borrows from the painting process, playing with arbitrary distortion of scale and colour or unexpected juxtapositions of content. Language has become a colour palette of words, linking and fracturing images or ideas verbally expressed. Items like best-before-dates collide with families, and Echinacea turns gothic. Like an Eisenstein montage, neutral images instigate the unexpected. To accommodate these images, poetry seems to be

IMAGINATION *in* ACTION

giving way to prose. Just as painting sometimes gives way to photography or print-making. Media and format are simply tools in the jump for the bone.

For me, whether crafting visual art or writing, meaning is found in translation, not replication. Source material passes through a perception filter searching for colour and implication. The possibilities are endless: less becomes more, small can become large, the prominent submerges, details are embroidered. Word images make giant leaps from cold to catalogue or from clean to murder. Green tries on fuchsia, yellow, lime...

# MERIKE LUGUS

Merike Lugus was born in Tallinn, Estonia. She has lived in Tallinn, Stockholm, Toronto, Philadelphia, Los Angeles, and Cobourg. She graduated from the University of Toronto with a BA in General Arts and an MA in Sociology. As a painter, she has had solo exhibitions in the Estée Gallery, Toronto; Galerie in der BlutGasse, Vienna; Galerie Beaux Arts, Toronto; Rader Galleries, Bellingham, Washington; and Art Gallery of Northumberland, Port Hope. In recent years she has turned to sculpture, her first solo exhibition being at the Art Gallery of Northumberland, Cobourg. Her first book of poetry, *Ophelia After Centuries of Trying*, was published by watershedBooks in 1998. Her poetry, articles, and reviews have appeared in *Poetry Toronto*, *City Woman*, *Avenue Magazine* and *Room of One's Own*. Over the past years she has read her poetry in Toronto, Gore's Landing, Cobourg, and Grafton. She lives with her husband, two successful dogs, and four cats in a century farmhouse near Cobourg.

## TRANSIENT THOUGHTS: EXCERPTS FROM A TALK GIVEN AT THE WALKING TOUR OF THE SCULPTURE SHOW, TRANSIENT STATES, ART GALLERY OF NORTHUMBERLAND, FEBRUARY 8, 1998

The body of this work was started roughly at the same time as my mother was starting to die, a little over two years ago. As many here know, it's a difficult, often disorienting time. For some reason my mother chose to tell me some things about my early childhood which I had never known, and it seemed as if my emotional world were turned upside down. My grip on my identity seemed so tenuous that I decided to see a psychoanalyst in Toronto to help me sort things out. I'll call him Dr. F.

The work you see here in this room, in my mind is so deeply connected with those trips to Toronto and with sitting in a dimly lit, warm room with a friendly stranger, that I thought: how can I talk about my work without talking about that? So, I thought I would read to you a few excerpts from the journal I kept during the course of both my analysis and the making of the pieces you see here. If I had to sum up what it's about, I'd say it was about seeking some sort of identity or psychic stability in this world. Why I jumped on the phrase "transient states" is because there IS no stability. We, everything, keeps evolving. Sometimes this constant change can send us into panic states, but if we're lucky we find something that grounds us. People to love, some meaningful pursuit, for example.

I've chosen some passages from my journals which I think say something about the creative process as well as explain some of the things I do. They're not in perfect chronological order.

## A world without words

Back to Dr. F.'s office. I have retreated into a space which I am unable to describe to him. He asks what would happen if I had to stay there forever. I say I would begin to scream. He asks what I would scream. And then I break down. I say it's pointless because nobody would come anyway. Nobody ever came. Nobody ever came! I cried and cried, repeating that nobody ever came. I felt very very broken, very small. Indeed, I had become very small. I had gone past Sweden in time and was into Germany, perhaps even Estonia. I was somewhere between zero and three years old. I see myself as a pair of eyes in the dark, watching, waiting. No wonder I had no words. Still crying, I said that I couldn't even be sure whether it really happened in this way or whether I was just making it up.

In the background I could hear Dr. F.'s soft but firm voice, You are not making this up. He said it twice and I believed him.

In tears though I was, I saw clearly how my confidence in my own reality had been challenged, how easy it is for adults to talk a child out of their own experience, or to deny its importance. Certainly everyone had suffered. Who could have guessed that such a young child could suffer so horribly. I was beginning to understand the very tenuous grip I had on reality. Words are the tools of historians. They had words and I didn't.

Until now I had never been sure that my memories were authentic, that they truly belonged to me. But without them I was not a complete person. Without this certainty of authenticity, I was at the mercy of other people to tell me who I really was.

No wonder I have such a deep mistrust of words and such a strong sympathy for animals. I think of the silence of my studio each morning. The freedom to move once I'm there, to choose this tool or that. The feeling of certainty. No need to rush. Eventually a shape will emerge.

## Dr. F. won't be molded

I feel tired this morning. I didn't sleep well. Spent all day in the studio yesterday working on sculpture. I watched a video on how to make a whole body mold to reproduce a human figure.

All night, it seemed, instead of sleeping, I was positioning Dr. F. in my studio as if he were a statue. He was hard, immobile, yet alive. I put him here, I put him there. It made no difference; I could not change his expression. It's in the nature of his job, I think.

Later he will ask me, what did you want me to do?

And I will answer: smile.


## The love of sadness

On radio, an interview with Doris Lessing some weeks ago: she was explaining how during a certain period in her life (in her sixties, I think) she "fell into grief." The state of grief lasted several years. She said what triggered it was listening too much to a certain kind of music. What kind of music? Music of the troubadours.

Next week, on the same program, the interviewer said he had been inundated with calls asking about music of the troubadours. Where could one find it? Everybody wanted to know.

So many curious people wanting to tempt fate. Or, so many people seeking to authenticate their grief.


## The Northumberland Hills

Early morning dream: There is a road with fields on either side, leading up and down hills. A black figure is in the distance going up one of the hills. A bomb explodes somewhere to the left. I expect there to be more explosions, thinking the war is not over. But there are no more. In the foreground, much closer to the dreamer than the black figure that is now reaching the top of the hill, yet smaller, fainter, almost ghost-like, is a family. My mother and we four children. We don't look like ourselves, but rather like the people in a painting I had done years ago of a family of refugees. Almost skeletal and exhausted, the mother's eyes are closed but she keeps on walking, holding on to the hand of the smallest child.

The family was fading. It made me very sad to see it so faint. Good-bye, dear family, I thought. I saw each face in turn, as we appear in the old family album, as we had emerged from the long journey through Germany, through cities that were bombed or were about to be bombed, our mother keeping her wits about her, trying to keep abreast of news of which way the war was moving. I was overwhelmed by feelings of love for each one of us…even myself. I feel I have a deep understanding of what each one endured, and the meaning of the expression on each face.

IMAGINATION *in* ACTION

The lone figure reached the top of the hill. She was silhouetted against a brilliant white sky. The dream did not reveal what was on the other side of the hill, but I didn't feel any fear because these were my own Northumberland hills, the ones I visit with my dogs so regularly. Oddly the dream is in black and white. They are my hills, but they are without colour.

Will there be colour, someday?

Why did I cling so long to a family of ghosts?

At the beginning of my journey with Dr. F., I was the ghost, and the past was strong and vibrant. A reversal in perspective has taken place.

I celebrate the occasion by taking the dogs for a drive through our hills. Certain patches and quiltworks of land I have grown to know well. I love the changes through the seasons. One stretch of land is almost bare earth of uniform colour. Only the different levels of wetness in the dips and hollows reveal the soft contours. From the distance it almost looks like a stretch of velvet. Another is defined by rows of bleached corn stubble.

Beethoven's violin concerto is on the radio. The second movement begins just as I get back to the house. I turn the car around and go back into the hills, where I want to be with my thoughts and this exquisite piece of music. Now it has started to snow, light snow like veils of thousands of brides. Veils of infinite depth covering my Northumberland hills. In this moment all feelings co-exist, love, hate, joy, sadness.


Who will shape me?

Thinking about Dr. F's role as my analyst. The image came to me: I am the malleable goo inside a bowl: undefined material that is refusing to take shape. The matter gets splattered as it is stirred (the natural activity of the brain) and tends to creep up the sides of the bowl, either inadvertently, or in an effort to escape. Dr. F. is the spatula that keeps scraping the sides and turning the goo back in on itself.

First time around, I thought he was the bowl itself. But clearly he's the spatula. So what is the bowl? My own body? My true self? An opportunity? The closest evidence of God?

Most obviously the image comes from working with sculpture in the studio, mixing plaster. I am refusing to take shape. I keep eluding myself. In the past I sensed it was dangerous to take shape. Best to be elusive, slip away, admit to nothing. Best of all, be a pair of eyes, nothing more.

## Art at the living edge

Early morning dream, after a satisfying day in the studio: a tree opens itself to me and shows me the interior of its bark, the rich living circle girdling the hardened dead part inside it. Funny I had never found this image before, all those years when I felt there was a huge empty hole inside me. The inner bark is the only living part of the tree, and yet it must protect even its dead history, for a tree can rot from the inside.

## The cheetah and the baboon

There was a series of photographs in *Life* magazine, years ago. A cheetah chases after a baboon. The last shot is of the majestic, muscular cheetah coming to a halt, its jaws open, its thick neck curved high over the crouching figure of the little baboon, who has turned to face its dominator. His whole body is one negative curve as though the physical impact has already hit. His fangs are bared but they won't save him.

I cut the photo out and often just stared at it. This is not the first time I think it represents my relationship with my father.

These two curves fascinate me, I tell Dr. F. The large curve looming over the smaller one. He smiles and muses that the curves are identical to the classic ones of the mother holding her child.

I wonder whether this ambiguity can be expressed in sculpture.

## My identity is creature

With Dr. F. beside me, I have had the courage to listen to the dreams and to begin my true narrative: what I believe defines me, is something beyond nationality, culture, or gender, and that is my childhood experience. Beyond everything, I come from the vast world of neglect, and yes, let's call it abuse. My strongest sense of identity is with the single mom raising her children. I am both the mother and the child. The experience of loneliness and bleakness has been by far the most defining, most influential part of my life. I have been, first and foremost, the lost child, and now, perhaps the reason I can write this at all, I am also a loved woman, a loving mother and wife. I have discovered gardening, and I am learning to be a good artist.

But tell me about Canada's treatment of single moms, and I become enraged. Tell me about neglected children, and I recede into a white space. So many wars going on simultaneously. Newspapers are full of warnings of how children are affected. Tell me about it. Tell me for how long. Tell me what is the "normal," from which war will divert them. Tell me how my whole life has been a diversion. From what? I think of all the children growing up in refugee camps, their parents' lives torn apart. From where will they find the material to build their identities?

I want to tell the whole story but I have no art to tell it and I have no art because I cannot see all the pieces, I cannot manipulate them into sequence. There are too many segments.

There is the woman in black who is immobilized.

There is the little girl who is still snow blind.

There is the mother who has nothing to give.

The wife who wonders if everything she says is deceitful.

There is the woman who wants to love and love well.

The woman who is frightened of her own rage.

There is the woman who is repulsed at the thought of her mother's feet.


## Garden of Eden

Yesterday was a most wonderful day. All the important people in my life were here under one roof, and I was surrounded by all that was dear to me, my dogs, my garden, my studio. At one point it occurred to me that this might be the zenith in my life: how could it get any better? All of us had just finished playing a game of Bocce that John and Val brought as a gift, and they went into the house to get dinner. I lay down in the grass to relax and stare up at the poplars and the dappled light shimmering through them. The dogs came to lick my face, I put my fingers deep into their fur. Their tongues made me laugh out loud. When I raised my chin to escape their tongues, I saw the woodland section of the garden, upside-down, how it was lit up by the evening sun. Deep red peonies, creamy goat's beard, ferns in the shade of the pagoda dogwoods, the bright golden elder in blossom to the right of them. Suddenly the dogs lifted their heads in unison and looked in the direction of the house. Their mouths were open, their tongues relaxed, panting lightly. I looked up at their beautiful heads, saw the sharp teeth inside the cavern of Maddie's mouth. Whatever they had heard or seen did not seem to disturb them, though they were alert. The house-wren chicks started making a racket inside their house when one of the parents arrived with food. The opening to the tree swallow's nest was mysteriously dark and still. The chicks had fledged at last.

Inside the house I could hear a lot of talking and laughing. Eventually Rod called to me. Time to eat.

## Choosing art

I tell Dr. F. about the wonderful program I had seen on PBS the night before, about a famous cellist, a Japanese Kabuki artist and Bach's fifth suite for the cello. The Kabuki dancer was explaining that he was familiar with many different forms of femininity in his dancing, and the one he wanted to evoke in his choreography for this particular music was something quite transcendent. He wanted to be not an ordinary lover to the cellist, but more like a bird that lands and sits beside him. This is a lovely alternative, I say. I would like to have that sort of relationship with him, Dr. F.

Is that possible? he asks, in a way that indicates it might be.

No, I say. This is too ethereal, too spiritual even though very beautiful. On my part, there has been too much passion during our sessions.

Impossible, I say again. But perhaps I'll find some other metaphor.

Coming to an end is always a difficult thing.

On the long trip home on the 401, some cello music on the radio reminds me of the Kabuki dancer. I think of him and his relationship to the cellist and to the music and I feel very proud that I have chosen art as a means of expression. Yes, it has been a good choice. There is so much more to live up to. A reason to keep stretching, to hold on to the idea of excellence.

Now, looking down at me from a glassed-in platform is the Kabuki dancer. His exquisite expression of pain and sorrow allows me to take my own seriously. He is the bird beside me. He embodies Art.

# MILT JEWELL

Milt Jewell began painting in 1961, studied briefly at the Three Schools of Art, but is essentially self-taught. His work became progressively more abstract until 1982 when he began figurative work. He has exhibited widely, and has taught art at the Three Schools, at Upper Canada College, and in various Scarborough schools. In the seventies he was founder/editor of *Artists Review* which featured reviews by artists, and he collaborated with poet Bruce Whiteman on a book, *12 Poems, 12 Drawings*. He has collaborated with the Modern Times Theatre Company, with the Canadian Electronic Ensemble and with Array Music. Since moving to Campbellford, he has helped with stage sets and props for Westben Arts Festival productions.

## THE CREATIVE MESS: EXCERPTS FROM A 1991 INTERVIEW

I paint because I saw paintings. I think we paint because we like paintings and want to do it ourselves. And I think you write because you enjoy reading. So you paint so you've got something to look at, as Barney Newman says, and sometimes you write so you've got something to read.

IN THE BEGINNING: I was twenty-three years old and I'd been playing football for ten years of high school and university. After the football season in the fall of '61 I went out in the country with a friend of mine who was an architecture student. He had the smallest little sketch-books you can imagine, and he would do these little watercolour washes and then take his drafting pen and draw into that and then the ink would run a little bit. They were very very simple little sketches. And so, we would go out in the country just to get away where it was quiet, and he had an old beat-up straw hat that we took turns wearing. It was very pastoral. He gave me one of these sketch-pads and a pencil. It was a revelation. There were a couple of barns a good distance away and I found I could get the very simple shape of the barn and the fields in front of the barn and the woods behind the barn. This little tiny drawing was really the first drawing that I was conscious of making and I got great delight out of it. I filled up that little book. Then I saw how he used watercolours, so I did endless watercolours of stubby beer bottles. You know, those stubby bottles, they were all the same, so that every one of my drawings was the same. An orange and a beer bottle, an apple and a beer bottle.

I just kept doing it. I don't know why. Suddenly I wanted to do it. I think that's a common experience. So anyway, I painted really badly but I started to look at paintings then and I found myself imitating painters. One of the first that I tried to imitate after the Group of Seven was David Milne. I did a lot of very loose watercolour studies, you know, where you use the watercolour brush in a very linear fashion, flat shapes and that sort of thing, influenced by David Milne. It just gradually came.

I went to England. I applied to the London School of Economics. I was a history graduate, and thought maybe I'd be a diplomat like Lester Pearson, but fortunately the London School of Economics turned me down. So I got a job teaching in a Roman Catholic secondary school in Camden Town and went to the Evening Institutes. It was a class of women painting geraniums in watercolour, but there was a tiny woman there who had trained at OCA. She'd studied with Lismer and others of the Group of Seven, so she was very interested in what I was trying to do, which was not geraniums. My responsibilities in London were minimal so I had a lot of time to read, and I went to the Tate Gallery a great deal. I was quite fascinated by Henry Moore. I would sit in a corner of the Tate Gallery and do drawings of all of the sculptures. This was my way of doing academic work, like the nineteenth century French used to copy the antique sculpture from Greece and Rome. I also picked up Herbert Read's two books, *Concise History of Modern Painting*, and, *Concise History of Modern Sculpture*. I think they're all wrong, but they were perfect for me, because they gave me a framework. All of a sudden I knew a way to look at paintings of the last hundred years. So I just kept learning, and the more I learned the more I wanted to learn, so I think I've just continually gone on from there.

THE CRAFT OF PAINTING: I've been studying art ever since I was handed that little sketch-pad. I've worked very slowly. Because I'm entirely self-taught, I've over-done virtually everything. At some point I read about an Australian artist who claimed that he had ground his own paints and stuck them in tubes, so I thought all art students did that. So I went to great trouble to acquire dry pigment and raw linseed oil and a glass muller and a glass sheet. That's how you make oil paint. A muller looks like a paperweight. It's a very heavy piece of cast glass, very solid, with a flat bottom, and the bottom's very rough. You need a rough surface to work on. Glass is the best. And you mix up a little oil with the dry pigment, whatever colour you want, and then you just put this glass muller down on top of it and go in a circular motion and grind the pigment very fine. You scrape it into a pile and grind it again. This is the way they made paint up until the advent of the modern roller presses. In Rubens' time, he would have a number of apprentices busy grinding oil colours for him all the time.

I was very interested in the whole craft of paint, so I made all kinds of paints. I got gum tragacanth and made pastels. They were awfully soft, but I used the same artist pigment and chalk filler and gum and mixed it all together and left it in trays to dry, and then I'd have a very soft pastel chalk that I could paint with. And I made watercolours. I used gum arabic. When I'd phone a big industrial company and they had these materials, it was too much trouble for them to sell it to me. You see, if I wanted to buy a barrel of gum arabic, they would bill me, but since I only wanted a little they said, "Well, come over to the lab, we'll give you a couple of pounds. You can have it," so in many cases it didn't cost me anything. So I made this watercolour and I had baby food jars and just put the water colour in that. I also got little tiny ice-cube trays and would fill those up and give them to all my friends. They would never use them. They would just frame them and put them up on the wall, a little tray with some handmade watercolour. I made my own gesso of rabbit-skin glue and chalk. Of course it was messy, but that was just part of the tradition. The equivalent process for a writer would be to carve wood-blocks and make books with a printing press like Gutenberg.

I taught life drawing at The Three Schools. I found that I could show them a few things, so that they had some idea of what a plastic medium drawing is, what the implications of marks on paper are, and why it is that some things come forward and others fall back, and show them a little bit of pleasure.

Because I'm self-taught, I did all kinds of things that were off the main track. I spent a winter doing Josef Albers' colour course. Danforth Tech had his *Interaction of Colour* in the library. A $200.00 book full of handmade silk screens; they thought it cost $2.00 so they ordered it, and when the librarian saw the book and its price she locked it up. I borrowed it for a weekend, copied out the exercises and spent months trying to do the exercises with crummy construction paper. I invested a hell of a lot of time, but I learned something.

In my ignorance I learned things that no art student would bother with. It's called creative misunderstanding. In my mishandling of materials I learned things that no one else would know. The best paintings often arise from abusing the medium.

You teach the right way to do something. It's up to the individual to try the wrong way.

PAINTING AND NARRATIVE: Paint for me is a way of thinking. So my interest in literature and my interest in music and dance and everything else, is looking for fresh ways to approach a painting. I get a lot of ideas from what I read and from what I see. Particularly in fresh art forms. That usually stimulates me a little bit and it's in the back of my mind somewhere when I go to do a painting.

Most artists look only at paintings. They don't pay attention to the other arts, except as entertainment. I get a lot of inspiration from other arts. My recent portraits are inspired by Jacques Ferron. I read his *Le Ciel de Québec* all one summer. He had all these people, F.R.Scott, Chubby Power, Paul-Émile Borduas, Therese Casgrain, politicians, poets, painters, churchmen, and he juxtaposed them in hilarious situations. Even Patterson Ewen is in the book. So I decided to paint portraits of people I admire and put them into landscapes and cityscapes. My paintings are really narratives.

*thoughts on creativity...*

CHOICE OF MEDIUM: I did sculpture because the painting was going very badly and there was nothing I could do. I didn't know what to do, didn't know what I wanted to do, and what I was doing I didn't like. For quite a long period of time I never thought of myself as a sculptor, but I did sculpture.

When I decided, in '81, in '82, I guess, that I wasn't going to do modernist work any more, that there was nothing much left to do, it was a field that had been worked over and re-worked over, and I wanted to go to something fresh, I grabbed hold of a pre-modernist, and the artist that I latched onto was Daumier. He was a caricaturist and a wonderful draughtsman, and he did some really interesting paintings, very small, some very very awkward, but they all had that wonderful life to them. Then I discovered that he had done a whole lot of these little clay portrait busts, so, while I still considered myself a painter, I found myself just drawn to doing sculpture like Degas and Daumier. I tried to find a slightly different approach, but their sculpture was in the back of my mind. It was partly just a frustration with painting. I knew what I didn't want to do, and I hadn't got a clue what I did want to do, and the sculpture seemed to be easy for me. I enjoyed looking at it after I'd finished it which wasn't the case with the paint. When I saw the painting I was just filled with despair, but I always had in the back of my mind that I was a painter.

Now, when I have this idea that I want to make a painting, I do pick subjects. There are things that I would like to see as paintings. I don't ever think, Well, I can't do this in wax, or I couldn't do this in watercolour. I just find that I work very differently in different mediums. I prefer the wax. It's very awkward and it's very slow, and it's clumsy, and I can't control it. When I get the painting to a state where it's really very ugly and I don't know what to do with it, the best thing to do is semi-destroy it, so that's when I lay out a sheet of watercolour paper over the painting, iron the back, and that smears things. I never consider that as the last step, but that's the beginning of fixing the thing up. You see, when I iron it, first of all, there's a lot of accidents. If I'm not careful, I put too much heat on and it really smears and then I'm in a real mess. That's when I always feel like I'm starting to paint, when I'm in a mess and try to paint myself out.

I realized that the best paint that you can make is wax. It lasts much longer than oil, is much more stable. It won't stand up very well in extreme heat or in a fire, but an oil painting won't either. The trouble with oil paint is it gets brittle, it's dark, it cracks, and the canvas support is far from ideal. I saw the mummy portraits from Fayum in Egypt. They were done in the second century AD when Egypt was really a Roman province. They were portraits and they would bury them with the people. The boards that the portraits were painted on survived for eighteen hundred years. The wax looks like it was painted yesterday. They're very very gorgeous.

So this was a safe way to make your own paint. There's quite a few artists painting in encaustic and they have widely different techniques for working on it. The trouble is, it's very awkward, it wrecks your brushes, they get all frizzy, you can't get really fine detail. If you want to rework an area you've got to warm it up, either by heating a knife or using an iron or a heat lamp. It is a struggle, but the struggle is kind of interesting, and I can do virtually anything anyone else can do in some other medium.

WRITING ABOUT ART: I did write, but it was out of a sense of duty. I really enjoy writing, but never feel I can do it very well. I used to write reviews of art shows for the *Artists Review.*

The art criticism in Toronto was pathetic, and I was not aware of the artists ever talking about art. They talked about how little money they had and how they never got any publicity. It was just the usual ranting that they tend to do, complain about grants and lack of grants and everything.

I just decided that artists should do it themselves. If they wanted to read some art criticism they'd have to write their own. Because *Canadian Art* or *Arts Canada* or what-ever it was, didn't seem to spend much time. There was a huge body of painters and sculptors and various kinds of visual artists in Toronto, and they would get absolutely no notice. It was almost like they were in a vacuum. They were invisible. So we put out this paper as cheaply as possible. It came out every two weeks, and we had an IBM Selectric typewriter which was very nice; you could erase easily. I would type out a two or three page review and I'd get one or two other friends to write something on a show, some-thing they were interested in, and we'd just go to the offset printer and print two hun-dred or five hundred copies. After I'd done five or six of these we got a Canada Council grant. It used to drive other people crazy because they tried so hard to get grants for their magazines. I had no knowledge of this whole grant business, so I was going to ask for a thousand. Well, there were a bunch of artists in this co-operative gallery I was in, ACT, and they were really sharp. They looked at the application and said, "Oh no, no. Ask for eight thou," which to me was an astronomical amount. The next thing I know, here's a cheque for four thou and a promise of another four thou in six months or a year. I managed to make that last for three years, and this was bringing out, you know, about twenty issues a year of this stuff, just typed on the machine, photo offset, we'd staple them together. That was the only writing I did. I did a lot of editing. Artists spell very badly. They don't know how to say things, but they know what they want to say, and I would help them to try and find the words. Sometimes I would correct the spelling and fix things up, and I've often regretted that I did that, because what they were giving me was not good English, but it was almost poetry. Very very beautiful stuff, and of course I'd fix it up to make it look acceptable. I think it was a big mistake.

The trouble was, it was so successful everyone wanted me to continue to do this as a service to the community, but I just wanted to concentrate on my painting. I was becoming known as the artist's friend, and I don't want to be the artist's friend. I want to be an artist.

It seems to me that you paint the things that you can't really put into words. If you can put it into words, why bother to paint it? Much easier, you know, to sit down and say what it is you've got to say, rather than to go in this huge roundabout way of giving us all these visual symbols for what amounts to a verbal statement of some kind.

Paintings can be read a number of ways. I don't know that paintings are necessarily vague. It's just that they resist verbal formulation.

I suppose it's impossible to really write about something visual. But that doesn't mean that no one should try. It's in trying to do the impossible… You try with your words to get as close an approximation to a visual sensation or a visual experience as you can.

I was always quite interested in Meyer Shapiro who was a wonderful writer. He wrote on illuminated manuscripts and things like that, but he was also very interested in modern art. So he's done a book on Cezanne. He was sort of my hero. Here was a model of a way to write three or four paragraphs about one of Cezanne's paintings, where you really did learn a good deal. He managed to see things, and draw your attention to the things that really were of interest. I don't think he gave you all the conclusions, but in the process he would give you a whole lot of things that most people would never have seen. They were there, but you had to look very carefully, and have a great deal of experience, to see why it is that behind the sitter's head the cabinet comes in at ear level here and goes out much lower on the other side, or a line that's not perfectly vertical, it's just off vertical a little bit. He would notice things like that. It wasn't strictly incompetence on the part of Cezanne, but instinctively or otherwise, it created a certain tension. Anyway, I've always felt that it's possible to talk in a fairly meaningful way about visual arts, but very few people do it.

METHOD: I start with an idea but it changes as soon as I start. I don't think I could make a mark on a board or a canvas or a piece of paper without a previous idea.

I say to myself, I've got four hours today so I'd better get started. I usually start with an idea, but the idea is always tentative. When I start this painting, I have no idea how it'll end up. In fact, I know for sure that I'm not going to be able to visualize what this painting will look like at the end. Sometimes I have a very strong idea which I will pursue for a long while, but eventually something else happens, so the painting always surprises me. But you know, I'm not really conscious of the process at all. What happens is, I work on the painting until it gets really awful, and then I stop and look at it and figure, How am I going to get out of this mess? So I just assume that when I start, I'm going to just blunder on for a while until it's really bad at a certain point, and then I have to try and fix it up. So all my paintings tend to be fixed-up paintings. I'm just trying to eliminate the… You see, what I have is a flawed masterpiece, and the idea is to get rid of the flaws. And then what are you left with?

# MONA HARRISON

Mona Harrison has always been interested in art, in one form or another. She was considered the weird one in her family because she read books. Now she writes short stories and poetry. She frames pictures, spins novelty yarns, creates jewelry, and enjoys photography. She and her husband live on a farm near Campbellford, where they recently retired from breeding award-winning Highland cattle. She still maintains a small flock of diverse poultry — for their eggscentricity, entertainment, and inspiration.

## PICTURES

She's been a long time gone, Emma Marie Harrison, née Marie Irma St. Croix. Nearly forty years. She'd have been eighty-eight years old next month. Two lifetimes for her.

Memories have dimmed over time, but I can still recall her face, her laughter. I see it in her photographs; in me, her daughter, and in Amy, the granddaughter she never knew. *My* beloved, beautiful daughter. Teasing blue-grey eyes thread through three generations.

Emma's favourite colour was blue. The soft, middle blue found on statues of the Virgin Mary. I chose a winter-blue satin lining for her whitewashed oak coffin, a tailored forget-me-not blue cocktail dress as her going away outfit. I was eighteen years old when I froze at the sight of her inert body folded on the bathroom floor like a discarded bath towel. Bruised horribly from the hemorrhaging of cirrhosis.

It would be a long time before I'd understand that her death was a release, and that in it, perhaps, she'd found peace. It would be a long time before those bruises would detach themselves from my numbed heart, allowing warmth and healing to penetrate my own dark coffin.

She was a farm girl once. I have a picture of her wearing dungarees, a milk pail in her hand. Walk with me to the summer pasture. I'll introduce you to the cows. The white one is Kalla Lily, named, in a way, after Emma. She loved lilies and roses. I have pictures of her with both.

Black and white pictures of a lovely young woman with a big shy grin. A face filled with love and mischief. One of how many children? Twelve? Sixteen? Born into a French-speaking community in Lac du Bonnet, Manitoba. To Emélie Fortin and Jean Baptiste St. Croix. Poor farmers. I have seen pictures.

She's here with me in my kitchen. The kitchen was her stage. I'd wake up Saturday mornings to the hypnotic smells of fresh baking. Homemade bread, cakes, pies. And "non-fattening" éclairs. Her apron, hands and cheeks dusted with flour; tendrils of raven black hair curling damply at her brow. Not even room left on the table for my small bowl of cereal. I know. I have pictures. Teach me how to make the buns in the muffin tins, the ones with three balls of dough. And tourtiere, always a Christmas favourite, with its spicy blend of beef, pork and veal.

Some weekend mornings my nostrils would catch the dark sepia scent of perked coffee. I would hear voices from the living room. Overnight guests, who'd played card games long into the night. I'd scavenge the kitchen for cold buttered toast and uneaten rashers of bacon amidst the detritus of dirty dishes, empty bottles and overflowing ashtrays.

I see her now at the sewing machine. Shoulders bent. Focused. Working on a party dress for me. Always a new dress for Easter, or the first day of school, or for Christmas. And sometimes for St. Patrick's Day. Nothing ever matched. She loved *all* colours. Didn't want to dismiss a single one. I know. My heart has pictures. Vivid with patterned fabrics and colours.

Red will always be her lipstick.

I see her in the victory garden. Still, head bowed. Like the painting "The Angelus." Thankful for God's bounty. My oldest brother Norm kneeling beside her. A faded photo has captured this moment in time. I can hear the birds overhead. Smell the warm earth. Taste the radishes.

Come to me another day. We'll walk again down paths remembered. We'll pick poppy-red geraniums in the park. Bobby-pin tissues to our heads and go to church.

Laugh till the tears flow.

*** 

I live on a small farm near Campbellford, Ontario. I'm a new writer, in my late fifties. I haven't painted for twenty years, and have recently resumed photography. The death of my closest friend was the key that re-opened the doors to creative discovery. Every day I'm reminded that life is a fleeting gift.

My first poem followed a photo session at Presqu'ile Provincial Park, where I was compelled to capture on film the faded beauty of red wooden shutters against a grey stone building. Once the pictures had been taken, the words describing the feelings that the images generated insisted I put them on paper.

Sometimes I'll be in the middle of the cow field, and something will spark my imagination, such as a dew-covered spider web, or the sunlight diffusing through the trees, and I'll almost run back to the house to put words to paper. It's as though the back burner is always on, and every so often the pot boils over and the words must find a home elsewhere.

Everything around me is a poem, a story, or a picture — from the horses and cats which I see as living sculpture, and the Highland cattle that appear as rugged and ancient as civilization, to each new morning sky, the changing seasons, the beautiful faces of family, friends, and strangers. Squash growing on the manure pile. Even the chickens which provide me with my breakfast eggs. The farm pond, the wildlife it attracts, the century maple and oak, the constant chorus of birdsong, the pulse of raindrops on the tin roof. The diamond-studded night sky, the whiff of smoke from a neighbour's woodstove…

Hokey as it sounds, I feel on occasion that I am a medium, and that the writing comes from somewhere, someone, or something unknown. When I re-read it, I wonder where the words originated…who *really* wrote them?

Many of my poems come to me in the middle of the night. Or at dawn, when I first awaken. They seem to slip out from a semi-conscious state, from my mind and heart, through my hand and pen to the paper. They are often heavy with emotion, imagery, and colour. I write poetry when I'm driven to express a feeling.

My camera captures moments in time. Flashes of colour and shape. Images I might need to write about later. Or ideas for pictures I might like to paint, although I haven't picked up a brush in years. Sometimes I think I take these photographs to verify the sensations that create the poems that inevitably follow. While each can stand separately, they also work together, and I like to see them displayed in tandem.

The poems with photographs are inspired by nature, light, colour, and patterns. But not every poem comes with a picture. Those without images typically hold the answer to an internal struggle or query. They paint word pictures of their own, where the reader is invited to fill in the blanks using his or her own palette. I hope that their vision will merge with mine to craft an even deeper truth. We'll explore together, as the reader becomes my camera, my paintbrush and my pen.

# MURRAY CHARTERS

Murray Charters is a teacher, musician and writer who has lived in the Brantford area for more than a dozen years. He was born in Toronto but worked and studied from London Ontario to London England. He was a professor of music history at Memorial University of Newfoundland before returning to Ontario. He now teaches for the Grand Erie school board and writes a weekly column about music for *The Brantford Expositor*.

## MUSINGS ON CREATIVITY

The following is very much just my own personal understanding of creativity and related matters based on my experience performing, arranging and sometimes composing music, teaching music both as a performance skill and as a quest for understanding through theory and history, researching and writing about music — especially the history of music, being an audience member, and finally becoming a writer for a small-city newspaper promoting, critiquing, and providing articles of general interest about music to a very wide, non-scholarly audience.

Two premises I must state up front. First, I believe we all see the surface of events and objects around us, but that some see more than this or beyond the surface. Second, I very strongly believe that our brains are completely unique one from the other and thus we gather and process information in entirely individual ways, but that there is enough commonality between some sets of brains that mutual understanding is made possible and even desirable.

Creativity, I believe, is a way of seeing the world. It can be an innate function of our brain's design, but can also be taught to some extent, or perhaps uncovered is a better term. Sometimes that uncovering happens spontaneously in response to a remarkable event.

The first level of expression for creativity would be appreciation for the concept that art of any sort is important to one's world. I think of this concept as going beyond the surface of the physical world and exploring connections between unconnected things, the emotional life created by things, people and events, and even something more than that which I will term spiritual. As we perceive the need for art in our lives, we resort more to reading, listening, having pictures on our walls, and studying live and recorded performances.

Such an interest can lead to the next level beyond appreciation, which would be some form of creation. I believe the first level of creation is empathy. I think that those who care to listen to and attend to other beings, objects and events are already demonstrating a creative response to the "something more" of my loose definition of art.

The second level in creativity is speaking. Here the choice of subjects and especially the use of metaphor would reveal a beyond-the-surface understanding of things. I feel an important element here is humour, for I equate the ability to see beyond the immediate with the ability to see all that is slightly preposterous about life. A more valuable element is the ability to explain things to others, revealing an understanding or appreciation that goes beyond the obvious, and an ability to understand how others do and don't see things. My second premise would warn us that no one is capable of explaining everything to everyone, for there are going to be those whose brains just don't receive messages that particular way.

Speaking leads naturally to writing, an activity that most do, but few do well. Just as empathy and speaking are abilities that we can foster and turn into careers, so there is much technique to be learned about writing; this is when we begin to take our interests and desires seriously and even start to use the word "creativity" more commonly, openly and legitimately. In a similar way many of us take pictures but only a few learn all the technical matter to create photographs, and some of those are still not for artistic purposes at all.

At this point I would bring in the concept of talent. My premise regarding different wirings of the brain suggests to me that some lucky ones have a wiring that naturally leads to an understanding of art in general, then of a specific art above all others, and then even to creation within that art. If that talent is very specific, perhaps there is not a lot of understanding by that particular brain of other forms of art outside the area of talent. But I feel strongly that brain wiring for art leads to some appreciation for all forms. The problem comes in the actual area of creation. Here specific physical skills may not have been bundled into the brain's software systems with the appreciation programs. Again, skills can be acquired, but this will probably not lead to such high levels of artistic creation as more natural talent may allow, and may lead to frustration for the artist.

I view creativity as a possible part of everyday life. Consider the old quip that life is a journey and not a destination. It's fine to mouth this, but to live that way involves elements of creativity. My father often said we would just explore around the next corner before heading back, and I loved that concept enough to continue it. He also would jokingly replace the "r" of explore with a "d," and I also think warmly of that added meaning. You just never know what may explode in your mind when you take time to look around that next corner. In Medieval music we have some lovely pieces from the Troubadours and Trouvéres of France. The name in both versions of French (Southern and Northern) means "finders," and the concept was that they just found their melodies much as the Greeks talked of finding a statue inside a rock. I like that idea very much, and feel it applies more widely. There is an element of playfulness to this way of looking at creativity that I think is exactly right.

I also want to comment on re-creation as well as creation. There is magnificent creativity when Bach writes a piece for solo cello and fascinating creativity again when

Yo-Yo Ma lifts those notes off the page and makes them dance and sing and say something just a bit different than what anyone else has thought of making them say. Similarly, when writing about an artistic subject, if the writer can reveal something more about that art, explain a bit about it to increase another's awareness, or otherwise enrich the artistic life of the appreciator, then I think something creative and truly artistic has happened. This is truly called creative non-fiction.

Naturally there are many examples of creative cross-referencing in the arts as well. Some paintings, by Bruegel for example, suggest boisterous, noisy activities. Similarly, some musicians often speak of colours when they hear music. Some talk of specific pitches or notes having a certain colour; others think in terms of keys and also of elements within a key having their own hues. Instruments also are capable of colours, and these can change depending on how the instrument is played although certain shades predominate in certain types of instruments.

Particularly interesting for me is the relationship between music and writing. Both involve creations that, unlike paintings, must be recreated across time, and thus in both one is aware of leading an audience along and giving them some surprises as well as some reassuring reference points along the way. Playwright Peter Shaffer, who is also a skilled classical musician, claims his plays can best be understood only by someone who is thoroughly familiar with the music of Mozart, for example. He may be right, as I adore his work.

In my writing, I think that I am very influenced in my choice of words from moment to moment by my musical awareness and interests. To begin with, I enjoy choosing words with an eye for their original or fundamental meaning — if I know it of course. I think part of this relates to the sense of music notes having the same meaning throughout time, and perhaps even to the idea of there being a fundamental note that influences the harmony sounded above it. On the other hand, single notes take on different meanings depending on the harmonies surrounding them and even the instruments playing them. In connection with this idea of additional meanings comes the much-lamented idea of the pun as being a verbal play on the sound of the word. In fact, for me puns occur immediately and spontaneously in response to the word's sound, much the same as I respond immediately and spontaneously to music.

More importantly, I often find myself choosing words for their sound qualities. This is not just onomatopoeia but more often choices of alliteration and rhyme. (I was delighted many years ago to find that Wagner wrote the libretti for his Ring Cycle operas in a free verse held together by various forms of alliteration.) I am influenced then by consonance, assonance and euphony in my simple prose essays intended for a general reading audience.

I am also aware that I frequently repeat words from one paragraph to the next like a musical motif that lends sequence and stability to my structure. Flow or continuity is a very important aspect of my serious writing, and I constantly reread to ensure that this is paramount. For me this concept consciously relates to the formal structures and more subtle repetitions used by composers to keep listeners, partly subconsciously, aware of their place as a long piece unfolds.

I sometimes begin my sentences indirectly, with supplementary information before getting to the main point. I believe this relates to a common nineteenth-century musical feature where a piece begins away from the main idea or home key and gradually reveals the facts to the listener. Some examples of this include the opening of Beethoven's First Symphony, pieces by Chopin, the opening to Wagner's *Tristan und Isolde*, and the symphonies of Sibelius.

In my writing I aim to explain how music works and affects us without any real reference to sound, other than through the subtle choice of words as indicated above. I cannot print musical examples and expect readers to understand them. Rather I try to write usefully about an aural art without using an aural element.

One way to do this is to focus on the impression that the music makes on listeners and then try to explain some of the sources of that effect. The first caveat here is that there is no one intended effect, nor should every listener experience any art in the same way. Art is in the individuality of the response, after all. So I can only deal with rather general effects if I am going to work this way. The first movement of Beethoven's Fifth Symphony is generally dark and foreboding, even angry on occasion; the last movement is bright and more optimistic. The directions of the opening, most outstanding and often repeated melodies are opposite to each other, the first movement descending, and the last movement ascending. That is a relatively simple but still profound example; profound in the sense that this observation can now be applied more broadly by any readers keen on learning more about how music affects them.

I am also influenced in my analysis of music by all the things that I have learned about analyzing architecture, painting or sculpture, and literature. In that sense I find there is much in common between all the arts, and in the way we look at them.

I particularly try to avoid the cliché of describing a composer's biography as a way of attracting listeners to the compositions. Biography is only relevant to very few pieces and very few aspects of music, and I refuse to go that easy route. Instead I prefer to look for patterns and reflections in the events of a person's lifetime, both in his own life and in the general events surrounding him, looking for resonances between those events and the person's artistic output.

When preparing my own performance, as cellist or conductor, I first and most fundamentally have a sure grasp of the form or structure of every piece on the program. In my presentation I am thinking in terms of speaking to the audience, trying to tell them a story that has no words. If the piece feels like a complete narrative to me in my practising, then I assume that this will be understood by members of the audience. I will convey a certain amount of this in rehearsal to my orchestra if I am conducting, but only to the extent that I am trying to create a uniform approach to the music. Even here I think it is important to respect each individual's appreciation of the art, although it is a conductor's job to bring all players to a common point in the final presentation. As a critic writing a review for the press, I also look for the integrity of the interpretation in terms of the entire piece as well as the entire ensemble.

It is not unusual for instrumental musicians to put in their heads words to certain rhythms and melodic phrases to help them retain the correct feel for those moments. Normally these are not just trite phrases but rather words loaded with meaning for the performer that somehow relate to what the performer feels about the music at that moment. It is my experience that these phrases are frequently shared in rehearsals of chamber music.

I also think in terms of colours when I am playing or when I am conducting, and have gone so far as to colour the music of a teen-aged student in an effort to get her to be more expressive. In this case the colours ranged from red through yellow to green and blue to suggest different shades of tension and relaxation. With my string students I also use a variety of consonants ranging from soft "SH" or "L" through "R" and "P" to harder "T," "D," and "G" or "K" to indicate the initial attack with the bow or by pluck-ing. To some extent these consonants are used as an actual technique of tonguing for wind instruments. In my case I am using the consonants more as a metaphor of the sound wanted or the effect to be created.

I am not a composer, but I have composed one short piece for violin and flute which came into my head spontaneously while thinking about the occasion where it would be played. There had been no plans for me to write a piece for this occasion, but I was deeply involved emotionally — the occasion was my second marriage — and I found myself picturing the event in my head several weeks beforehand. This led to the sound of this piece suddenly appearing, unbidden, when I was otherwise engaged in the mundane household task of washing the car. In picturing the scene I suddenly heard an initial sound and saw where that sound would go. I did not see the whole piece all at once, but the initial idea from which the rest would flow and also the basic form were apparent at once. I was compelled to stop what I was doing, sit down at the piano and work out the details. The whole event of spontaneously visualizing this music and then rushing to get it down before it disappeared had me in a state of high agitation. It was a happy excitement, and I felt very pleased with myself but also curiously honoured or blessed to have been given this gift.

Similarly, when arranging a piece, I often listen to it over and over in my head over a period of several days, and then ideas begin to flow about what I might add around the initial idea to make it my own. Occasionally these ideas come quite quickly, togeth-er with the initial thought of doing the arrangement, usually inspired by hearing the tune. Once, at a weekend conference that also evoked some strong emotions, I heard some words at the Friday evening introduction that suddenly inspired me to create a solo arrangement of a Beatles tune related to those words. This was not a music conference and there was nothing external that suggested such a response; this was simply my very personal response to some words that moved me. The musical material took hold of me and constantly ran through my head over that night and the next day. The surprising result was that, although I had no opportunity to practise, I confidently performed the music on my cello for the first time ever at the Sunday farewell gathering.

As with many performers, after I perform, certain sections continue to pop into my mind over and over. Also, when I have migraines, one trite little phrase will get stuck in my aching head and be an aural part of the agony. In fact, I have music going in my head a great deal of the time, sometimes to the point of personal irritation — which is one reason that I often listen to something like CBC Radio Two where I do not know what is coming next, but where there is always other music to distract me from the self-generated tunes.

Often these pieces come spontaneously with no apparent connection to external events, just pre-existing sounds I suddenly remember. Sometimes the piece reflects the atmosphere or scenery or event around me. But very occasionally I will just invent a bit of melody in response to my mood. I have never tried to follow these up and write them down except for the one instance described. I don't believe mankind is any the worse off for that.

# NANCY JANE BULLIS

Nancy Jane Bullis is a Toronto-based author/lawyer, poet, spoken word artist and broadcaster. Her publications include a chapbook, *Leather Lattice* (1994), a full-length poetry book, *The Eel Ladder* (watershedBooks, 1999), and a novella, *I Think It's Time To Give Up On Henry* (LyricalMyrical, 2006). Her radio program, *HOWL*, airs on CIUT 89.5FM and features interviews with authors, poets and songwriters. Nancy co-authors non-fiction reference publications in tax law and business compliance. She performs spoken word with the PoetiKs, a trio that includes Michael Morse on bass and David Story on keyboards. Nancy is wildcard champion of the 2002 Big Mouth Poetry Slam and has been on the Toronto poetry scene since the early eighties. Nancy embraces life with gusto. She is currently working on a novel.

## EVERYTHING STARTS WITH A THOUGHT...

All thoughts have rhythm
some thoughts have words others have sound waves outside my head

Thoughts that are heard are my music my soul's best friend
I sing and play to hug me inside

Thoughts that have words save my life
I write every day my heart breaks to repel what lurks and surrounds me

These are the seeds planted
not all seeds grow

Some die on impact or fester or transform into music from words
words into music

I am an organic beat box a liberated rhyming scheme a be bot paradiddle
Be bot be be    bot be bot bot    be bot be be    bot be bot bot

Some spin in perpetuousity
inside my head

Some die on impact because I don't record them then can't remember
these are the ones I miss most
the excuses are endless yet creatively finite
the doctor the bills the cats are screaming on the computers

Ideas that fester are caught in a cobweb waiting for who knows what
their demise or their glory a one-way conversation that I don't quite get

Some thoughts are gifts
a deadline I've said yes to without knowing why or where to unwrap them
not all thoughts turn out well the first time and
reattempts have been known to occur

Some thoughts become poems short stories or songs through improvisation
honed and edited reworked to be in the right place at the right time

Some thoughts are born in a newspaper TV news report or in conversation
something my mother said my brother said a guy passing by my
front lawn said stops me rolls out and rocks me in repetition or
a vowel sound just fascinates me like
v-a-s-t vast or brouhaha

Some thoughts sparkle and ignite shooting stars that dare me to catch them
if I can and when I do throw me back in my chair talk to me tell me
their stories... parachuting turtles impersonating Elvis ... a bracelet of
goat toenails serving me quandary ... clamouring cymbals crashing in my
cochlea ... a winking eyeball warns me he's shy ...

These thoughts are rare and the ones I like best yet
all thoughts have merit all thoughts have promise because
everything starts with a thought ...
even you

~

# NORMAN RAVVIN

Norman Ravvin has published the novels *Café des Westens*, which won the Alberta Culture and Multiculturalism New Fiction Award, and *Lola by Night*, which is now out in Serbian translation. His story collection *Sex, Skyscrapers and Standard Yiddish* won the Ontario Arts Council K.M. Hunter Emerging Artist Prize. His other books include *Hidden Canada: An Intimate Travelogue* and *A House of Words: Jewish Writing, Identity and Memory*. He is the editor of *Not Quite Mainstream: Canadian Jewish Short Stories* and co-editor, with Richard Menkis, of *The Canadian Jewish Studies Reader*. His short stories and non-fiction have appeared in journals across the country, as well as on CBC radio. A native of Calgary, he has lived in Vancouver, Toronto and Fredericton, but now lives in Montreal.

## ALL MY CAFÉS: WRITING AWAY FROM HOME

I grew up in an area of southwest Calgary that did not readily produce writers. Business people, professionals, and golfers were on offer, along with the odd M.P. The neighbourhood, developed in the 1960s just south of the spillways of a man-made reservoir, could easily be characterized as suburban, although the city has swept far past it, making it seem well within the urban core. As an adolescent, I had no notion of our family as suburbanites. We were simply placed on the landscape — the house with its peaked roof under the prairie sky; the hills of a golf course behind the caraganas in the back garden; and the houses of our neighbours, neatly tended, except one yard across the road from us where five kids lived, their detritus spread about the grass. This bothered one of our neighbours — the wife of a meat-packing executive — so much, that she made it a point of pride to take the long way behind the house with the messy front yard, so she wouldn't see it on her way home. A short bike ride away there was a big mall, but mall culture didn't exist then as it does today. The place was entirely wholesome, with a restaurant with swivellng naugahyde stools, a bowling alley, a single screen movie theatre, a coin and stamp shop, and dyed chicks at Easter time.

No single influence was paramount in my adolescence — not sports, nor school, nor TV, nor any other slice of popular culture. My father gave me a transistor radio the size of a fat paperback, which I kept tuned to an AM station where a DJ, who called himself Johnny Apple, played the hits. I lay in bed at night — in summer, when it was still bright out, you could hear the older kids in their nearby yards — and let the stuff seep in. There was nothing avant-garde about this radio fare, but it cycled the world through my bedroom: Haight-Ashbury, Motown, even the descendants of the Brill building in midtown Manhattan.

Our house was entirely free of cant about the importance of literacy. It was, however, full of books, magazines and newspapers. In my childhood, Calgary had a morning and evening paper. We must have subscribed to fifteen magazines, including *The New Yorker* and the Sunday *New York Times*. I was not told to read any of these, but inevitably, like a highbrow Johnny Apple, they brought the rest of the world into the house. I have the clearest memory of the fat beige elastic bands that came wrapped around the Sunday *Times*, as if they themselves had some talismanic value, binding what the paper had to offer, from real estate prices on the Upper East Side to the crossword puzzle, which was far too erudite for me. *The New Yorker*'s enticements included cartoons and the magazine's colourful covers, which I collected, as well as short stories in odd, obtuse tones by the likes of Bruno Schulz and Jamaica Kincaid. It was impossible to know, spread out on the rug, reading, what these stories were about. What was clear was they emanated strangeness and surprise, a geography of faraway places and times. I didn't know for certain if Jamaica was a man or a woman. And it didn't matter for a story to work its magic.

In addition to the reading matter in my childhood and adolescence, and the music on the radio, there were story-tellers. My father told jokes, not stories. His father was a newspaper reader and probably never told a joke in his life. We had baby-sitters whose reason for being seemed to be to shut up any tendency toward playfulness and irony. But my mother told colourful stories about family members, most of whom had been born in Poland and went on to live fairly eccentric lives in North America. One uncle — a pawnshop owner on Vancouver's Cordova Street — was murdered in his store by two men, recently sprung from prison. There was an aunt in Glendale, California, who was not above pulling rolls of carpet onto herself in hardware stores, in the expectation of a quick settlement. A poetry-writing uncle in Baltimore, who had dreams of being a clothing designer, abandoned his family. It was a rich vein that I would come to know better upon moving, for my first year of university, to Vancouver. There, my mother's mother lived alone in a white stucco house bought in the mid-1940s. My grandmother was the real thing — a story-teller par excellence. We arranged a routine. Three times a week I came for dinner (on Sundays I ate both lunch and dinner at her house, with time in between for studying). In exchange, I was an all-purpose presence: I drove my grandmother to the vegetable store; I scrubbed her wood floors in the old way, with steel wool and kerosene; before Passover, I stood on her kitchen counter, head high in the heat at the ceiling, and brought down her holiday plates. But more importantly, I excelled at listening. In her stories there was a certain amount of repetition, and there was an enervating tendency to worry about family members, whose behaviour didn't please her, and over whom she had no control, but there was gold, too. The gold consisted of stories of prewar Poland, which relied on finely-detailed memories of small-town Jewish family life north of Warsaw. These offered a portrait of rootedness in place and custom that could not be replicated amidst the safety and prosperity of postwar Vancouver. Her stories conjured a deeply *other* world, a world of dreams, which had been destroyed after my grandmother's emigration in 1935. In this world of dreams, her father took her in a horse-drawn buggy to check on property he leased, where he farmed peat moss — a common heating fuel — and she fell off the back of the wagon into the snow. A cousin who'd gone to the *mikve*, the communal ritual bath, on a brutally cold day, caught his death on the walk home. Cossacks rampaged through the town, threatening rape and pillage. At some point, the chaotic juggernaut of the Bolsheviks arrived. Remarkably, she described these things with the clarity of a realist, the detail of a documentarian, and without the characteristic rancour and cynicism of many Jews who fled eastern Europe. Her tone of voice, a critical observer might comment, was appropriate, unguarded, unwavering. Prewar Poland was the real world for her. She recreated it for me over tea and honey cake in her yellow-painted kitchen, with its view of the backyard and its cherry, plum, apple and pear trees, perfect emblems of Vancouver's distance from everything left behind.

In my second year as an undergraduate at the University of British Columbia I found my way to a Creative Writing workshop. I don't remember why, but I might have viewed it as an offshoot of the literature classes I was drawn to for their free-wheeling discussions. I had no sense of myself as a would-be writer, and I never considered becoming a Creative Writing major. In those days there was no romance associated with such a decision. Toronto agents did not come calling after the sexiest grads. And something about a BA in Creative Writing seemed to me supremely impractical, one step less real-worldly than the BA in English and History that I was pursuing.

The writers who led the two Creative Writing workshops I took were patient, low-key men. They were senior faculty, and seemed steeped in authority, ease and experience. I can't remember much being concretely taught. One of the two thought that verb forms ending in *ing* were weak. But their instruction was rarely more proscriptive than this. Like all workshops, a good deal of time was given over to participants, who tried their best to be civil as they stumbled about, judging whether their classmates' writing "worked." For some reason, I remember an argument breaking out between two would-be writers over the effectiveness of the word *refulgent*.

These, amazingly enough, were the days of the mimeograph machine, and we read each other's work in the light purple copies we printed in the department lounge. Of the two instructors, the one who had the strongest impact on me returned lengthy and detailed comments, in numbered paragraphs, beginning with the most substantial issues. He typed these on a manual typewriter. Students received a carbon copy of what he had to convey — a violet typescript listing what was successful and what was not working in a particular story. I still have one of these. I must have kept it because I valued it above all the others I received. It is the instructor's response to a story called "My Father and the Sky," a romantic, folkloric thing, set on a prairie landscape that might have been Saskatchewan or the Polish plains. The story's atmosphere was influenced by a woodcut I'd Xeroxed from a library book, picturing two men in workers' clothing, engrossed in a chess game. From a corner of the room a bird oversees the game's progress. The story had at its centre a family story, told often when I was a child by my mother. In this way, the "real" story — the thing that had in fact happened — was embedded in a largely fanciful, in some way archetypal narrative. The instructor's violet typescript allowed that the piece included some good writing. It suggested I read a book by Walker Percy called *The Moviegoer*, which he thought shared something with what I was trying to do.

The outcome of these suggestions, however unconscious, was the notion that I might become a writer. Not that I was one yet. What I was was an undergraduate living in Vancouver's West End, who rode a second-hand bike, but, as well, had inherited a giant blue Buick convertible, who jogged on the Stanley Park sea wall, drank great amounts of coffee, and smoked the occasional Gauloise to join in with a best friend who had taken to rolling his own out of a little packet of tobacco. Life was simple and challenging in the most benign way.

In all I've described so far, writing operates as an extension of what might be called real life. It is a tool for extending or deepening such things as family talk and history. In addition, writing enriched my daily routine, gave it colour and texture it wouldn't otherwise have had. In particular, there was my inclination to write in cafés. I'm not sure how I arrived at this habit. Coffee was itself a new pastime, having been picked up as an excuse to spend time in a particularly lively campus lounge. I was routinely meeting friends in such places, and studied in them. It might be, too, that I was not a homebody, period. I spent long days on campus, so it was natural that I would cast around for a place to write in the course of a day's ramblings. This should not be taken to suggest that I spent a lot of time writing. I didn't. But as the day neared when I was expected to turn in a story for mimeographing, stapling and distribution, I stopped at a place called Café Madeleine, at the bottom of the West Tenth hill up to UBC. The coffee there was especially good — it came in a glass cup and saucer, and was a dark French press blend that I don't encounter in cafés and restaurants anymore. Making each cup was labour intensive, and required a mysterious series of bangs and roars behind the espresso bar. The café was stocked with oddballs and beautiful losers — flophouse dwellers, would-be gurus, fanatical smokers, amateur composers, and students with their fat, softbound editions of Hegel and Sartre, who used their discussions of consciousness as a prelude to a night on the town. Sitting in Café Madeleine was entirely sensual — the taste of the coffee, the clouds of cigarette smoke, the Indonesian recipes the owner had learned from his mother across the sea, bike gear piled behind my chair, and the crisscrossing from table to table as the regulars made an effort to socialize without completely interfering with whatever guruizing or studying or writing one's neighbours had come to do. It was my left bank by the Georgia Strait. Café bohemia amidst the muffin stops, 7-11s and granola breakfast joints.

These early scenes of writing were clearly a source of community and a way of grounding myself in a city where I had not grown up, where my main points of reference were the university, my grandmother's house on Willow Street, and the sea wall where I ran. Much of this life was evanescent and would vanish when the short, fortunate time of studenthood came to an end. The café was a point around which one circled, approached, and upon which one could always rely.

My decision to focus on the short story, rather than the other genres on offer, was in part caused by the expectations of the workshop. But the short story leant itself to the belief that writing might take the place of a day job. Like chopping a cord of wood, or cutting the front lawn, or painting a room, the story demanded concerted attention, it had a through-line, and it was finite. A realistic market existed when I was starting out, much of which has fallen away in the last twenty years. In some cases the return was okay. If you were patient and kept at it, stories might pay the way, at least in spurts, through a sale to a magazine here, a contest or radio broadcast there. It would be nice to remember what this sort of free-wheeling, youthful idealism felt like, but I don't. It's gone, like the ability to run the ten kilometre sea wall in Stanley Park on a whim, or to ride blithely up the West Tenth hill into the November rain.

In my early adulthood, writing had a great deal to do with idealism, as well as with some vague sense of youthful rebellion. Here my sense of what writing meant to a suburban kid from Calgary, who came of age in the 1980s, comes clear. The act was never associated with high culture, nor with a tradition or community of Canadian literary output. Even the Jewish writers I'd taken an interest in came from the faraway unknown, in Montreal. If there was a place I viewed as the capital of writing, it was the lower half of Manhattan. Writing did not help me position myself for a career, nor did it satisfy some need to link up with other media workers, whether they be film makers, journalists or TV writers. Writing was a way around the formulaic life. It offered an alternate community, a new set of rituals, and a unique kind of freedom, even if that freedom was only available for short periods of time at a café located in one of Vancouver's ever more prosperous west side neighbourhoods. The peculiar relationship between cafés and a yearning after alternatives to the everyday appears routinely in work by writers who practiced their craft under the thumb of the Soviet censor. In a wonderful story by the Albanian writer Ismail Kadare called "The Albanian Writers' Union as Mirrored by a Woman," he signals the collapse of independent life in Tirana by the shuttering of the city's cafés.

Some of the constituent elements, then, of those early formative years, were the pursuit of a strange sort of freedom, a ragtag band of marginal freelancing colleagues, and no long view to speak of, beyond the next grant application deadline. Something worthwhile seemed to be getting done. There was a craft to be learned — a dedication to approaching the form (in my case, at this early point, that of the short story) from different angles, using varied voices, with new flourishes, and then by paring things back, sometimes consciously emulating models or imagining a whole new approach, working from one's own point of view or from some entirely other vantage point, focusing for a time on setting, then on dialogue, or atmosphere, or character. This combination of inwardness and the more practical goal of a craft appears in almost any kind of valued work. It is what is shared by writing and the work of a good auto mechanic, or that of an architect whose buildings are as pleasant to look at as they are to enter.

It goes without saying that once one is busy writing, one is reading. But my search for models of stylistic, atmospheric, and narrative possibility often went beyond novels, short stories or poetry. I looked into books of paintings and photography, at the lush mysteries of an Impressionist portrait or the strange juxtapositions of a Soviet-era collage. Such images exuded narrative possibility. They suggested the spark of sensuality, or irony, the kind of nostalgia or idealism on which a day in a character's life might turn. Movies had some of the same power, but were overdetermined. They were narratives themselves, so one took things from them unconsciously — a manner of talking, or the look of a foreign time and place. A certain kind of road movie impressed its shape on me without my being aware of it, along with the type of character who is at odds with him or herself, and is embarking on an adventure of abandonment and self-recreation. The two film makers I am now most aware of having fed me this material are Wim Wenders and Jim Jarmusch. It is surely no coincidence that both tell stories that bridge new and old worlds. In Jarmusch's breakthrough oddity, *Stranger Than Paradise*, a couple of losers in down-and-out America are transformed by the arrival of a cousin from eastern Europe. Wenders is constantly at play in the surprises created when America and Europe overlap. The most memorable image on this theme in his oeuvre is that of a disheveled Dennis Hopper driving a great, white 1950s Thunderbird through Hamburg's narrow streets in *The American Friend*.

A certain kind of popular song has become a model too, of what good fiction can accomplish. One often hears that smell is the supreme trigger of memory — the wisteria in a childhood garden; the leather seats of your father's car; the peculiar and now largely segregated scent of second-hand smoke produced by a particular brand of cigarettes. But a song opens itself in even more dynamic ways, in part because it is built of another's memories, sensations and movement. Songwriters can be story-tellers themselves — Tom Waits, for much of his early output, turned the Beat aesthetic to musical ends. But the right gathering of voice, lyric and accompaniment can evoke specifics that are not narrative per se. Rather, they are the constituents of narrative. I return again and again to a Lloyd Cole song from 1995 called "Like Lovers Do," which is as perfectly wistful a representation of summer as I could ask for. If I let the song take me into itself, a story of summer inevitably appears. The music of Thelonious Monk, with its angularity, its irregularity and irrepressible humour, is redolent of a New York City afternoon. And then there are the cool, rambling improvisatory tracks on Miles Davis' *Kind of Blue*. These are inescapably evocative for me of a Montreal winter street in the city's Plateau district. Music, in these instances, has an incantatory power — there is something archaic and inexplicable about the way the imagination flowers under its influence. In Bob Dylan's memoir, *Chronicles:Volume One*, he describes the phenomenon this way: "Sometimes you could hear a song and your mind jumps ahead. You see similar patterns in the ways that you were thinking about things."

So, if a café plays awful music is it any good for writing? Not for me, anyway. In fact, the whole package must be right, and the likelihood of this happening has been downgraded by the weird new phenomenon of businessmen and women meeting to cut deals in their local Starbucks. The ever-presence in cafés today of cell phones and laptops — recently, I watched a man set up a full-scale printer on a spare chair — adds to the sense that these spaces have become proto-corporate sub-offices. So one moves on.

It's possible that café-hunting is nothing more than a failed effort to recover lost youth, lost idealism, lost time. Still, in Montreal, where I've lived for the past eight years, I occasionally walk into a place and think, *Hm. If I just sit down right now I could write a novel at that table over there.* One such café exists, too far across town from me, on Rue Hutchison, on the fringes of Montreal's Outremont district. There, amidst the flats of diehard Péquistes, the University of Montreal students, and the Belzer Chasidim, it offers bowls of excellent café-au-lait, Serge Gainsbourg on the airwaves, and a patio under leafy trees in summer. But there's no escaping where I come from: if I feel awkward ordering my *croque monsieur* in English, will I move with confidence from the white bowl of coffee to the white page before me?

Discovering the right café is my only hang-up with regard to writing. I don't "sweat blood" when I work; I enjoy revising and appreciate a good editor; I'm happiest and healthiest when writing is an important part of the day. I write longhand, because that's how I've always worked, and treat myself to a fountain pen so that the physical act has a satisfaction that a ball-point can't supply. The computer enters into the process as a printing machine: I enter my early drafts and then print out repeated versions, editing on the page, reentering corrections and changes. In this way, I create complex paper trails, with pages of material to be attached, little scraps where ideas are scribbled before being included in the larger project. These methods are as much generationally influenced as they are idiosyncratically personal. I was a graduate student before computers came into common use, so I did all my apprenticeship work — whether it was an essay or a short story — on lined paper in blue ink, to ready it for the typewriter.

The connection between writing and health is crucial for me. Long periods without the time to work are disheartening. I wake thinking: "I've lost myself," "I'm swamped," "I've sold my soul." The return to a project calms all this manic muttering. My attentiveness to an audience is secondary to these considerations. But the longer one writes, the more natural it is that a sense of readerly expectations enters into the process. One wants to hear back, to know that the work has moved out into the world and gained a life of its own. There is great satisfaction in hearing from a reader that they settled into the pages of your story and found themselves moved to thought or memory or surprise. This kind of bond between writer and reader is not exactly friendship or intimacy, but it has qualities of both. The goal is not to be admired, but rather to bask in the rare solitude of the act, and look forward to the surprise of a readerly response.

The scene of instruction, then: a vanished Vancouver café in summer, which gives way, years later, to a scene of accomplishment, as one comes upon a reader who looks past the pages of the work to contemplate the movement on the street beyond.

# PAULA LATCHAM

Paula Latcham is a painter, sculptor and printmaker living in Toronto. She studied at the Ontario College of Art, then at Accademia di Belle Arti in Florence. She has studied Japanese, has a Bachelor of Fine Arts from York University, and a Teaching English as a Second Language certificate from the University of Toronto. She has taught art at various schools and community organizations. In 1987 she received the Xerox Canada Inc. Award for her etching. Her work has appeared in numerous group and juried shows, and solo exhibitions have been held at Gallery 76, Samuel Zacks Gallery at York U., Pages Books, and in Creemore Ontario. Her poetry and reproductions of her art have appeared in *Waves*, *Wordseed* and *Art News*.

## TO WORK ON PAPER

I've always loved paper; the different thicknesses, textures, sizes, colour ranges..., a source common to both writing and drawing.

I write with a variety of fountain pens, using inks of many colours. With a fountain pen I apply less pressure. There is a flowing effect; the ink and words flow.

My conscious respect for paper was realized when, as a first-year OCA student, our class was instructed to buy hard-cover blank-page books, open them at various positions — both prior to and following our visual efforts, and then place the pages in the snow. An experiment, I now guess, which was used to encourage us to work on creased broken-down surfaces, and to not over-value our work, but note the process by which it was executed.

Our class and instructor developed this definition of art. I found it on one of those pages, still legible — not having been damaged by the melting snow of more than three decades ago: "...form, as it is present in the fine arts, is the ability of making clear what is involved in the organization of space and time. Through consciousness man converts the relations of cause and effect that are found in nature into relations of means and consequence..."

I believe that all creativity comes from the same source, a combination of the heart and mind, spirited through one's soul. Sometimes the art work starts out as a necessity — a looming guilt that I haven't accomplished all that I'd set out to do. Other times it just happens. And then, other times I'll have an idea which I contemplate and then say I'm going to do that.

Whether it is strong or wispy, the hand has contact with the paper, copper, clay, canvas — and the message is blended with technique and calculation. The starting point could be a squiggle, branch or leaf, the reflection of the sky, an abstract thought, the pattern from a floor tile. I do my work without concern for the result, the culminating end-product. What is crucial for me is that I do it. I think that my painting and drawing are related, but the sculpture is considerably different, because there's much more of a tactile expression in sculpture.

How does it happen that one line has merit and another is non-convincing or lacking strength? As in a sentence that lulls along, with its boring grammatical correctness, never taking a chance. As predictable as watching a trampoline jumper always leaping to the same level, afraid of falling. Boundaries need to be assessed and then stretched.

To facilitate the stretching task, there is such a vast variety an artist can put into practice, noting that the preparations enhance the artistic processes.

For Japanese calligraphy an ink stone is used to blend the ink. I grind the hard stick, controlling the consistency and shade by adding more or less water. There is the physical sensation, the sound of the grinding.

With printmaking a grinding process is also employed — both throughout the preparation of the plate, and the incising of the stylus across the shiny copper. The ink is prepared and applied, the excess wiped away, and dampened paper placed on top of the plate, ready to be pulled through the press.

Mixing the paints is a truly gratifying task — a palette knife cutting in and blending the butter-like texture on a pane of glass, or, with watercolours, the tip of the soft brush stirring around an intensified or paled version of a desired colour.

I became interested in writing when I went to Italy in my fifth year at the art college. I spent just as much time on my journal as I did on my art. Concerned that someone might read my personal thoughts, I decided to write in French. and now there are parts I can't understand without a dictionary. Later I began keeping a journal at home, this time in English.

My poetry evolved from my journal-writing. A few lines would catch my interest and they would gradually evolve into a poem. A friend liked them and saved them; otherwise they would have been lost.

I had always enjoyed poetry. My mother had an anthology of poems and used to read them to me.

Painting might give me an idea for a poem, and vice versa. For writing and drawing, the thinking modes are different. They might be spontaneous but are different, because, when drawing I am also manoeuvering my body and there is quite a physical movement going on; whereas, when doing gesture writing I am still. Perhaps it's a mental/physical activity, exercising various parts of the brain. (I'm talking about random writing where I don't have an idea ahead of time.)

There is an anticipated mood resulting from the chosen subject matter for both drawing and writing. For example, a sleeping child could evoke gently-drawn and shaded lines or descriptions, whereas a moving figure might command jittery bold lines.

I do different types of drawing. Some involve and command more physicality, and less planning goes into them. Whereas, when I do a sustained drawing, the concentration is more intense, yielding different qualities.

Drawing from a model is physical. They move so quickly, with perhaps as few as two minutes to work before the next pose. Such expenditure of energy can be exhausting but invigorating to the work.

While in Italy, I painted many scenes in watercolour, and lately my interest in landscape has returned. I paint at Centre Island and High Park and in the greenhouse at Allen Gardens.

Occasionally I work from the outside in, but more often from the inside out, with the thrust from a focal beginning.

The lines cross each other over and over again. I often make composites from many gesture drawings — using oil and watercolour format. The work can be built up and layered using opaque or transparent coloration, but it is the quality of controlled experimentation that makes me so fond of etching processes.

Usually, I aim for an open, unfinished feel to my work, which allows viewers to move in and participate, making the painting their own.

I used to draw the dance students at York. Later a friend who is a choreographer invited me to his studio to sketch the dancers during rehearsal — that experiment sparked some poetry — the association I had with my life drawing.

Writing and painting are similar in that they both result from the desire to express oneself. A dancer, whom I know, wants to paint. Many poets paint, and a lot of painters write. With all art the restraints remain ongoing: one piece will influence another — as do the various techniques. Overworking can obliterate the qualities the artist strived to develop — but risks must be taken.

Creativity

Remember when you
were young in
school.
You housed your
words with lines
that
surrounded the words,
going up and long for
the capitals.
It confined the space.
The words had no
room for roots.

They strangled in
their air nests and died.
And the teacher asked,
why is your sun coloured
green.

# PENN KEMP

Penn's publications include twenty-five books of poetry and drama, ten CDs of Sound Opera and Sound Poetry as well as Canada's first CD-ROM: sample pennkemp.ca, mytown.ca/pennkemp/ and myspace.com/pennkemp. Since Coach House published her first book in 1972, Penn has been pushing text and aural boundaries, often in collaborative and participatory performance. Her videopoem won Voice Award, Vancouver Videopoem Festival. mytown.ca/poemforpeace/ includes many of 117 translations of Penn's "poem for peace." Through Pendas Productions, Penn edits poetry book/cds, http://mytown.ca/twelfth/. The League of Poets proclaimed her a foremother of Canadian poetry.

## HOW POEMS COME

What fun to discuss why I create, how I create, where it comes from and what forms it takes: naming the Spark of Creativity. Writing celebrates the moment, the ongoing collection of moments, luminous and mundane. My intention is to name and describe the source of creativity for my work in writing. What is emerging is the outline of a mythology that lay below my conscious awareness but resonated in communion with world mythologies. Reading between the lines in my notebooks reveals webs of affiliation with those larger stories. The dreams and guided visualizations recorded in my notebooks guide me. Tracing this mythology is my life's work. Invenio. "I come up", "I discover", becomes "I invent" and "I create".

How does the psyche gather enough courage to express itself? My energy and attention acknowledge and solidify events. Attending to particularities of time located in daily events, I witness the emerging pattern-making of my life. In return, lines light the page, lift that white emptiness into the purple flag of memory, understanding the press of time. Words fill the blanket loss of the past with quilted pockets of meaning.

For me, the psychopomp to the source of my creativity is the Muse, or Anima. She is the Lady of Origins, the alchemical prima mater. How do we recognize the emergence of Anima in our lives? For me, the Anima implies animal, plant, mineral, inclusive of all the other kingdoms, queendoms. Anima reaches into the depths and is transformed even as she transforms me. This hermeneutical practice leads us to explore mystery. Anima is what James Hillman calls soul, the low-lying vale, swamp and water. Her presence is a shimmering web I have come to identify as a certain luminosity of change, muted colours and forms. She is shape-changer, the shadow between seasons, between polarities. She is dawn and dusk. All subtlety and evasion, her effect is indirect, caught on the periphery of vision, a dream flicker. Her element is water and a play of light. But her essence is fire, the phosphorescent spark in the deep sea. Her power is as great as it is unnoticed and pervasive.

The Anima says so much, in word and image, that it feels as if I have spent my life preparing to write this piece. I want to stay with the moment as the location of writing, because it is in the eternal present that Anima lives. I like to write from the totality of the consciousness of the moment, investigating into what I do not know.

My task is to retrieve some connective thread in my biography out of the myriad of stories, the endless winding back to origins that this kind of interpretive inquiry demands. Anima teaches me to spin. I take it for granted that the mind creates its own version of the past with each selection of personal history it chooses to highlight. I believe we are in the process of inventing our own history as well as our future by the way in which we hold the only moment of power that we have — the present moment. The present is the time of choice; it offers the possibility of change. And so, I try to be mindful of how I choose when aligning my conscious intention to the larger sense of destiny that Anima offers. To follow each clue through the labyrinth, beginning from the entrance underground, I scrutinize the threads of familiar thoughts that loop in circles. I need to discriminate between the loose ends that need tying and the line of inquiry that will lead me into something larger.

What is knowing? How do we know? I want to know Anima, life as it exists, not as it is defined or described. I want to experience knowing for the moment, in time not in myth. I want to articulate my subjective experience in a way that can be heard. My psyche may not be ready just yet. To protect the depth of my experience, I will not force this articulation. Carpe diem. Often we try to say something too soon, or say it too late when it is assimilated and forgotten. I am discovering the small things that are ready to be revealed, rather than thinking too large, trying to define the Goal.

When I look back at my biography with Anima as guide, the perspective is new but she herself is deeply familiar. I have met her before, at key points in my life, in dream. She is prompter, pushing and pulling consciousness on, up, out. It is easier to define what she is not or to laden her with adjective describing the shifting veils she surrounds herself with, than to name her. She is no mirror to me. She is completely other, though we know each other inside out. I do not know whether she is aware of everything that has happened or will happen. I do know she carries the weight of possibilities and probabilities, which waft like feathers in my peripheral vision, for me to grasp as I can. She leaves it to me to figure out how to become what she envisions. Anima holds up a thousand mirrors to demonstrate that what we concentrate on we become. Each mirror presents a possibility that I can enact if I choose.

Anima is the emerging impulse of intention, the intention not just of my conscious mind, but of something larger and shadowy, unknown and perhaps unknowable. I believe she offers the plan of my life, the blueprint I carried before conception. And so my perspective of events, when aligned with hers, is suddenly and subtly vast with possibility. She leaves it entirely to me as to whether I pick up the skeins of intention.

Anima does not, like Ariadne, offer one connective thread that would lead me to the plot line that would make sense of my life, but to a thousand multi-coloured strands that I must braid and weave myself. We are co-creators. As psychopomp, she is flippant, a raised eyebrow, a shrug of the shoulder. What's it to her whether I perceive her gifts as schemes to entrap me or a design to elucidate? She is Godiva, earth goddess, not a White Knight. She entrances; she does not rescue. She has no need to teach, no need of me. But she is delighted to dance, to play, to come into my consciousness as co-conspirator, breathing with me into more abundant life. Where? In the space of the moment as it is lived.

My work is to acknowledge her presence throughout the period of transition in my life and to pay homage to her as the power of change. My choice is whether to flow with her or to resist. Resistance means a stiff neck and a paralysed body. I never know the price of change, but I am learning to trust and to leap into the new. My choice then is when and how, not why and not even where. Exactly where I am leaping is the mystery and the challenge Anima posits.

The risk is large, because I am writing into empty space, without knowing the parameters of the essential question I want to ask. Anima as guide demands acute discrimination, because she appears to have no regard for what I consider to be my welfare. I have learned that the archetype in her push for evolution has no concern for human frailty. I am afraid of delving into old pain, old stories, without coming to clarity and resolution. I am afraid of being bogged down in my own morass. But I trust that in time the question, if not a ream of possible "answers," will be clear. I want a mélange of all my realities in the text — dreams, fantasies, physical symptoms and their emotional equivalents, calls and inquiries down the long halls of the mind, the labyrinths of mind.

I observe my body as it collapses internally, caves in at the heart. As I write, my heart palpitates. The middle of this essay is a dark woods, cedars drowning in a marsh. I cannot see the forest for the trees of question. I cannot see a way out, only further in, down, examining all preconceptions. The word "clue" seems to be the clue, leading me out of the labyrinth. I recognize my "signature" as the connective thread. No matter how far I look back, to birth and beyond into "past" lives, the result is the same. The longer the retrospective view, the more consistent and detailed the imprint. But, although I see, I do not understand; her words are muffled. I do not easily translate visual images into meaning; they prefer to stay as they are, as direct knowing without any need of words. And yet my profound belief is in the possibility of words as translation from that source. And as communication. I often seem to be on the brink of hearing, of saying something really important that I can't quite hear. My writing is a way of moving toward that sometimes, "exstasis," and away from the sense of apocalypse. In

IMAGINATION *in* ACTION

"exstasis," there are no words. Yet. Although I seem about to break through an old pattern into a new realization, all I can record is the process, not the main event.

In my writing, I often look for a natural, organic order, hoping that it reveals my own individual sense of form, my imprint. I don't follow the standard Aristotelian method of Introduction, Plot, Climax and Dénouement, logical coherence and conclusion. I don't want to tidy things up at the end, as if I have solved the problem forever. I am not looking for an easy synthesis. I do not even want to record here what the Anima offers. Instead I want to mirror the way my mind works in response to her: bursts of insights and new snarls, hiatuses and new bursts. In reflecting on the patterns of thought, emotion and action that I uncover, I see how I came to cluster the particular incidents into groups. I look anew at the particular events my mind has pre-selected and delivered as thematic clusters, with ready-made opinions, judgements and assumptions.

How do I interpret what happens? What do I take for granted? How do I come to recognize the process of intuition? What makes understanding possible? What is the process of discovery? I believe that who we are is defined by our limitations and boundaries, a progression of understanding. How do we use our limitations as gifts? How do we recognize sensory triggers? How do we make use of those triggers to recreate immediacy?

For me, the difficulty in writing is often that it is a spiral of inquiry more than a line. There are times when my mind appears to be going in a circle, falling into familiar traps, repeating old stories, evoking lassitude and boredom. On the bottom loop of the mind's spiral, I can only trust that my desire for knowledge and understanding will provide enough impetus to reach the next level of consciousness. Prigogine reports that the time of maximum chaos is unpredictable: the dissipative structure can swing either way, into chaos or into new order. This is the moment of trust in the face of what, to the old order, seems to be the direct threat of annihilation. What makes change possible? How can we escape old habits of holding information or receiving perceptions? The answer for me is attention.

How does poetry happen? I try to address this question in the poems themselves, leading the reader through "a landscape of dreams, images, and sounds, and then back out again." Here is the poem that describes for me the place/source of poetry...it's from *The Lunar Plexus*:

> There is a band of words just above
> the ineffable fabric of love that allows
> for poetry; a slim arc over the abyss of
> pure being that roils below, that royal
> knowing we aspire to by drowning
> self consciousness in a whole blue

that is sea, that is sky, one and the same.
At last, alas, the loss of letters on the tongue
in the circumferenced web of time all present
now. The numbers churn on, press forward
as if progress were real, progression royal, all
things aspiring hold their breath toward
reality for the sake of all sentient beings.
Although there is always time for the typing
of lines on the screen, there is hardly a moment
for editing it back down and over to you.
Lobbing the poem over the net: love all

Poems like pommes don't fall far from the tree. And the tree is the source, that tall trunk of our body with its roots in the earth and its branches in the sky. How do poems come? The particulars of concrete observation is the inspiration of the spacious present. Poems that drop into one's head are a rare gift. I wait for those moments, though it may be one in a decade. I listen to poems in dreams, even if they seldom seem to transcribe. I follow a trick of language, a phrase that catches my ear, till I can tease out parallels into a poem. I'm caught by the alchemy of the linguistic tree, the glamour/grammar of transformation. I follow the form of a poem that delights me, letting its form sink into new riffs. Art follows the track of art.

I'm delighted by synchronicities that confirm the trail of words. As I write, I'm half listening to José Carlos Samoso, speaking with Paul Kennedy at the Blue Metropolis in Montreal, on *Ideas*, CBC Radio One, April 24, 2006. He says, "Writing is the only form of magic we have left, because we can create something out of nothing. We can create a world. You are inviting the reader to participate in that strange ceremony..." Yes! Follow the magic...

Poetry's role in the world is to connect us, heart by heart. Poetry can change the heart as well as the mind in a way that heady argument or debate never can. The sound of poetry carries its meaning. That sound resonates in our bodies and hearts, as well as our minds, connecting all the parts into a larger sense of wholeness. Sound poetry is a variety of wail that allows for any eventuality. Sub-verbal, sounding explores languages in widening waves of individual expression. Whatever the subject, it is great fun to create and perform. Such communication can resolve the tension between inner and outer worlds through vocal play. Sounding is our first and perhaps our last resource for creative expression. For years, I have been exploring in workshops and performance the outer limits of soundscapes, using variations on primal sound patterns to release original voice.

Sound poetry has been my medium of expression and communication, but its source is subliminal and so surprising. Inspiration comes literally, from the breath, and the way the breath forms sounds, shapes its own meaning as waves carve out niches in a sea cave. Sounding explores the realm of the senses along the edge of skin till the immediacy of experience resonates with possibility. Soundscape explores the primal areas of the human psyche that are beyond the reach of words and ideas at this juncture of the threshold, on the surface of skin, looking in and out. Sounding is play grounded in a spacious awareness of word-hoards and an acute attention to syllabics. One of the things that sound poetry does is break language down into component sounds, and probably some sounds that are usually made only by cats in heat or me in labour. Sound is how we discover language; learn to communicate with our world.

Sounding is a process by which private space can explode into performance. Utter, utterly. Inspiration and expiration are interdependent. As we let go of breath, there is the interval between the worlds, when anything is possible in the silence between the notes. Life is no longer circular. We are suspended, between serial events. Change happens every time a breath is taken; a new cycle begins at the entry into the body. Sound and language are only possible through breath. In the gap before meaning, first language emerges.

Sounding is a hoot! It's an invitation to jump into the well of sound and splash vocal possibilities. My notion of sounding started with the labour of childbirth, in sheer amazement at the inhuman howls emitted from a mouth that insisted on its own expression. The screams I uttered were beyond my ken. Grounded in that direct experience of the female body, my experiments continued in hearing and echoing babies' exploration from babble into language. In playing with my children, mirroring their sounds back to them, I continued to stretch vocal possibilities. In travelling, I try to mimic the sounds of languages foreign to my tongue, my mouth. I can trace my sounding back to our itinerant music teacher, Mr. Golding. Admiring my height, my expressive face and my ability to memorize the words, he asked me to stay in the Grade Five choir, in the back row, and to mouth the words. Sounding is such sweet revenge.

Language dazzles me, that will o' the wisp that I might follow into the mire, just for the pleasure of the treasure hunt. A phrase might catch my ear, a feminine rhyme perhaps, or a juxtaposition of sound and sense. I like to scrabble past all the layers of accumulated leaf mould into the root of a word, its etymology. Or its associations through what pops into mind. My book on teaching writing is called just that: *What Springs to Mind*. At sixty-two, I'm not very interested in expressing emotion, though I can still work up a rant on demand. But I'm fascinated still by the ineffable, the wisps at the corner of thought and feeling, the outer boundaries of perception. I'm intrigued by what I don't know, other dimensions of understanding, a sense of spacious presence.

Poetry as my primary medium is a wide vessel that can spread over into music (new and experimental music, to be sure, through sound poetry) on one hand and art on the other, through concrete poems. My father was a painter who helped to establish the art scene in London, Ontario. As I was growing up, painters from the Group of Seven and Eleven would stay overnight; I would serve them drinks and listen in to their stories. At first, I too wanted to draw, and had a talent for fast-flowing line. My father took me in hand and set me tasks. I was to draw the yellow bedroom lamp. What interest did I have in this plain object that was so visible to everyone? What I wanted to draw was magic, the figures I envisioned in imagination, not the humdrum daily. Worse, Dad instructed me to study the Bridgeman book of anatomy. I wanted the flow of silk dresses, canopies, shrouds and those wonderful mediaeval veils flowing down a lady's back. No structure, no bones for me, thank you. So I turned resolutely away from art to poetry.

I might have learned something from Bridgeman, after all. And to typesetters' chagrin, I love to place words in a poem aesthetically, for the sheer pleasure of composition, as if the page formed a canvas on which to balance the words. Such a space allows for breath, for emphasis as notation. I look for a larger sense of structure, an architectural frame when I edit, when I'm shaping a bunch of poems into a book.

Another inspiration is causes, anthologies of celebration and recognition, a tribute to a beloved poet or a collection around a theme. I'm conscious of an audience if I am trying to communicate something from within out, the definition of education. If I am writing an essay for teachers on teaching creativity, the vocabulary I use is very different from the words I'd use in a writing workshop for children, even though the exercises I conduct are almost the same. If I am writing a play, I'm much more conscious of community, usually because I rely on my director, Anne Anglin, for the theatrical line, that skeletal structure I'm conscious of lacking. I'm still not very interested in the bones of plot, though I've learned to respect the necessity of form and its Aristotelian pleasure. Our culture delights in the satisfying of subject, verb, object. Beginning, middle, end. All very contained. But those boxes do not describe or delineate my reality.

How do I decide which medium to use? I've supported myself as a writer since 1970. How? By tracking the money as well as inspiration. If there's a pilot programme at the Canada Council that interests me, for example, then I might apply for it, rather than an existing programme in which I'm competing with more established writers in their field. With a new programme, the rules have not been laid down, nor silos erected, so I can help determine the turf. If there's opportunity in the schools to teach, if a play is commissioned, if I'm invited into a collaboration, that's where I go. That free lance has to be as flexible as a willow, and as difficult to wear down.

Poem power! Random Acts of Poetry, everywhere! Liberate the lanes for poetry, the alleys for allies of our verse! I'd do almost anything to lift the word off the page, including raves, ongoing! My Muse delights in play, in the dance of possibilities. As the source of creativity, she transforms life's experience. From this material, I develop an abundance of ideas and images, an enhanced awareness of structure and form, and more ease in showing or performing work. Although my focus is on writing, the techniques can be applied to the visual arts as well. No initiation required. The Muse is enthusiasm and inspiration itself!

# PETER THORN

Baby-boomed in 1947 in Southampton, England, to Welsh and Yorkshire parents, Peter Thorn immigrated to Canada in 1957. He discovered music on a crystal radio set. He played guitar in garage bands during his school years, and then retired for decades. With his wife, he co-ran a picture framing and art business since 1979, and raised Highland cattle. Peter met other musicians in the local pub, and re-discovered the urge. He currently plays guitar with the Bad Poetry Blues Band. And he still colours outside the lines.

## ... FROM A NOTEBOOK

I am a guitar player. I like the guitar, its sound, its feel.

I like to play it, to move its strings and make sounds and music.

A natural extension is to play tunes, then to write tunes.

Perhaps given access, all are creative.

Perhaps given access to the tools, the creative spirit will express.

> Paint
> Engrave
> Print
> Write
> Sculpt
> Muse
> Music
> Dance
> Spin/weave
> Discover

The appreciation of beautiful things; horses whinnying, covered in ice and snow, soft nuzzle. Independent Highland cattle, snow-covered in the blizzard, like huge cottonballs, like huge sheep, nonchalant. Breeding to improve. Do they need improving? Only for man.

Honing a Haiku.

*****

Came home the day after payday
and your coat wasn't on the peg
and the stove wasn't cooking,
and as I was looking
I knew you'd gone.

*****

Woke up this morning, looked around for my blues.
Couldn't even find 'em; now I got nothing left to lose.

*****

Gettin' old, feelin' cold. Think I'll take this hand and fold.

*****

My road to hell is better than yours

*****

CAIRO

On a road to Cairo I stopped in a little store,
bought a pack of cigarettes, maybe a little more.
Went on back (to your place) stayed a year or more,
ran out of cigarettes one day, went back to the store
...picked up my mail,
heard the train on the rail
whistling...we gotta go.

And I'm on the road again to somewhere.

*****

Look out your window you'll see I'm gone.
Too many miles on the road, too much time on the clock.
At the crossroads on a cold and windy dawn,
And I never saw the Devil...

but I heard him close behind.

\*\*\*\*\*

I don't exist well in cyberspace.

I prefer face to face.

\*\*\*\*\*

May 11, 2005

Play it live, and the moment is gone forever.
Record it, and it could be there forever.
Be careful what you wish for.
It could haunt you forever.

\*\*\*\*\*

Summarize, realize, trivialize.

\*\*\*\*\*

To discover a piece of the past you had written
and lost and forgotten;

Like recalling a ghost you had met.

Create confusion and delusion,
at what cost, and to whom?

And the conclusion... is no resolution.

\*\*\*\*\*

*thoughts on creativity...*

## SUITCASE (fall 2005)

Came home from my job on the nightshift
for a cup of coffee before my job on the day
and I found my suitcase on the landing
and my key didn't fit my front door.

So I'm standing on the sidewalk
with my suitcase in my hand
and nowhere to go to
and no one to understand.

And the suitcase don't hold much
just the dust of years
and it just goes to show you
that you can't take much when you go.

*****

Hope you bounce when you hit bottom.

*****

IMAGINATION *in* ACTION

# PHLIP ARIMA

Phlip Arima is a poet and short story writer living in Toronto. To his credit, he has three books and an audio CD. He has performed more than one hundred and fifty feature readings, and his poetry videos have aired on national television. To learn more about him and his work check out www.phlipari-ma.com.

## WRITING SCULPTURE

My writing process is like sculpting with clay. A clay sculptor starts with an armature, a semi-flexible structure that acts as a skeleton for his sculpture. He bends the armature into the position he wants the torso, legs and arms. Then he starts adding clay. He pushes clay into the centre of the armature to give it solidity. He puts a mound of it around the feet to give it a foundation. He layers it on to the torso and limbs, building up mass on the skeleton.

As he works, the sculptor keeps turning the sculpture, working it from every angle. He adds some clay here, takes off a bit there. He pounds some into place with a block of wood, carves another part smooth with a wedge. Then, turning the sculpture, he sees he must add some clay to another spot or take some off from a place where it no longer works. He keeps developing the sculpture, round and round building it up by adding and subtracting clay; pushing and carving and pounding it solid until he feels he's done.

When I write, I start with a vague idea or a neat-sounding phrase or something equally simple and flexible. This is my armature. I then start adding words and phrases. Sometimes I use a phrase that conveys an idea. Sometimes I use a phrase because of the emotion it evokes. Sometimes I stick a word in just because I like the way it sounds, because it feels right. Idea, concept, emotion, sound, tone, feeling, etc., are the shape and texture of the clay. Like the sculptor, I keep building it up by adding and subtracting words until I feel I have a complete, fully-realized whole — a finished piece of writing.

# RENEE RODIN

In the sixties Renee Rodin moved from Montreal to Vancouver where she raised her three children. She ran R2B2 Books, along with its weekly reading series, from 1986 to 1994. Her visual work, mainly photographic, has been shown at galleries in North America and at the Venice Biennale. Her essays, poetry and fiction have appeared in periodicals such as *The Capilano Review, West Coast Line,* etcetera, and her books are *Bread and Salt,* a collection of prose poems, (Talon, 1996), and a memoir, *Ready for Freddy* (Nomados, 2005).


## THE QUEEN OF RESISTANCE

"Boredom is the dream bird that hatches the egg of experience."
—— Walter Benjamin. *Illuminations: Essays and Reflections*

I don't know how to be creative or even get a tiny grip on the process. If I knew how to go there, I'd be there all the time. Wanting to make something, whether it's by writing, cooking, painting or knitting, all seems to come from the same place. It has to do with nerve, impulse, some visceral energy I can't control. When I choose to act on it, follow it, where it takes me is always unpredictable, and even when I think I know the ending, it never turns out the way I expected.

Writing is like kneading clay or carving wood until something emerges. All you have to know is that the shape is in there. Still it throws me far more into crises than raptures. I'm the queen of resistance, an ace at avoidance. I'd rather be doing anything else in the world than writing, and let myself be distracted by the most mundane things until I finally connect with the writing, and then there's nothing else I want to do.

Boredom played a big role in my life when I was a child; time could drag on endlessly and I was often trapped in tedium. Now time has sped up and I'm seldom bored any more, but boredom has morphed into resistance. While boredom can't exist without resistance, resistance can operate entirely on its own, and be more stealthful, byzantine. But both take enormous energy. Both block points of entry to becoming engaged. Both insist on "emptiness" between involvements, demand that ground lie fallow until it is ready to be seeded again. Both are valuable, because it's in the making of something, whether that be an object or a connection, that you find your way through them.

For a brief period, when I was in elementary school, writing was one of the few things I could do easily. Maybe it had to do with living in books. And not being self-conscious. Also, I was lucky to have teachers who loved what they were teaching; they kept me loving poetry and literature too.

Creativity begins in the unconscious. We're all born with urges to transform our environment, and we continue to make things and think creatively all our lives, unless we are thwarted.

Making babies is creative. Probably, because I won't know till after I'm dead, and doubt I'll know even then, my most creative period was when I did the least amount of writing. It was when I was a single parent on welfare with kids so close in age they were almost triplets. Raising children, no matter what the circumstances, requires creativity so that you can help them grow to their full size. So does eking it out with money and other resources to help you not fall between the cracks.

When my kids were little I rarely had the space to decompress and focus on writing, except for fragments which were sustaining because I could come back to them. I still feel everything I write is in fragments which I could work on forever if I let myself. Later, when the kids became more independent, I opened a bookstore. Making it attractive, interesting, and keeping it going like any other business took creativity.

At the store I ran a reading series where I met other writers. Most of them were far more accomplished than I was, but just as insecure. It made me realize how important support is. That we all need it. Especially novices, no matter what age, because we all start at different times. Not that publishing should be the primary aim of writing, but it never occurred to me that I could write a book until Stan Persky encouraged me to put a manuscript together.

I'm more or less reconciled to my speed and style of writing. Initially it comes spurting out until it's a total muddle, a blur I can't see through. Then I put it away and hope with time and distance I can decipher it. When I begin to whittle away, often my favourite parts are the ones I have to discard. They've become the biggest obstacles, the idées fixes that I've clung to at the expense of everything else.

I sweat over every word. Then I sweat over the work again and again to make sure it doesn't look belaboured, forced. I'm not prolific because I get hung up on perfection. I'm always trying to get it right. As if such a thing exists. When I can't bear to look at the piece any longer, that's usually when I decide it's finished. Once I risk letting it go I'm happy to forget about it and let it land wherever it's going to. I'm always startled to find out that someone actually read something I wrote. From my point of view I know what I'm writing about, but I'm surprised by what another person might tell me, how they read it.

In order to write, I have to make my mind go blank, stop obsessing about my responsibilities and anxieties, remove myself from myself and everything else. Disconnect. Not turning on the radio to hear the latest news can take a supreme effort. When I'm in a period of writing I like to be engrossed in page-turners and to watch tons of movies, usually on TV. If I could be magically whisked into theatres I'd be there every day. Immersed in other worlds. Sometimes I can do this with music or silence.

Smoking used to be a good way to kick-start my mind. But that was then. When I had a typewriter I thought I was addicted to white-out which I'd sniff every time I had to correct an error. But now that I use a computer, I think it's actually writing I'm addicted to. It feels weird not to do some writing every day, even if only e-mails, which it often is.

Daily living and maintenance require a lot of attention, but these days I'm able to keep most of my time clear, or at least stay flexible, to be available if something fires me up and I want to respond to it. This is hard to do if you're constantly taking care of other people. Or if you're at a job that eats up everything you have. Though it has its own financial challenges, I feel privileged to be able to live the way I do.

When I'm not involved in a project I always think, "That's it. I'll never write anything again." First it throws me into a panic; I become an invisible blob to myself, shapeless. Then it's a big relief. I want to celebrate that I got rid of a bad habit, something that was oppressing me. But it's a phony kind of freedom, because what's really oppressing me is my lack of expression, and in fact I'm just waiting for whatever's percolating to surface so I can write again.

Grappling with writing gives me some respite from the barrage of external events and my own internal loop. It gives me a chance to discover what I'm dealing with, and some semblance of control. Writing is a kind of release, I just don't know of what. Or where the on/off switch is. When I'm writing, life takes on a weight I can carry. All parts of me seem to fit together better. It's a very temporary experience.

If I over-analyze my relationship to creativity I'll jinx it. And it's precarious enough as it is. All I can say is, there's no feeling in the world like writing, the high of getting it down. Telling it.

# RICHARD HARRISON

Richard Harrison is the author of six books of poetry, among them the
Governor-General's Award-nominated *Big Breath of a Wish*, and *Hero of the
Play*, poems in the language of hockey, re-released in 2004 as a Tenth
Anniversary Edition. He was one of the commentators in the CBC's 2006
series, *Hockey: A People's History*. Internationally published, his poetry has
been translated into French, Portuguese, Spanish and Arabic. Currently
Richard teaches English and Creative Writing at Calgary's Mount Royal
College where he also teaches a course on Comics and Graphic Novels.

## WHEN PUSH COMES TO PLEASE

Most of my published writing is poetry. Most of my drawing is graphic as in "graphic
novel" — comic book art. I've been writing poems for thirty years, and my first book
came out twenty years ago. My drawings have appeared in my self-published, black-
and-white comic books, and on posters around my college advertising a course in the
comic book as literature. Mostly, though, they stay at home. I hear other artists say that
the photograph is another approach to the images of the text, or the sculpture is another way to dance, but I've never found it myself. I've longed for it. I know that if I had-
n't been captivated by my father's recitations of Dylan Thomas and William Butler Yeats
in my childhood, or, later, by readings of their own work by Patrick Lane and Alistair
MacLeod, and said not only, "I love this," but also, "I want to do this, too," I'm sure I'd
have made my artistic gamble in favour of following the great comic book story-tellers
of my childhood — Jack Kirby, Steve Ditko, and Bob Kane — instead.

For many of my comic book-artist heroes, I later realized, the relationship
between the stories they drew and the stories scripted over them was often a combat
zone. But for a while, I understood comic books to be a world where the things you
drew were one-half of a complete creative vocabulary. You drew the mouth that you —
or someone you trusted — put the right words in; the face, the arms, the movement
of the body on the page, as in life, made up part of the communicated whole.

I chose words, though, over drawings, as the medium in which to do what I think
of as "my work." Not that I don't, in fact, obsess in much the same way over the content of my drawings and my poems. It wouldn't take much for anyone to see the connections between my publicly displayed poetry and my private collection of supermen
and wonder women. I think every poet's work can be seen as defining a cluster of
words, turning those words over and over until they are fully and completely known.
It's a lifetime's work. And you could probably boil down my collected poems from
their beginning to the key constellation of "father" (the first among these), "son," "hero,"

"faith," "soldier," "war"; and then note how, later, my wife woke me up to "woman," and my daughter, bless her, re-created "word." I keep looking at all the ways in which my father is represented to me to see if I can unlock the mystery he represents. It doesn't matter whether it's a war film, Batman, a hockey player, a poet, a painter, or the direct invocation of the man himself, I keep looking until I think I know, until I think I get it — that outwardly expressed inner sense of decision and strength that I identify with the concept of "man." Then I lose it, and look for it all over again.

Dad hated comic books and loved poems. He kept himself sane, I think, during the Second World War and the "Malayan Emergency," one of the first of the post-colonial wars to follow it, with all those memorized words from the great writers of the English tradition. All soldiers keep something from home with them to remind them they are human beings with families and peace to return to. It's the something they love not for themselves in the small sense of the self, but something, like a holy book (however secular its content) that says "this is the place I preserve." Shakespeare did that for Dad. So did Robert Browning. And Tennyson. Dad gave me a love for the word, the sole creation that needed only to be thought in order to exist and which could only be lost if the self who had it in him was killed. For my father, poetry was the external object whose existence was identical with his own — it was him and not him at once.

Comic books were for kids; long after I should have outgrown them, I kept up my readership. Dad used to quote St. Paul's "When I was a child, I spake as a child" lines from the Bible. I can't tell you how many times I threw away my own drawings and sold for dimes comics that I've much later bought back for fifty or sixty dollars apiece. Now a comic book has won the Pulitzer Prize, and the Anglo-American world has woken up at last to the form's literary value; this despite the fact that a century ago, Goethe himself was a fan when he first saw Rudolph Töpffer's "words and pictures art." But prejudice dies hard, and Dad grew up in a world that saw comics as either a childish pastime, or the kind of corrupting, violent influence that we often think video games or the Internet are today.

Yet many artists take up forms their parents or their culture actively disdains. The war between my art forms isn't about their history, any more, I think, than it is about their content. Their history does not explain why when I turn my hand to a drawing, all thoughts of writing utterly disappear. I don't mean retreat the way they do when I've been working on a poem and got to the point where I have to walk away from a problem that I know I can't just bulldog my way through. I take in the air, or read the paper with a coffee beside me. I know that somewhere in my brain my mind is dreaming its way to the words that will just come back out in the right order and surprise me with how easy they look when they finally arrive. No. I'm talking about obliteration, about the blank page that's waiting for a face or a hand to be drawn there and then another and another, about an activity that, in the doing, I don't care if I ever leave. Only in drawing's enforced absence does the urge to write return.

And maybe the urge to write is what enforces the absence of the visual art; maybe writing's first act is always to push away the rest of the world in order to make space for writing. Maybe my sense of the tension between drawing and writing is what everyone feels when they have to stop doing something in order to write. I remember Sharon Berg's lovely, painful line (which I've only heard her say) to the effect of, "How do I explain to my daughter that I have to shut the door on her in order to write how beautiful she is?" Maybe what's at war here are art and time, art and the world.

But I don't think so. When I'm with Lisa and/or our children, by and large, I don't feel like I'm taking time away from my writing. And though that could be because I love them, the fact that I love them is not enough to explain their compatibility with my poems. My family makes me a better man than I was before I was married and before Emma and Keeghan were born. It's not a stretch to say that my better writing and my best books have come since then just to prove it. When I teach, I, too, am doing something I love. The classroom is a creation renewed every day. And in the way that I believe all the best creations are, it's collaborative.

So what do teaching and parenting and poetry-writing have between them for me that makes this cross-fertilization real? I think it's this: every word you're reading right now I'm saying out loud as I type it — including the words I typed in and took out when I went back over the page. I'm constantly talking as I write. Those who've overheard me outside any of the offices I've had over the years make fun of it. Toronto poet Jim Smith once wrote a series of prose-poems based on his experience at a writers' retreat that he and I attended at the same time. His room was next to mine. In the poems, he imagined me as twins: my secret was out. There were two of us, and we talked all the time, though he could never make out what we were saying, and only one of us was ever seen in public. My twin, my poet, was bed-ridden and never left the room. I love that image of myself, of poetry, of essays, of writing — being present in a voice I use to speak to myself at a volume that only reaches the inside of the door.

When I draw, though, I say nothing. I am amazed how creaky my voice sounds when I'm done and have to reconnect with the world. If I answer the phone, the person on the other end of the line asks me if I was asleep. I draw and draw and I realize that while I'm in that place I draw from, the door is silent and no one knows I'm there. I've escaped. I'm in hiding. In its own way, the sweep of the pencil over that page, not to represent a sound but the contour of a muscle, the fold of a sleeve over the arm, the twist of a hand neither open nor closed, is a disappearing act. It is not the meditation I find in a poem, though, though it seems, as I write this, easy to confuse the two. The poem pushes me; the drawings please. The poem that needs me to write it demands something that I am not capable of but I'm the only person in the world who can try. Yet though I know that in trying to make *this* poem, *this* writing the best it can possibly be, I am always in that place between achieving my best and knowing there is better to be done. I have faith that poetry is infinite and has room for me to enter further.

If that ceases to happen, I'm done as a poet. But while I love what I look at when I finish a drawing, I don't love it in the same way. I know I'm only training my eyes to be pleased with less than what could be. But "less than what could be" is just fine.

And all that says something about me, something that thinking about each single art on its own could not show. I seem to believe that the art that pushes is superior to the one that pleases. I seem to value the created object over the experience of creating it — maybe I value the object over the experience every time. I don't have much patience for things that aren't intended to last. I fear what vanishes. I'm drawing a lot these days as my parents become increasingly ill, as the wars that genuinely disturb me, perhaps because of their resonance with the imperial war my father helped fight from the imperial side, creep closer and closer to the centre. I don't yet think of myself fearing dying — though I worry about my children when I think of it — I do worry about dying having left nothing behind that lasted no matter how much happiness I found in the making of it.

My arts are at war because each one stands for something the other rejects — and it isn't their content, though one pushes deeper into my adult life and the other revisits my childhood fantasies. Nor is it, I'm thinking now, their relationship to time and personal pleasure. Both please me, though I think of only the poems as having a life outside my own. It's what each of them calls up in me in their creation. It's about who I am. And I'm a talker. Words create me as I create them but pictures do not. In rendering the only art I want to draw — figures designed and produced by others — or figures very like these — I've drawn on the kind of silence that isn't the silent part of speaking; it's the silence of not saying something of your own. No matter how pleasing my visual art is, I *say* nothing in its creation. It is amazingly tempting to rest here.

I wish I could point to some really radical or cool claim to artistic fame, like spearheading a "don't ask, don't tell" initiative for poets in the military, or teaching a platypus to paint. I did make a stab at adapting digital camera technology to give sight to the vision-impaired, but the constant firing of the flash made it impractical. No, instead I've become a dabbler. Does that make me a Renaissance man, or merely a jack of all trades? I've cartooned, put out a politico-musical fanzine (and suspiciously had a lot of my mail arrive opened), played in bands, punk mainly, from age sixteen to about thirty (I still do the odd interview, believe it or not), had photographs published, worked as a graphic designer, done window dressing, joined in the movie boom in Toronto as a set dresser (that's the furniture job, not the wardrobe one), and, like most people, I've written a few movie scripts I've yet to sell. (They're damn good, tho', I must say.) I'm working on a music book as we speak. (Actually, we're not really "speaking" here, are we...? Oh well, it's just an expression.) It's been a full life.

## THE DEATH OF ARTIE FELLOWS

Int. Flo's Diner - Day

The place undoubtedly held some kind of homey charm when it first opened decades ago, but it long ago sagged into its current existence as a drab adjunct to a dumpy motel on a sparsely-travelled two-lane highway to anywhere but here... so here it sits, lost in time and Texas. "Hank's Garage," an aged and dusty whitewashed cinder-block eyesore with three bays and a pair of dated gas pumps, has been cut out of the scrub across the road. Three men in oil-stained coveralls bearing stitched tags with the name of the garage's apparent owner, sit at a window booth, and make up the bulk of the noon rush.

ARTIE, an obese vulgarian, balances a mouth-stretching hunk of pie on his fork, and deftly crams it into his mouth.

ARTIE

Bullshit.

A bit of his pie is messily spat back out, punctuating the statement.

RUBE, a hunched and emaciated man in his fifties, pulls his coffee back from his lips.

> RUBE
> Christ, Artie... swallow first, will
> ya?

Artie looks up at STEVE, clearly the newbie at the garage, with his relatively less-stained coveralls. Swallowing maybe half the pie in his maw, Artie continues to spew forth, ignoring Rube.

> ARTIE (to Steve)
> What the heck *you* know 'bout
> writin' movies?

> STEVE
> Actually, there's a surprising
> number of books on the subject.

> ARTIE
> I ain't an idiot. I know they got
> books 'bout 'postrophes an' crap...

Artie leans forward and points his fork non-threateningly at Steve.

> ARTIE (cont.)
> ...what I mean is, what the hell *you*
> gots to write 'bout?

Steve nibbles on a french fry thoughtfully, then grins smugly.

> STEVE
> Life, essentially.

> ARTIE
> Life... whadaya mean life? Whose
> life? *Yours?*

> STEVE
> (with a laugh)
> Actually, I'm writing about Hitler.

Rube takes a sip of his coffee and smiles, his pose virtually unchanging, elbows on the table, mug clasped in his rough hands, never returning the mug to the table once it's been lifted.

> RUBE
> It's funny, ya know... 'bout them 'postrophes. Mebbe with alla us wearing "Hank" on our chest, we oughta take the 'postrophe offa the sign.

Artie and Steve both follow Rube's gaze through the dusty window, across the street, to the "Hank's Garage" sign... Hank's *with* the apostrophe... then look back to Rube, who's chuckling away, clearly amused with his observation. Rube taps the embroidered name-tag on his coveralls.

> RUBE (cont.)
> See... we's all Hanks.

Artie and Steve share a perplexed look, then try to ignore their companion.

> ARTIE
> (sarcastic)
> So you's a historian now, too?

> STEVE
> No, but I did research it. Anyway, the script isn't so much about "Hitler" the historical figure, as "Hitler" the man. The part of him that mirrors the rest of us. Where the hatred and evil come from... that sort of thing.

Artie snorts dismissively, and instinctively looks to Rube for agreement, but finds him, disconcertedly, still chuckling away to himself.

> RUBE
>
> 'N fact, why they even gotta say
> "garage." Fool kin see it's a garage.
> Should just say "Hanks."

Rube laughs a little harder for a moment, then settles back into a distant smile.

> ARTIE
>
> Chrise on th' cross, Rube, yer
> startin' to scare me.

> STEVE
>
> Anyway… you just kind of try to
> bring life to the people that you're
> writing about. You bring in the
> people you've known, the things
> you've felt as you've gone through
> life… I try to project them onto the
> characters, make them real.
>> (beat)
> Look, take Rube here…

Rube perks up a bit to the conversation, hearing his name and all.

> STEVE (cont.)
>
> …you've never seen him eat
> gazpacho…
>> (sighs)
> …it's cold soup, Artie… what do
> you think, you think he'd like it?

> ARTIE
>> (laughs)
> Naw.

> STEVE
>
> That's all you've got to do. Let's say
> you were a character in my script…

ARTIE
(muttering)
Better not be.


STEVE
…I can have you doing anything I
want. The more of a bead you get
on the character, the better you
know just how they'd react in
different situations.


ARTIE
But you's doin' this on Hitler.


STEVE
Yeah… that's right.


ARTIE
So what… you gonna have Adolph
Hitler sittin' here eatin' pie?


STEVE
Maybe he liked pie.
(the joke dies)
Look, try to imagine Hitler; he's
sittin' in a dilapidated Bavarian beer
hall in the twenties… expounding
his ideas to skeptical friends.


ARTIE
So yer the Hitler in this, right?


STEVE
Well… in a dramatic sense…


ARTIE
(laughing)
I knew they was something funny
'bout you… Adolph.

Artie roars loudly, pulling Rube into the fun.

>                    RUBE
>           Yer taller than I thought you'd be.

Rube suddenly looks at Steve with concern.

>                    RUBE
>           You ain't *really* a commie, is you
>           Steve?

>                    STEVE
>           Fascist, Rube. Hitler was a fascist.

>                    RUBE
>           So you's fascist, then?

Artie laughs even louder.

>                    STEVE
>           For fuck's sake Rube, I'm not a
>           fascist, okay? We're talking about a
>           story. I'm an *art*ist, not a *fasc*ist,
>           okay?

>                    ARTIE
>           Thought you said you was a writer.

>                    STEVE
>           A writer is an artist, you boob.

>                    ARTIE
>           Whatever you say... Adolph.

>                    STEVE
>           And I am an artist... I draw, I play
>           guitar...

ARTIE

That figgers. Mebbe ya should write
a song 'bout Hitler instead.


STEVE

Trust me, it's been done.
(beat)
Why do you find it so threatening?
Or is it just the artists themselves
you don't like?


Artie stands up, and pulls a couple of crumpled bills from his pocket, throws them on the table...


ARTIE

Mebbe it's just you I don't like.


STEVE

Rube here paints, did you know
that? And wait... Hitler painted too.
Maybe *Rube* is a fascist.


ARTIE

Ask me, yer *both* a couple a freaks.


...and heads for the door. Steve turns to get the last word in, even if it *is* to Artie's back.


STEVE

You know, those girlie magazines
you're always reading? Artists took
those pictures. Think about that next
time you whack off!


Artie sucks a bit of pie caught in his teeth, then leaves without looking back... The slam of the door finishes the exchange. Steve slumps down in his seat.

STEVE

It's funny when you think about it.
Frustrating as guys like him are, I
don't think I'd have the drive to do
it otherwise. The writing... the
music... I guess it's kind of
cathartic.

Steve clues in eventually to the odd look Rube is giving him.

STEVE (cont.)

You okay?

RUBE

You said you wasn' gonna tell 'im
'bout my paintin's.

STEVE

Sorry, I guess it slipped out. He just
really ticks me off.

RUBE

Shoutin' at the dark don' make
it any brighter, ya know.

Rube stands...

RUBE (cont.)

He really ain't so bad. We bowls
together... takes me to the Legion
Hall... I needs him to drive me, on
account of I don't have a car.

...and begins fishing in his pocket for money.

STEVE

Don't worry... lunch's on me.

Nodding a quick "thanks," Rube turns to leave, then turns back.

RUBE
Funny, eh? Me bein' a mechanic,
an'…

Steve easily finsihes the thought for Rube, clearly having heard it repeatedly.

STEVE
…not having a car. Yeah, I know.
(he smiles)
I'll see you back there.

Once Rube leaves, Steve leans back, lost in thought for a moment… then quickly grabs
a pen from his pocket and begins writing furiously on a napkin.

CUT TO:

CLOSE-UP — STEVE WRITING ON A NAPKIN

*WRITING*
Story idea - "The Death of Artie
Fellows: a confluence of fatal auto
shop catastrophes."

# ROD ANDERSON

Toronto-born Rod Anderson graduated in Chemistry from the University of Toronto and then spent twenty-eight years with Clarkson Gordon (now Ernst & Young), chartered accountants, latterly as managing partner of the Toronto office. During those years he was author or co-author of several arcane textbooks on auditing. In 1983 he left that profession to spend full time writing. His poems, reviews, and short stories have appeared in various literary journals. His one book of poetry, *Sky Falling Sunny Tomorrow*, was published in 1989 by Wolsak & Wynn. He wrote the libretti for Peter Paul Koprowski's one-act opera, *Dulcitius*, and Harry Somers' full-length opera, *Mario and the Magician* (an adaptation of Thomas Mann's novella — performed by the Canadian Opera Company in 1992). Since the mid-1990s he has been a late beginner at composing music. Some people can't decide what they want to do. Recent performances have included two choral pieces performed by the Oriana Singers in Cobourg in 2004 and 2006.

## LET THE DOG DO IT

Why create? No doubt different people have different answers. I've read a few commentators arguing that most people who say they wish they'd been writers really don't want to write but want to "have written" — that is, to have the status of the acknowledged writer. But I'm sure that phony position is a minority one. Even if the status of writer is viewed as a "satisfying accomplishment," the essential emptiness of that position reminds me of a wonderful quote from Henry Miller: "The true adventurer must come to realize, long before he has come to the end of his wanderings, that there is something stupid about the mere accumulation of wonderful experiences."

I like creating because the process feels good — not in the sense that chocolate tastes good to the body, but rather that this process tastes good to the mind and spirit. The process is mind-expanding and gives one a share of epiphanies (even if the piece of writing itself turns out to be less than successful) — epiphanies that one cannot reach by rational thought alone. Certainly I have felt that way about writing poetry and short stories and I feel that way now about trying to compose music.

How does one go about it? No doubt everyone has a slightly different technique — though they probably can be grouped into similar "families." My way is not to wait until there's a burning message or melody demanding to be let loose (because I find that happens very infrequently, what with the distractions of daily life) but rather to simply make the quiet time and space available — staring at the blank page or the blank score. I really do admire Margaret Avison's lines: "waiting quietly at/home upon occurrence" suggesting the cultivation of a certain degree of passivity. (If one is too active, no new ideas or insights can break thorough the frantic noise of one's activity.) A book I liked (I've now forgotten the scientific authors) compared the mind to a radio receiver. When it was well tuned, programs would flow into it — but you wouldn't be able to find those programs by taking the radio apart with a screwdriver (or looking through the brain's neurons). It is a question of cultivating an openness to insight. Which is not to say, of course, that good craft isn't essential as well — but someone (can't now remember who) said something like: "technique alone without soul is empty."

The other problem with creating is to keep the left-brain critic (who never could create anything anyway) out of the way while the right-brain tries to fumble its way into a new creation. This is talked about to some extent in Gabriel Rico's wonderful book, *Writing the Natural Way*. I find I have to say to the left-brain, look I'm just doodling around —this isn't serious — probably nothing will come of it — so don't waste your time looking over my shoulder. Not till the poem or short story or musical composition is well along the way (perhaps half done) do I begin to admit that this indeed may turn out to be a serious endeavour — in which case the left-brain's editorial and critical skills will indeed have their role to play. But premature criticism is stifling. One can imagine Shakespeare starting off "To be or not to be," and the left-brain critic jumping in and shouting: "Hey, you can't start a sentence with an infinitive; very bad form; bad bad bad; start again."

Where does it come from? Who knows? But I have a sort of optimistic faith that it's out there and we discover it more than *create* it. This ties in, I guess, with mystic ideas that we are all connected and while we may think we're separate (as one wave may look at its neighbouring wave as a separate entity) we're really all connected by the sea of water beneath us.

I believe one must pay attention to the audience. It's *not* valid to say something like: "I don't write for an audience; I write solely to please myself, and if someone else wants to listen in, that's fine." I'm not saying you look to the audience for inspiration, or what idea is in vogue this month, or what will sell or get the highest popularity ratings. That, of course, is all junk. But one does, after receiving the initial inspiration, have to *think about* the audience. One has to project over the footlights or the communication won't work — and would then merely become a diary of personal therapeutic thoughts, and not art. Art surely has to communicate and communication requires considering the situation of the recipient of the communication. Therefore poetry or short stories can't be so abstruse that no one except the author understands them; music can't be so apparently cacophonous that no human ear can make any sense out of it.

Indeed, I have found that the predicament of reaching the audience meaningfully is somewhat similar in all the arts. When I play a new piece of music for Merike, she may say things like: "I think the second part changes too abruptly from the first," or, "I think the second idea could have been taken farther," or, "I wish I'd heard more of this part." She wouldn't know how to meet her demands technically. For that one needs knowledge of harmony, melodic structure, rhythm, progression, serialism, etc., etc. But the audience doesn't have to be expert in stagecraft to know whether the play "works" or not for them. Similarly, I may look at one of Merike's paintings and say things like: "I wish that transition from the image at the left to the colours at the right could be a little more gradual," or, "I wish I could understand a little more clearly what that surreal, exaggerated leg was supposed to be evoking," etc. I wouldn't know how to meet my demands technically. For that, one needs knowledge of brush techniques, colour relationships, how to create sharp edges or blurred edges, layering effects, the use of various media, etc., etc. But the language we use to critique each other's works is more similar than the quite different technical knowledge of craft used in responding to the critique.

But how to balance creation and study? One great problem with creating is that there is always so much ignorance in one's own head that sometimes it would seem wiser to spend one's time studying to try to limit that ignorance a bit. But the trouble is, if you go down that route, you never create anything at all — because there is always so much to know which one doesn't yet. I try to divide my time: say 1/3 studying and 2/3 creating. But one ultimately has to accept the fact that one is ignorant. Scholarship is a wonderful activity, and scholars who delight in learning are to be applauded. But scholarship and creating are too different things — though both important. I do not aim to be an eminent musicologist, nor a brilliant performer. To accomplish even 5% of either task would require a lifetime of learning and/or practising. What I want to do is create. I realize I must learn some things, but I don't want the learning drive to take over as an end in itself. And to avoid that, one has to be willing to create while still inevitably somewhat ignorant.

We need feedback to hear our mistakes. We all know that creative drafts have to be revised and revised and revised. That's what makes the computer so great — one doesn't have to type the whole story or poem over again from scratch on a typewriter, or write the musical score over again from scratch by quill pen. One can take the earlier draft and revise it (cut, change, add, etc.). Listening to one's own work can be humbling but also educational. Looking at the printed text, one is too tempted to say, "Yes, I know it stumbles a bit there, but that marginal note I made is going to fix all that." But listening to a taped version of oneself reading one's poem or short story can be illuminating. "I can't believe I make that same stupid mistake every time I read that poem. On fifth hearing the problem is now becoming more and more obvious to me."

Similarly in composing music, I find the world of MIDI and synthesizers wonderfully educational. In the old days, you wrote a string quartet, and then you had to wait for four string players to agree to come and play the work before you could say, "Oh,

I hear now that the second movement isn't really working." The advantage of the synthesizer is that it can play back the MIDI file (in effect, executing the score) in a way that admittedly doesn't perfectly simulate a live performance but is *good enough to show one one's own mistakes*. "OK, that's not working. I'd better revise it. That other part is good but I didn't go far enough with it; I've got to push the envelope farther." You could say that a genius like Mozart doesn't have to do that; he could hear it all in his head perfectly anyway. Yes, that is the desired end — but how does one learn how to get here? By profiting from hearing one's mistakes.

The other advantage of synthesizers is that they facilitate creative ideas. I know you can say that a true musical genius can doodle something on the piano and imagine instead a flute or a trumpet. But if you're a non-genius, how do you climb that hill? The same notes on a flute or trumpet invite different development, different ornamentation, different directions than those notes on the piano. So doodling on the synthesizer keyboard when it's set on flute sound suggests different ideas than doodling on a piano. I've found it a really wonderful learning tool. I know some professional musicians look down their noses at MIDI, because if badly done it is much much worse than a live performance. But as an aid to the composer in working out ideas, I find it invaluable. Many of my compositions on my website (www.rodmer.com/RodMusic/RodMusic.html) are mp3 files of my various synthesizers playing the MIDI files and only occasionally, when I've been fortunate enough to have some group perform them, mp3 files taken from the actual live performances.

Writing and composing: do they help or influence each other? Probably not. But one interesting thing is when one does *both at once*. When a writer writes the words and a composer composes the notes there is always an *uneasy alliance* between them. The writer wants the words to be understood. The composer wants the musical structure to be perceived. The two aims are often in contradiction. When one writes both the words and the music, as I have done a few times now, one is negotiating with oneself, and the trade-offs can be much more successful and sometimes lead to transcending inspirations as a problem is being worked on. Imagine how writing a poem would be if one person were in charge of writing all the verbs and another person in charge of the nouns. That is a bit like the uneasy alliance between writer and composer.

I don't decide on a subject or theme. It isn't a decision. I play around and eventually the ideas percolate from the material. Or maybe I'm merely tuning the radio and, when once tuned, the ideas will start to flow in from some mystical unknown place. As someone said, "intention endangers creation." Creation involves a little bit of (hopefully divinely inspired) playfulness. Earnestness, intention, rational decisions as to what to write or compose, all stamp out that playfulness and kill creativity in the process.

Are my choices instinctive? Absolutely. Of course that doesn't mean that rationality and knowledge of the craft doesn't have its place as well. But the image I like is that of an expert skier at the top of a hill of moguls. He/she does not say: "Well, let's see.

I think I'll jump over that mogul nearby, and then ... and then ... and then ..." No, this would be a horrible way to proceed. What you have to do instead, is push off from the top, *keep your knees loose*, and make *snap, instinctive decisions* as you proceed down the hill. Of course, experience will guide some of those intuitive decisions no doubt, so learning, practice, and the making of mistakes are all essential steps along the way. But in the end it is intuitive decisions that rule the creative process.

Or, on the other hand, one could always let the dog do it, as in these excerpts from "Poem by Madeleine."

> Number Two Dooropener
> asked me to poem write for him.
> So here is it. But look — be on outwatch.
>
> ...
>
> Hey, the Dooropeners have turned the day off
> and are going up the steps into the darkness
> so time it is to beat the Zeph upstairs to get
> the best place on the bed
> which is always a good way to nose up
> important thoughts as I am doing now
> with the soft featherstuff under my ear
> so that I can hardly that ear feel at all whereas
> the other ear is feeling still a little
> which makes me realize that the
> important conclusion is…the right conclusion
> well I'll just nap for a few minutes
> because I feel very happy right now
> as in fact I generally feel
> and everyone is here close by
> my dogfriend Zeph and the two Dooropeners
> even if their legs sometimes in the way get.
> There the other ear feels not at all now
> which leads…will lead in the morning…to…

# SONJA DUNN

Sonja Dunn is the author of eight books of children's rhymes, chants and stories, as well as works on videotape and audio cassette. Some of her poems for adults appear in *Uncivilizing*, Insomniac Press, 1997. She is a poet, story teller, and performer, instantly recognizable in her many-pocketed story skirt, as she strums on her guitar and encourages her audiences to sing along and participate. She is a former teacher, actor and drama consultant. For twenty-nine years she hosted *Sonja Dunn and Company*, a TV show with CBC Sudbury. She has written, produced and hosted TV shows on the arts for Rogers Cable Systems. She was born and now lives in Toronto, but travelled throughout her childhood, attending fourteen elementary schools across Canada.

## EVERYTHING IS CONNECTED

BACKGROUND: Due to circumstances beyond my control I was born in a house at 22 Wolseley Street, Toronto, on January 26th, 1931. My parents came to Canada from Ukraine in 1926. Most of my relatives were displaced persons who came over after World War II. When I was six my mom died and left my brother, Ronnie, and me in the care of my dad. My adult poetry addresses the sadness that ensued.

My mother tongue is Ukrainian, and although I don't read and write it as well as English, I still speak Ukrainian fluently, mostly with my relatives. Bill, my husband of fifty-four years, eventually learned to understand what we were saying, probably in self-defence.

After my mom's death, my dad and I travelled across Canada, with Toronto as our base. During those nine years I attended fourteen elementary schools in Ontario and Quebec.

The culmination of my life, so far, is represented in my work, whether it be writing, teaching, performing, or painting. Things happened to me in stages: school, growing up, life-guarding, being a telephone operator, teaching, acting, getting married, having children...

ON TEACHING: I didn't plan on being a writer. I was a teacher and wrote rhymes, plays and stories for the children in my classrooms, mostly rhyming poetry. I found that the quickest way to memory was through repetition and rhyme, and through enjoyable experiences. One can learn a song much faster than a prose passage. Children memorize instinctively.

Crackers and crumbs
Crackers and crumbs
These are my fingers
These are my thumbs...

I chanted it two or three times, and then the children were chanting it, running out the door, waving their fingers, "These are my fingers, these are my thumbs..." It was rewarding to watch them perform my poetry.

I taught everything from junior kindergarten to the university level. When I taught drama at university, I often correlated language, music, art and movement, bridging as many art forms as possible for the final result. I would give the students a text to read and then segue into action, beginning with tableaux and moving into dialogue, maybe saying, "Why don't you make a tableau out of one of the significant parts of this poem?" or, "Act out what the witch did with Rapunzel's cut-off hair?" They would add music and art, and when it all came together we would get a three-dimensional effect. They were learning to write their own stories.

ON WRITING: Where does the writing come from? For me, it just comes. I'm compelled to write. When the muse gets me by the short hairs I can't stop, and when it comes I can't edit it. It has to come just the way it is, all mixed-up. Sometimes disorganization isn't so bad. I might have to take out or put in a word or two, or make some other changes. That's how it works for me.

Often my writing is like a dream. You know how a dream happens all at once. BAM! It's all there, at the same time. It doesn't happen in sequence. When you wake up you can remember the whole thing as though it all took place at the same moment.

Well, that's how it is for me in writing. It all happens at once, in no order, and I change it around or fill in the blanks if it doesn't make sense. It works for me. That's what's important.

I have to grab my pencil and paper before I forget my thoughts. They have to be written down right away on a serviette or a brown paper bag, my arm, the dashboard of my car, or whatever is handy. I understand many other writers do the same thing. I envy those who sit down at nine a.m. in front of the computer and start to work. I'm humbled by them, by their discipline and commitment.

ON RHYMING POEMS FOR CHILDREN: My background includes years of folk singing, some of it on a television show in the sixties. Many rhythms come from Ukrainian folk music which I learned from my dad at home and in Ukrainian school, as well as Gregorian chants which I heard in church. Many of those rhythms come out in my poetry. I also have a lot of kids' poems that don't rhyme. Some are cross-over poems that work for adults as well. When I perform my poems for families I find that the parents also get involved.

My latest book called *Math Chants* is all about mathematical terminology for primary children. I took words like symmetry and integer and made poems to illustrate their meanings.

ON WRITING FOR ADULTS: My adult poetry and prose differ from my kids' work. I have sixteen unrhymed poems published in *Uncivilizing*. This collection was shared with James Reaney and several other Canadian poets. The poems deal with my family, memories of my friends, the tragedy of Baby Yar, where the Nazis shot and buried innocent Jews, gypsies, the infirm and children, anyone they felt unsuitable:

> It is said that beneath us
> we can find brains
> babies' shoes
> nannies' embroidered blouses.
> Under us lie
> the ravaged.
> Nakedness made them invisible.

Travelling is a great catalyst. There is something about visiting a strange new land that is especially motivating. Ideas come from many sources. Customs, language, food, and all the sights lend themselves to poems and stories. On a journey to the Gobi desert I heard the sand singing, and from this powerful experience a poem was born. A series of hilarious incidents that happened in a cemetery during the reburial of an uncle, turned into a humorous story published in *Kobzar's Children: A Century of Untold Ukrainian Stories*, a recent collection about Ukrainian immigrants. Sad people, sometimes. At the moment I'm inspired to write a story about my Ukrainian wedding...

ON PAINTING: I don't consider myself a painter, but it was important at one period in my life. After my children were born, painting was an outlet for me. Watching my son in a high chair eating jello, and getting it all over, making such a dreadful mess, I thought I should make a mess too. I bought oils and canvases and brushes, and painted many scenes from memory: the llamas in Peru, mariachis strumming on guitars, Peruvian men playing their little flutes. Now the paintings don't have great perspective. They might be called whimsical, and I have kept them on my walls.

So now, about the creative mess. I guess that's what I'm talking about. This potpourri gets into some kind of form, and it may even be a hodge-podge, but the form is an expression of something creative. I'm not that much of an artist, and don't know all the lingo. But what I do know is that I did paint at one time, and enjoyed it. My work started out representational, and, inspired by Jackson Pollock's drip paintings, became more abstract.

I almost started painting again after I saw Joe Rosenblatt's show. When I look at an abstract work, I think, "I bet I could do that," and then, in the back of my mind, I think, "Yes, but I didn't do it. I didn't think of it. The artist thought of it." So that stops me.

ON ACTING: I acted professionally in Sudbury Theatre Centre, and I also acted in many amateur plays. My favourite role was Auntie Mame; it was the most fun, and the most challenging was playing Martha in *Who's Afraid of Virginia Woolf?*

I learned to act from my father who was a professor of Ukrainian language, orchestra, violin, mandolin and viola. He directed Ukrainian choirs, and at one time he played the violin with one of the first orchestras that performed at Massey Hall during the depression, for fifty cents a night. Jobs were scarce for immigrants; as a musician he was lucky to be able to earn a few dollars.

ON TELEVISION: There was a time in my long life that I was completely and happily immersed in television. I fell in love with TV. It was the perfect venue to promote all the things that mattered — children, education, performing, the arts, and working with significant people, places and events. Opportunities presented themselves and I embraced them. My debut happened by accident at a party in Sudbury. I was playing the ukulele and leading a sing-song, "The Darktown Strutter's Ball," when a local producer from CKSO-TV asked if I could play and sing any Christmas carols. I couldn't, but said, "Sure." So I went home and learned "Good King Wenceslas" which had only a few chords, and BAM, I was on television. I also took up the five-string banjo and played "Go Tell It on the Mountain." Soon after he asked if I could sub for a regular performer who was going on holidays. This was a daily show, and again I said, "Sure. As long as it's after school because I teach all day." The TV crew shot a fast-forward of me running out of school, jumping in my car, zooming through town, and tearing into the TV studio. I sat down, clipped on the mike, and said, "Welcome to *The After School Show*."

After the regular fellow came back, I wrote, produced, hosted and performed my own television program, *Sonja Dunn and Company*, a CBC/CTV affiliate, which was broadcast out of Sudbury, and received throughout northern Ontario. It ran for many years.

I have a very curious nature which was useful when I interviewed many famous and interesting people, such as painter William Kurelek, film director Alan King, film producer Bruce McDonald, songwriter Gene McLellan, Paul Thompson of Theatre Passe Muraille, and writer Sylvia Fraser. I also interviewed Milton Acorn, W.O.Mitchell, the actors Paul Kligman and Diane Hyland, and Paddy Crean, the man who taught sword-fighting at the Stratford Festival. He was Errol Flynn's double in the movies.

As well as my own show, I sometimes did two other shows a week.

I moved back to Toronto in 1980 and had my own show, using the same name, with Maclean-Hunter and Rogers. That's when I interviewed Pierre Berton, and many Canadian children's authors. If a guest didn't show up I filled in with stories, poetry and folk songs, or talked about Canadian books. Improvising was a challenge that I enjoyed.

I was on *Mr. Dress-up*, and CBC, and on YTV with Rosabelle and Tansy, as well as various radio shows.

PUBLISHING MY FIRST BOOK: While I was teaching I was writing poems, raps, chants and songs for my pupils. These were hand-written on experience chart and construction paper. The head of Pembroke Publishing, who published my first three books, looked at my manuscript aghast and said, "No one delivers a manuscript in a brown paper bag labelled *The Tall Girls Shop*," and I said, "Well, you asked me if I had any chants and rhymes, and I said yes, so here they are." It was my portfolio.

I have never learned to type, so everything was written longhand. It was part of my creative process, printing on scrap paper and brown paper bags. One great poem was written with the kids in the class on forty-foot-long mural paper which was rolled up to present to the publisher. She shook her head.

ON PERFORMING: Performing for a live audience is, in itself, a creative process. My venues have been varied: schools, libraries, television, festivals, concert halls, altars of churches, The House of Commons, Ontario Place, armed forces barracks, and even a Hallowe'en poetry reading in a cemetery.

A performance is tailored for an audience, be it for children, families, teachers, librarians, hospitals or senior homes. There are times when, during a performance, one has to change horses in the middle of the stream. Once on a school visit, prior to my presentation the children had prepared readings of several chants and songs that I was going to present. This was very rewarding as I appreciate hearing children perform my work. So, presto, some changes had to be made on the spot.

Teachers often ask for a specific theme: conservation, fairy tales, nutrition, explorers, friendship, etcetera. I search my books for suitable material. For example, on the environment:

> Don't throw your garbage
> out on the street.
> Keep our planet
> clean and neat.

They might ask for a poem on conservation:

> Save our deer
> Save our fish
> Save our land
> That's our wish.

Or space:

> McMoon
> McVenus
> McMars
> A hamburger stand
> in the stars.

The whole process is creative: the original poetry, the preparation and the performance. It just naturally goes together.

The next part of the creative process might be for the audience to illustrate a poem or presentation. One enhances the other. The process goes beyond the original story. That's what teaching is about, developmental learning.

STORYTELLING: It was so much fun telling stories in the classroom with the kids that I just kept doing it after I retired from teaching. At one time I belonged to the Storytellers' School of Toronto, although my kind of storytelling wasn't fashionable in the eighties because I used a lot of actions and participation. That's not the type of storytelling that was being done at that time. I'd read a poem about scary Hallowe'en witches and they would respond with an "EEEEE" between each line.

> On Hallowe'en the witches fly
> EEEEE
> They sail on brooms across the sky
> EEEEE.

These were all grown-ups and I think they thought I was crazy, but they participated vigorously and with great enjoyment.

When I began to tell stories I incorporated rhymes because I felt that made them more effective.

ON AN AUDIENCE: Why do I write? Primarily I write to communicate. I want people to enjoy it. Writing for myself would be somewhat like baking a cake, eating a piece, then hiding it in the cupboard, not sharing. Or writing a poem and leaving it in a drawer.

When the muse is heavy on my shoulder I am compelled to write, and yes, I do want to be read, but I don't think about that when I'm doing it. The whole process is instinctive.

COMPARING THE CREATIVE PROCESS: I believe there is a powerful connection between all the arts. Everything is similar, everything is together. Not only in poetry and music. In all of life: people, music, art, drama, writing, reading, poetry, stories, plays, acting, architecture...

Creativity. That's the magic, the spark.

When I have an idea, I've got to write. The magic begins and I pick up my pen...

# STAN ROGAL

Stan Rogal was born in Vancouver and now resides in Toronto. His work has appeared in numerous literary journals and several anthologies in Canada, the U.S. and Europe. He has published fourteen books including two novels, three short story and nine poetry collections, the most recent being *Fabulous Freaks* from Wolsak and Wynn. A third novel, *As Good As Dead*, is forthcoming from Pedlar Press. As a playwright, his plays have been produced variously across Canada.

## APART, A PART

Begun.

OK, not the brightest or prettiest or even most original of opening lines — "Call me Ishmael," a ghost in the background, sounding — but, at least, setting sail (sort of), and already arrived at *some place* with a quote and an allusion in tow. Which is the way with us form/genre jumpers: we are curious about far too many things to not want to try our hand.

Meaning, I never set out to be a royal pain in the ass for anyone. It simply happened. In fact, I was quite happy to be a short story writer and leave it at that. Only, my world shifted and I shifted along with it. Like I had a choice, right? Wrong. From a marriage break-up to quitting a job (a career!) to slouching toward university later in life, and, what is it they say? Those people; those folk? A little knowledge can be a terrible thing. It can, yes, but the terribles can contain their own form of personal beauty as well. Ask anyone who has suffered through, whether slings and eros or any other type of pseudo-sado-masochistic: it is a kick, outrageous fortune or no.

Which brings me to poetry (or *brought* me, as I'm nine published books into it): this series of seeming unrelated circumstances. I was never into poetry as a kid and had no interest in writing it. Most poets we studied were dead and to all intense purpose, so was their work: *the Gray Hairs*. No amount of memorizing or reading aloud would alter this situation. A slight inroad was made around grade ten when my English class was visited by a student teacher. To my memory, she was young, beautiful, animated; very much a hippie type, sporting a cast from a skiing accident on Grouse Mountain which was autographed and adorned with flowers, paisley patterns and love beads. She played Leonard Cohen songs for us on a portable record player and told us that this, also, was poetry. I didn't come fully around, though it was nice to have someone place verse in the land of the living, especially in the sphere of pop culture.

Years later, at SFU, beginning a BA with a major in English, a professor/poet of mine would provide a key element as to what made a poem different from most song lyrics. Coincidentally (though, perhaps not so much so), it was Leonard Cohen, again, who was referenced. His song, "Suzanne," ends with the circle complete: "She touched his perfect body with her mind." Whereas the poem ends on a very different note: "She touched *her* perfect body with her mind." Eureka! This single change serves to subvert, not only the movement of the poem's story, but the expectations of the audience. A great thing for a poem; not so when you're trying for a hit song. My prof explained that the media, in order to sell, aims for lowest common denominator (*demon*-inator) and, as happy, nicely-completed endings are more easily consumed and digested generally, best to keep to the formula. Which spells bad news for anyone trying to make an honest buck in the poetry racket. It was this same prof — d.h. sullivan — who convinced me to write poetry in the first place. He said that working in a compact form, where each word was important and the rhythm of the language was everything, would naturally help my fiction. He said: "Like poetry, your prose should be so tight, you can't squeeze a cigarette paper through."

I gave it a whirl and continue to do so. My first collection of poems dealt with shadows and the shadowy world, and came together as an elective course. I presented the raw material to Dorothy Livesay, who was writer-in-residence at the time. Her comments were invaluable. She told me that while she enjoyed some of the pieces, some of the imagery, she felt that, overall, the poems were a bit too metaphysical for her taste. I nodded politely, thanked her and left her office, having had no idea what the term "metaphysical" meant, never mind how it applied to my little poems. I was off to the dictionary and off to a few philosophy courses that finally led to a minor in the discipline, a further result of which was a fictionalized introduction to my book of poems, *Geometry of the Odd*, by Andrew Marvell who welcomed me among the ranks of the metaphysical poets.

Theatre was a similar happy accident. I decided to take an acting course in order to better read my poems aloud in front of an audience. That was it; my one ambition. Next thing you know, I'm on stage performing Mamet, Shepard and adaptations of Kafka; I'm directing Pinter and Albee; I'm writing skits and one-acts; I'm bashing out full-length plays; I'm entering my plays into contests, and eventually I'm mounting my own plays in various festivals. This is farther down the road, time-wise, after the move from Vancouver to Toronto, and "mounting my own plays in festivals," not primarily as a creative function, but because no one appeared eager to mount them for me. Note: I use the word "mount" in its widest form and meaning here; with proper intent. Chalk up a second minor in theatre.

There's a joke that goes: "How many actors does it take to change a light bulb? Answer: six. One to change it and five to say, 'I could do it better.'" Which is probably what initially sparked me toward most of my artistic endeavors: I did feel I could do better than most of what else surrounded me. And, let's be utterly honest: I don't see much point in doing this type of work just to be a clone or maintain the *status quo*.

There's enough of that going on, which is why we have TV, Hollywood, the Best Seller list and so on and so forth down the line. Within this vein of attempting to stand outside the crowd, the phrase, "finding your own voice" was an interesting and familiar concept, though it never fully made sense to me, or included enough. Moreover, there was something almost mystical-seeming about it, as if this "voice" was somehow apart from you, or worse: a gift from God/the gods. Where did that leave the rest of us poor sons-of-bitches slaving away at our so-called Art? Besides, I assumed that even the most banal writer/artist was in touch with their own "voice," so what the hell did that prove? Simply that there were an awful lot of "voices" out there that sounded alarmingly the same, churning out the same product *ad nauseum*. Certainly, I was banal enough within my own uneventful life and generally a quiet sort of guy who liked to keep to myself, so…? No, I was more enthralled by, "finding your own *signature*," a phrase presented to me by a former theatre prof, Peter Feldman. The implication is that you are responsible for creating your signature using whatever sources are available (including your own form of banality, of course); you create that thing that stamps a work indelibly and recognizably yours and yours alone, though with obvious references and allusions to whatever's gone into the pot. In other words, you work for it, same as you do your Art.

As an overview, my work is an attempt to deal with grand ideas or issues, set within a very personal arena. The poems: *Sweet Betsy From Pike*, placed the folk song in Canada, with the principal characters traversing the country, unheedingly wreaking ecological and environmental havoc in their wake. *The Imaginary Museum*, referenced works of Art and Mallarmé's idea that everyone has "an imaginary museum" in their heads. *Personations*, which centred around the notion of "maleness," and, can one be a well-rounded, caring, sensitive, intelligent human being and still be a "man" in the sense of maintaining an identity separate from "woman," and, if so, what was it? *Lines of Embarkation*, using science as a stepping-off point, was especially influenced by the book *Gödel, Escher, Bach* by Douglas Hofstadter. *Geometry of the Odd* dipped into chaos theory. *Sub Rosa* offered various interpretations/transformations of eight paintings by Jacquie Jacobs. *In Search of the Emerald City* compares the artistic journeys of poet Arthur Rimbaud and painter Vincent Van Gogh with the Hollywood journey of Dorothy/Judy Garland in *The Wizard of Oz*. My most recent collection, *Fabulous Freaks*, revolves around the theme of freaks, monsters and celebrities.

Some singular influences on my poetry (in no particular order) include: Jack Spicer, Marjorie Welish, John Berryman, Richard Brautigan, Judith Fitzgerald, Arthur Rimbaud, Kenneth Patchen, Stanley Cooperman, J. Michael Yates, Viktor Schlovsky and Anne Sexton. Add to this the Beats, the Surrealists, certain Black Mountain types, the letters of Lorine Niedecker/Louis Zukofsky, the literary theory course I took at York U…

Through it all, I imbue the work with various discourses, from fairy tale to myth to science to academia to art to street vernacular and so on, all in an effort to collapse time and space in order to make everything appear alive and lively here and now. Obviously, some of this arises from my background as actor and director, which may explain my predisposition to the present-tense verb. In all of this I'm certainly not alone, though it makes for a seeming tight crowd at times.

My fiction also tends to bounce around. Short stories within collections move from naturalism to realism to noir to magic realism. My first novel, *The Long Drive Home*, was very much in the vein of *Film Noir*, complete with soundtrack. My next novel, *Bafflegab*, was a pseudo writer's journal containing a thin narrative line. Another (unpublished), is an epistolary novel in a female voice. *Tell Him You're Married* is a series of linked short stories. *As Good As Dead* is a more stream-of-consciousness type novel that will be published in the next year or two, the small press gods willing.

So, there are recognizable overlaps within my *oeuvre*, but, the big question is: what is/are the difference(s)? Moreover, are there specific criteria for deciding what becomes a poem, what a piece of fiction, what a play? For me, the answer is yes, and it entails a combination of subjective and objective items. Since I've been writing for so long, part of it is simply a feel for the material or subject matter. Another is mood: can I really face looking at a stack of two or three hundred white pages with the intention of filling them with words? Part of it is the form itself. For me, poetry remains a compact form, and like Nietzsche, who said: "I want to put as much into an aphorism as most writers put into a novel," I want to do the same with my poems. Which is why, I guess, many of my poems are constructed along the lines of collages: I take a skeletal theme, adorn it with other objects which may or may not appear to readily suit the theme, then scramble, bend, contort until the whole becomes greater than the parts. Picasso called collage the greatest art invention of the twentieth century, and the vision of a bicycle seat and handlebars becoming a bull has always fascinated me, both as an image and as metaphor for the creative process. Next is to use words and language themselves as so much clay. Why use several words when a few will do? Why a few when one will do? Can't find the right word? Manufacture your own. Finally, bust the balls of narrative in order to allow the reader room to interpret.

Fiction allows me to relax a bit more, as well as work with developing characters, settings, relationships, dialogue and so on. It's also an opportunity to play around with narrative in a slightly different manner. There is a clearer through-line for the reader as one is "story telling," but there are other devices one can use to upset expectations: false clues, unreliable narrator, plot twists…The novel involves plots and sub-plots and even sub-sub-plots. Then there are the various genres and genre-bendings to experiment with and employ for whatever literary end, and a piece of realistic fiction can easily and almost unperceptibly evolve toward magic realism or horror.

Plays are meant to be performed live, which means thinking in terms of actors, directors, lights, sounds, stage directions, props — even of audience and what will be expected (though not necessarily) reactions. A play on its feet can become a quite different animal than a play on paper and a good director can say: we can cut this or that line or even this scene and convey to the audience with a look or a sound cue or whatever. Having been through this process, I try to think ahead to the production aspect, which often has some directors muttering obscenities under their breath as they are used to playwrights being totally transparent and explaining absolutely everything within the body of the text. Again, my plays tend toward being absurdist/expressionistic dark comedies where things are rarely ever what they seem.

In closing, I also enjoy collaborating with other artists and allow them to do what they do best in order to have it affect my work, whether it's merely for a cover image or use inside the book or designing a set or putting a piece of music to a poem or story or play.

Shakespeare said: "The play's the thing." I would say: "Play's the thing." And if an artist can't play, who can?

# STEVEN McCABE

Steven McCabe is a Toronto-based poet and visual artist. He is the author of four books of poetry: *Hierarchy of Loss* (Ekstasis Editions 2007), *Jawbone* (Ekstasis Editions 2005), *Radio Picasso* (watershedBooks 1999), and *Wyatt Earp in Dallas: 1963* (Seraphim Editions 1995). He co-authored and illustrated a chapbook *Orpheus and Eurydice Before the Descent* (Lyrical-Myrical Press 2006) He has illustrated books and magazines with fine-line ink drawings, created public murals, and exhibited paintings on canvas and paper. Currently Steven McCabe is creating sequential drawings with text, a project which might be called "a graphic novel." He teaches art & creative writing workshops.


## TO BE A POET: A WRITER WHO IS NOT A WRITER

Ideas (inspirations) either germinate or arrive with blinding speed, begging to be realized. There is no way of knowing which is which until it occurs.

My third book of poetry, *Jawbone*, deals with art, creating art, and the "dementia" of love.

In this article I hope to discuss something of what goes into my creative writing process.

Normally I have several projects on the go simultaneously. I feed my "political" work with on-line "blogs" and news services which fuel paranoia, unfortunately justifiably. My erotic or love poems are inspired by my continuously evolving "romantic" relationship. My interest in absorbing and regurgitating mythology and cultural anthropology also involves reading as research.

My poetry is influenced by the fact that I am a visual artist and "see" things. Some of this makes for good poetry and some not. I don't worry about that while I'm writing. I leave it up to the revision process, the editor and editorial decisions. This morning I woke with the image of a tree "growing" coffins, and began writing. The themes included mortality, the underworld, a capitalist conglomerate controlling third world water supplies, and other details including a reference to Goya. While writing the poem I stopped myself from wandering off at certain points: for example, at the village near the grove where artisans from "south of the border" paint "ghoulishly carnivalesque scenes" on the wooden coffins for a small fee. I made a decision to *not* go into detail about the subculture of this village. I felt that this would detract from the flow of the poem. The poem is five pages long. I added it to the box of poems I have yet to type and present to my editor.

I work with an editor who is non-intrusive and highly sensitive to what I am trying to "paint" with words. She sometimes gives me a list of words I have overused and need to forget.

I try to remind myself that I never need to explain "why" something happened in a poem. That the "because" doesn't matter. That the "is-ness" of something is all that matters. That I do not need to "situate" everything I speak about as if I am cross-referencing the history of suicide with pomegranates.

The process of writing poetry is highly personal. No one rule applies to each and every person. I have heard some very funny advice over the years while attending readings. I only listen to those whose poetry I admire. And usually the best advice about writing is found in the writing itself: e.g. "How did she do that?"

My editor once took a hundred-line poem where I worked to juxtapose/blend Mayan mythology with a story about painting my bicycle as a boy to make it invisible. (Believe me I had my reasons.) She reduced the poem to nine lines. She kept the essence and discarded the window dressing. "What can be discarded?" I ask myself.

I am interested in poetry with layers of meaning, imagery, emotion, history… I do not care for insipid, middle-of-the-road poetry. Neither do I care for vapid, bellowing "Let's wake up the whole hospital"-type stuff.

Poetry is not raking leaves. Neither is it showing off a new tattoo. On the other hand, perhaps

*Poetry is raking leaves off a new tattoo.*

It strikes me that art and science are closely linked in the examination of life, physical reality, complexities of the human being, nature and space. Applied science gives us ziplock bags and formica. Applied language produces advertising. But poetry is a way to view the ineffable. To escape the inescapable. To escape the ineffable. Like a pottery shard celebrating erotic visions found frozen in lava. Maybe poetry is a tool that changes shape every time you use it. As a way *out* of pain. As a way *into* love. As a way *into* pain. As a way *out* of love. I appreciate the explanation of Orpheus in the Cocteau film *Orphée* as he is being examined by the underworld judges: "A poet is a writer who is not a writer."

I have never had writer's block or a lack of ideas. Not all of these ideas, or first drafts or fifth drafts make it to the finished stage. I have a friend with a theory about therapists: you visit ten, you meet three you like, you choose one. Perhaps poetry is similar: a poet finished ten poems, three appear to succeed, and in the end only one is included in the manuscript.

It only makes sense to me that thirty-five years of being a visual artist informs my twelve years of being a poet. Even if I begin with a phrase that appears out of the blue, it is accompanied by at least half an image; an arm, a scene, a movement of colour. These visuals have an emotional texture or feeling. This feeling creates a context. A mood. The deepest personal reservoirs of loss fall like rain over prehistory which sits like a lizard above the dying fire. Like Mark Rothko's painting, words import and export a somber and joyous glow, somewhere in the brain.

My personal history of being an expatriate and war resister also affects my work. Even if a poem is not political I view it as being non-neutral. It exists in opposition to everything "they" have planned for this world. If I was in a communist country "they" would, no doubt, be the "central planning committee." Living in a capitalist democracy, my poetry reflects an "otherness" to the all-pervasive bank commercials on television, the Dow Jones average, the vast expenditures poured into war preparation, etc...

An unpublished poem of mine, "Poetry Product Placement," deals with selling space in a poem to a product manufacturer. This poem spoofs the prevailing gimmick in movies of prominently placing products for our "benefit."

My first book, *Wyatt Earp in Dallas: 1963*, dealt with three themes intertwined: universal mythology, political reality, and a folk legend. I began by making audiotapes set in a jailhouse in Tombstone, Arizona. I had a feel for the west, having grown up in the middle-west state of Missouri when cowboy themes and "the western" were popular in movies and television. As a boy I visited the house where Jesse James was shot dead, and we visited caves searching for civil war memorabilia. One of my earliest memories is of sitting on a sun-drenched wooden floor at Sunday School, crayoning a Noah's Ark colouring book.

In my early teens I was profoundly moved when President John F. Kennedy was gunned down in Dallas, and this book also reflects my feelings about my parents and what they were going through at the time of the J.F.K. assassination. Both of my parents were creative, but frustrated with the situation life had given them. By intertwining these themes in a book-length narrative poem I was also able to indulge in some speculative storytelling.

The audiotapes gave birth to visual art expressing the theme of Wyatt Earp interacting with the myth of Noah and the universal flood; for example, a papier-mâché sculpture, "When Wyatt Earp Wears His Noah's Ark Hat the Pimps Shudder." (The pimps are meant to be weapons dealers.) Inexplicably the Kennedy assassination entered the fray, triangulating the motif. I began rewriting history, reversing time-frames, etc...

I mounted an exhibit at Pteros Gallery, Toronto, rehashing visually the basic ideas. Included with the paintings, sculptures, and collaborative art works was an eleven-minute video titled *Widow* featuring "Mrs. Kennedy" wearing her pink outfit from November 1963, and interacting with art, nature, and the "wild west." Since the Pteros Gallery exhibit in November 2003 commemorating the fortieth anniversary of the assassination, I have filmed two new "Mrs. Kennedys" for the film *Widow* which I now consider to be a work in progress.

My two books subsequent to *Wyatt Earp in Dallas: 1963* have not had such an exhaustive related visual treatment. I do hope to create some specifically and richly-illustrated poetry books in the future however. Currently I am working with another writer retelling the story of Orpheus and Eurydice, with plans for fine-line ink drawings.

Sometimes while painting I will play one song from a CD on "repeat" numerous times, and get it stuck in my head. Then I find myself writing poems to the tune of that song for days.

My work takes me all over Toronto and I use public transportation most days. I write on buses, subways and streetcars. I don't care who looks over my shoulder, but I feel compelled to explain, as they glance at paper layered with pencil, pen and marker at all angles, "This is just a rough copy, okay?" I feel compelled to explain but I don't.

Once I spent seven hours in the bath writing, and stumbled out of the tub temporarily blinded, not by poetic genius, but from evaporating chlorine.

I sometimes wake up with a phrase in the middle of the night and kick myself the next morning if I haven't written it down.

Even hearing a so-so poet read his/her work will kick-start new word combinations. Reading a great poet like Neruda, however, both humbles *and* offers the possibility of language as more than just words.

# SUSAN L. HELWIG

For several years Susan Helwig produced and hosted the literary programme *In other words* at radio station CKLN-FM in Toronto. Her broad-
casting stint closed with a flourish as she talked to David Gilmour about
*Sparrow Nights*. Her work has been widely published and anthologized
throughout North America, from *Acta Victoriana* to *Zygote*. A lifelong obsession with food has started to pay dividends with the inclusion of one of her
pieces in a book on Appalachian home cooking. She nourishes her musical
appetite by singing in the alto section of the Toronto Choral Society and
coaxing pop tunes from her 1911 Martin Orme piano at home. Her first book,
*Catch the Sweet*, was published in 2001. Her second collection, *Pink Purse
Girl*, was launched by Wolsak and Wynn in September 2006.

## MOST OF MY FRIENDS WRITE

But most of the time, I don't really feel like a writer myself. Oh sure, I've had two
poetry collections published (*Catch the Sweet*, Seraphim Editions, September 2001; and
*Pink Purse Girl*, Wolsak and Wynn, September 2006 — hurrah!), but I don't sit down on
a daily basis and carve out some poems. I don't even sit down on a weekly basis.

Hey, I never wanted to be a poet in the first place. I wanted to be a famous novel-
ist (emphasis on the famous). I assumed I would have to build up to this by writing
short stories so I signed up for a beginners writing workshop with Carole Leckner in
the fall of 1988. I was thirty-seven years old and approaching my "best before" date.
There was a federal election going on, around the issue of Free Trade. Change was in
the air. The time was at hand. Now or never.

The last night of the Leckner classes, we were each encouraged to present some
of our work to the group. I read a couple of poems. Well received. I demurred. "I really want to write stories," I said. "No one reads poetry any more." Leckner chastised me
for this attitude.

In the ensuing years, I gave short stories my best shot. I even got one published in
1994 (in *Grain*). But finally, I had to conclude that perhaps it was not my métier. I
turned back to poetry, where my muse stood waiting. I was forgiven for my dalliance.

These days, I write poems in church, during the service, when the only paper
available is the Sunday morning bulletin. I scribble outlines, taking them home to flesh
out later.

## When Dot Huffman dies*

When Dot Huffman dies there will be no more coughing. Silence will fall over the church like a warm towel after a shower. People will look round their pew, not spotting the difference, and think, new carpets, the minister has shaved his moustache, maybe it's snowing outside. At the scripture, when Dot used to cough the most, they will hear the story of the woman at the well as if for the first time; when Jesus says, drink of the water I give you, and never thirst again, they'll think, what a wonder, why haven't I heard that before in all its quenching splendour, how the mind can wander, and there will be Dot, not coughing.

Or I write a poem on the bicycle, on my way to work, jotting a word or phrase onto the margins of the *Auto Trader* I've grabbed from the box, as I wait for a green light.

Poetry seems to nose in on me when I'm busy doing other things.

My nightmares involve a spacious well-lit room, a clean desk, reams of paper, endless time — and no ideas.

I still write the odd prose piece — for example, meditations for the church bulletin (the same bulletin that I deface with my Sunday morning scratchings). These are spontaneous, unexpected, unpressured — and the bulletin editor falls all over herself thanking me for my contribution. If only all my words fell on such welcoming ground.

* from *Pink Purse Girl*, Wolsak & Wynn, 2006

# THEA CAPLAN

Thea Caplan has worked as an addiction consultant and found that the drug-dependent, although destructive, are tremendously creative. She has a post-graduate degree from Carleton University, Ottawa and is a recipient of the Woolwich Writing Fellowship at Columbia University. Her short stories have been widely published in literary journals in Canada and the U.S. and many have been anthologized. She has published book reviews for literary journals and *The Globe and Mail*. She lives in Toronto where she sails, mentors gifted students, and is working on developing community-based solar energy. Her novel is almost finished.

## DAYS AND NIGHTS IN WHITE SATIN

Why does the sight of a woman selling fruit stimulate some people to write, or to paint? For many, the woman barely registers but for some visual artists/writers she is the subject of new work. Why? Do these artists choose their subject? Their medium? What compels artists to create art?

What human society has *not* created artwork? From the petroglyphs scrawled on caves to Seurat and Andy Warhol's soup cans, art — or perhaps, individual creative expression of something new and of value — is a manifestation of human society. But why is artistic expression universal? What is the motivation? Is it a need? If so, what need does creating art fulfill? And what benefit does the viewer receive? What need is nourished for the viewer?

Artists speak in terms of feeling moved: affected, intrigued, frightened, upset, joyful, passionate; something jolts them out of the status quo; something — the crosshatch of lines on a woman's face — sparks their interest or curiosity; it niggles, it haunts, and they need to express themselves (sometimes symbolically or obliquely), access their feelings, or confront their fears. We are sentient beings with highly developed brains which compel us to make sense of chaos (perhaps invent order), to understand, and be understood. We want to produce something worthy of the situation, worthy of us, that is unique — that only we, a breathing speck in time — could do. A gesture at immortality. As John Lennon said: "My role in society, or any artist's or poet's role, is to try and express what we all feel."[1]

The need to share feelings propels art (and other things), but why? Joy, anguish, confusion, anger — all emotions — are the stuff of art. Why did Edvard Munch paint *The Scream*? And why did this painting of existential anguish have such an enormous and enduring impact on viewers? I believe artists channel their feelings and emotions into creative endeavours in an attempt to process, understand and cope with passionate feelings. An appreciative viewer is moved by the artwork, touched: someone is speaking her language, she is understood, for that moment she is not alone. And although it seems trite to find comfort in not being alone, think of the enormous relief and validity that people feel when they realize that other intelligent, attractive and interesting people are also… angry… alcoholics… sad… victims… ill… lonely… abused. *Why did this happen to me* gradually becomes a softer drumbeat, the compelling echo fades to… *Someone is listening to my pain, someone cares*, and later, *Where do I go from here, what I can do.*

Because we humans are not the mightiest of beasts, we are small, naked, no match for a medium-sized dog, to survive we have had to adapt, form groups, co-operate, make a society work — we have had to communicate well. Linguists say we are hard-wired to do so. Art is a powerful medium of communication, of communion: it unites. Art can entertain, inform, ridicule, condemn, irritate, mobilize — it is a mighty instrument. It can bond individuals into powerful groups which serves our primal need to belong and be safe. Every day we are bombarded with advertisements, messages and propaganda. Why? Because it matters what we think and feel.

To know oneself and be known. To feel — whether it is pain or joy, to feel emotion, unlike the rock. I know a depressed person who is so overwhelmed with sadness (a mishmash of chemicals?) that he doesn't talk, listen to a conversation, read a book, view art. He sits on his bed and moans. He has no interest in, no sense of wonder or curiosity about what is happening outside of him. His failure to do something productive or interesting further depresses him. Life is happening without him, in spite of him, he is nothing. *What's the point?* his eyes say. *It's hopeless.* Contrast that with what Einstein answered when asked about the key to his success. "I'm just curious,"[2] he said. Could creativity be a conduit of hope as Press[3] suggests, and/or is it the other way around?: hope is the conduit of creativity.

Creative people, fueled by curiosity, driven by challenge, thrill to the joy of creating and understand that part of the artistic process is trial-and-error, not "failure." Fear of failure is a death knell to creativity. We become self-conscious, and of course, the blank page mocks us, how stupid we are. We hesitate, pull back, give life to our doubts: we do not risk. The *thought* of freedom of expression strangles us. We *know* that what we are thinking, the tack we are considering is the wrong one, silly, boring. *Stop now, before you waste time.* The blank page wins. But what happens when creativity beats the finger-wagging monkey on our back?

It was Monday, and on Friday morning at eleven a.m. I would be putting my beloved dog to sleep. My big beautiful black and white collie, Pinocchio, could no longer eat or stand. A friend offered to come with me to the vet's, and I said no, but there was something she could do. I asked her, a painter, to come over with some stretched canvases. "I want to paint," I surprised myself by saying. The next day Suzanne arrived with paint brushes, overalls and a hug. By then I'd become a bit self-conscious. "I don't know why I want to paint," I said.

"Why don't we open some wine," she said, laying down some canvases on the kitchen floor.

"I'll put on some music." "Nights in White Satin" was Pinocchio and my favourite. For thirteen years, whenever I played that song, he'd dance around me, or maybe I danced around him. Whatever, we danced and sang and ran around the house, laughing. This time I cranked up the volume. Pinocchio, lying on the kitchen floor, didn't move. "Poke," I said, and his black ear lifted.

We got down to work, opening cans from our last house-painting job. We drank red wine to the Moody Blues and I produced the measuring tape and started pencilling. "I want the lines to be straight, my hand is wobbly," I said.

"Oh, it doesn't have to be straight," Suzanne said.

"But I *want* the lines straight."

Suzanne poured me more wine. "Have some," she said.

I drank it down, pencilling in very straight lines. But I couldn't get the paint to go on perfectly straight. My hands trembled and the cheap bristles developed a cowlick. "Relax," Suzanne said. "That looks good." She pointed to a big smear of Benjamin Moore Dijon over November Rain. And it did, look good.

"The hell with these lines," and I gave her the measuring tape.

"Great," she said. "Is there any more wine?"

I could tell she was hiding a smile. I said, "I bet you couldn't wait for me to get rid of that tape measure." Suzanne laughed.

I flung some Honey Harbour at the painting. The dribbles looked good, had panache. I flung some more, more wrist action this time. It was inspiring. I also made some dashes with the brush on the other side, to balance things out. I was getting the hang of it, Suzanne was saying, "Here we go, here we go." My husband opened another bottle of wine. I got some small plastic cups and poured paint in them. I just picked colours, this time I included blue, a royal muddy blue. I tiptoed around cans and wet brushes to get to Pinocchio. "Hi, bunny." He licked my hand. "Poke," I said, "I don't think you ever painted but let's give this a try." He looked up at me and in the reflection of his eye, I could see myself. I dipped a paw into the paint and stuck his paw on the canvas. When we lifted his paw, Suzanne and I said in unison, "Yes." I swear my sweet sick Poke smiled. I did it again, into Barley, the paw went. The long collie fur left a muffled, tantalizing trail. We were on a roll. "Here goes, Poke, are you ready?" I dipped his nose into the latex paint and brought the canvas up to his soft face. And the dog smiled again. There is only one nose print in the world like his — and I have it. Gorgeous blue ridges.

By midnight Suzanne and I were zonked, drunk and rather pleased with our five canvases. At some point in the evening my husband had popped in and snapped a photo or two: Suzanne and I look out of our heads, but happy; I am holding the photos now.

That Friday, Pinocchio is gone.

I had wanted to bury him in the backyard, but no one wanted to help me dig the frozen ground. I could wait until spring, but I thought having him in my basement freezer might bother me (I now think I was wrong), so my Poke ended up in an urn (I keep calling it a *toil*) in the dining room (I did not want to be one of those women who keeps ashes on the fireplace mantel). He's gone.

It's more than a year since Pinocchio … and I am in an art and frame gallery with my Pinocchio's paintings. Without preface, I show the proprietor two paintings. I want to know if they would look better framed. I know I am not objective. She looks at one, reaches for the other. She is quiet for a moment. Then she says, "I love his work."

I am stunned.

"I really do," she says.

I am silent.

"Look at the balance, the composition." I am reeling, hot and cold. I hear words like subtlety and breadth, surprise and warmth, transition, brush strokes. I clearly remember her saying, "We can't keep him in stock."

"Who?" I manage to get out.

"I — I can't remember his name. It's on the tip of my tongue. I just can't remember. We sold him two days ago."

"I don't think it's him," I say.

"Who? How do you know?"

I don't want to cry, break down in front of this woman. "I just know. It's not him." She looks at me, funny.

"I know." My voice scares me.

"Did you do these paintings?" she asks, her voice the colour of White Dove.

I shake my head. My voice has left me.

She looks concerned, her hand is on my shoulder, which is shaking.

"They are beautiful," she says.

I raise my eyes to this kind woman. "My dog did them," I tell her.

"He's very talented," she says.

"The sad thing is, I didn't know he could paint. And now he's gone."

She smiles at me, says nothing.

Notwithstanding the gallery owner, I don't think my and Pinocchio's paintings are masterful art. But I do think, that that night something creative came out of the dark. Once I threw away the tape measure and forgot about painting within the lines (such a cliché but I mean it literally here), I did feel as if I transcended my parochial self, was swept away on a magic carpet (another cliché!) and flew above my grief. I let go and let luck? a cascade of neural chemicals? take over, and created something, perhaps a work of art, perhaps not, that I had one hell of a good time doing — and which offers me comfort still. I think that is, essentially, the benefit and value of creativity.

When we are our most creative selves, when we get *out* of ourselves, when we transcend our ordinariness, our routines, when "flow" transports us and taps both our conscious and our subconscious selves we make magical connections. We feel absorbed, intense, euphoric, weightless, we are flying. We have the power to entertain, challenge and reward ourselves. Our work, our life, has meaning. The psychologist Mihaly Csikszentmihalyi, who studies creativity, believes that the special state of flow, "involved enchantment," is an antidote to the evils of boredom and anxiety.[4] I think of my severely depressed friend curled into his pillow, who does not lift his head, does not see the old woman selling fruit and wonder about her.

Solitude and rumination and reflection are the lifeblood of the creative. We need to stare out of a window and daydream. Einstein found music. "Whenever he felt that he had come to the end of the road or a difficult situation in his work, he would take refuge in music,"[5] recalled his son, Hans Albert.

But it is tough for the artist to produce work that is appreciated and valued by an audience. Tastes, perceptions and fads can run havoc with one's creativity, and pocket-book. It's no easy feat being an artist who is true to himself in these material times. Consider what this artist said:

> "What am I in most people's eyes? A nonentity, or an eccentric and disagreeable man — somebody who has no position in society and never will have, in short, the lowest of the low. Very well, even if this were true, then I should want my work to show what is in the heart of such an eccentric, of such a nobody."[6]

Of paramount importance, this artist said, he wanted his drawings to *touch* people.[7]

It can be depressing, and indeed it was for this artist. But touch us he did. We are all richer for having seen Vincent Van Gogh's paintings and drawings. (Though he only sold one painting during his lifetime — he was thirty-seven when he committed suicide — his portrait of Dr. Gachet sold in 1990 for more than 82 million dollars, but shortly before his death, when he received accolades for his work, he became distressed. He was probably bipolar; during his last manic phase he was prolific and artistic, but the following depressive phase did him in.)

It's a conundrum. Kay Redfield Jamison, professor of Psychiatry at John Hopkins School of Medicine and an expert on bipolar disorder — and herself bipolar — refuses the drug dosage recommended by her psychiatrist as it renders her too flat and not creative. Instead, in a cost-benefit analysis, she risks a few manic episodes a year (she has given health and financial power-of-attorney to two trusted colleagues), and her professional integrity and creativity are intact. She sometimes finds gold in her manias: "...ideas are fast and frequent like shooting stars, and you follow them until you find better and brighter ones."[8]

And in the end, I think, that's what you do. You take your meds (if you need them and to the extent that you do), eat, sleep and love as well as you can, but even if you don't do anything right, creativity lurks; let go, it's there, waiting; open your eyes and find the wonder within you.

[1] Lennon, John. *John Lennon: Drawings, Performances, Films*. Wulf Herzogenrath and Dorothee Hansen, eds. Ostfildern: Cantz, 1995

[2] Ann Hulbert, "The Prodigy Puzzle," *New York Times Magazine*, Nov 20, 2005, Section 6, p.108

[3] C. M. Press. "Psychoanalysis, creativity and hope: Forward edge strivings in the life and work of choreographer Paul Taylor," *J Am Acad Psychoanalytical Psychiatry*. 2005 Spring; 33 (1) 119-36

[4] Csikszentmihalyi, Mihaly. *Flow: The Psychology of Optimal Experience*. New York: Harper & Row, 1990

[5] Arthur I. Miller. "*A Genius Finds Expression in the Music of Another*," *New York Times*, January 31, 2006, D3.

[6] Van Gogh, Vincent. Letter to his brother Theo, 21 July 1882

[7] Ibid.

[8] Jamison, Kay Redfield. *An Unquiet Mind*. New York: Alfred Knopf, 1995. p.67

# CONTRIBUTORS

| | |
|---|---|
| Adam Dickinson | St. Catharines |
| Adrian | Princeton |
| Allan Briesmaster | Thornhill |
| Antanas Sileika | Toronto |
| bill bissett | Toronto, Vancouver |
| David Livingston Clink | Thornhill |
| David Lee | Hamilton |
| David Peacock | Oakville |
| Deborah Stiles | Truro |
| Edith Hodkinson | Owen Sound |
| George Swede | Toronto |
| Holly Briesmaster | Thornhill |
| Honey Novick | Toronto |
| Jacqueline Dumas | Edmonton |
| Janet Calcaterra | North Bay |
| Joe Blades | Fredericton |
| Julia Steinecke | Toronto |
| Kathryn Collins | Victoria |
| K.D. Miller | Toronto |
| Ken Stange | North Bay |
| Kent L. Bowman | Toronto |
| Kristin Andrychuk | Kingston |
| Marjory Smart | |
| Marvyne Jenoff | Toronto |
| Mary McKenzie | Toronto |
| Merike Lugus | Cobourg |
| Milt Jewell | Campbellford |
| Mona Harrison | Campbellford |
| Murray Charters | Brantford |
| Nancy Jane Bullis | Toronto |
| Norman Ravvin | Montreal |
| Paula Latcham | Toronto |
| Penn Kemp | London |
| Peter Thorn | Campbellford |
| Phlip Arima | Toronto |
| Renee Rodin | Vancouver |
| Richard Harrison | Calgary |
| Rob Mallion | Toronto |
| Rod Anderson | Cobourg |
| Sonja Dunn | Toronto |
| Stan Rogal | Toronto |
| Steven McCabe | Toronto |
| Susan L. Helwig | Toronto |
| Thea Caplan | Toronto |